D0209124

The Economics of Work in Japan

LTCB International Library Selection No. 3

THE ECONOMICS OF WORK IN JAPAN

KOIKE KAZUO
Professor of Human Resource Management
Hosei University

LTCB International Library Foundation

Transcription of names

The Hepburn system of romanization is used for Japanese terms, including the names of persons and places. Long vowels are not indicated. Chinese terms are romanized using the pinyin system. The Wade-Giles system is used, however, for certain place-names outside mainland China. As for the romanization of Korean terms, the McCune-Reischauer system is used.

With regard to Japanese, Chinese, and Korean personal names, we have followed the local custom of placing the family name first.

This book was originally published in Japanese in 1991
by Toyo Keizai Inc. under the title
Shigoto no Keizaigaku.

English translation rights arranged with
Toyo Keizai Inc.

Published February 1996 by LTCB International Library Foundation
1-8, Uchisaiwaicho 2-chome, Chiyoda-ku, Tokyo 100, Japan
Tel: 03-5223-7204 Fax: 03-5511-8123
This book abridged from originally translated English manuscript.
Translation and production by Simul International, Inc., Tokyo

Printed in Japan
ISBN 4 924971-02-2 C1336 P3000E

CONTENTS

Preface to the English-Language Edition

This book presents in broad outline my analysis of Japan's labor economy and human resource management. I focus on work—highlighting the way work is done and the formation of work ability. Work is an important part of life with a profound impact on the way people live. In researching it, I visit workplaces and listen to the people who work there. The observations of workers who have spent many years at their jobs are tremendously compelling. Their work underpins Japan's present standard of living. It is my hope in writing this book to forge an understanding worldwide of how work is performed in Japan.

This book has two main purposes. The first is to show that Japan's labor economy has a lot in common with other industrialized countries' and to thereby present a counterargument to the sometimes overwhelming Japan-is-different thesis. Many people overseas claim that Japanese industrial society is different. Japanese labor practices are unique, they say, its labor market is uncompetitive, and its workers put their company's interests first. Japan, they add, does not play by the same rules as the rest of the international community, and unless it changes its ways the rest of the world cannot compete with it because the rules of international free trade do not apply. Sadly, this argument originated in Japan, where it persists in some quarters. But the analysis of good-quality data discloses many more common aspects between Japan and other countries than it suggests, something made all the more clear through detailed observations of how work is performed at workplaces. There is no mystery in the way work is done; it is quite straightforward and therefore universally comprehensible.

Despite the high degree of similarity an examination of work reveals between Japan and other industrialized countries, differences do exist. Indeed, there are aspects of work in which Japan leads other countries. And it is the second main purpose of this book to explain these aspects. They include the means by which skills are formed; the nature of those skills; and the intensive, long-term competition that stimulates skill formation. Skill refers to the know-how needed to deal with changes or problems for which it is difficult to standardize or document procedures. Ongoing competition encourages the widespread acquisition of know-how.

Let me explain these two purposes further. Japan's labor economy is central to the Japan-is-different argument. The argument refers to Japan's distinctive system of permanent employment, seniority wages, and enterprise unions and especially to the group-centered way of thinking that, despite Japan's lack of domestic market competition, makes the Japanese economy very competitive vis-à-vis other countries.

A lot of excellent statistical data is available in Japan. Using it, I demonstrate that those in Japan who enjoy so-called seniority wages are only part of the workforce and that the workforce in Japan consists of diverse groups (chapter 1). I also point out through a comparison with other industrial countries, for which data has only recently become available, that Japan is not alone in having a seniority wage curve; it is a feature common among white-collar workers in Western Europe and North America. What is distinctive about Japan is that the seniority wage curve also applies to blue-collar workers, a phenomenon that I refer to as white collarization (chapter 2).

Permanent employment is examined through a comparison with recent Western European statistics on length of employment. I demonstrate that there is a group of immobile, long-term employees in Western Europe similar to that in Japan and that the length of employment of blue-collar workers in large Japanese corporations is like that of white-collar workers in Western Europe, further evidence of white collarization (chapter 3). In chapter 7, I examine another aspect of permanent employment: dismissal. Contrary to popular belief in Japan's permanent employment system, but as expected, dismissal does occur even in large firms with labor unions if financial losses continue for two years. I show, moreover, that Japan's voluntary redundancy form of dismissal predominates for white-collar workers in the United Kingdom, the United States, and Germany, again indicating white collarization, and that it is only now being extended to blue-collar workers in the United Kingdom and Germany, making Japan a trendsetter.

My examination of enterprise unions takes place in chapter 12. Statistical comparisons of strike activity and a look at organizational structure and function reveal that the basic organizational unit of labor unions in the United States and Germany is the enterprise or the plant and that there are no major differences in the functional separation of roles with respect to wage negotiations and so on.

White collarization epitomizes the merits of the Japanese system. What underlies white collarization, as seen in the wage system, employment, and dismissal, is skill on the shop floor. In this book, the skill that is the source of Japan's competitiveness is called intellectual skill: the know-how to deal with problems and changes effectively. Efficiency does not increase simply because of the increasing sophistication of machinery and equipment. The world is beset by uncertainty. Problems and changes are frequent. Consumer demand alone changes constantly and, for the most part, unpredictably as to when and to what extent and for what product. No one can know precisely what products will be in demand and how much will be sold. How well an enterprise responds to qualitative and quantitative changes has a major effect on efficiency. This requires complex, sophisticated know-how.

Production lines, meanwhile, are never problem free. How well problems are handled is crucial. If not dealt with, line machinery will continue to make defective products, ruining quality and efficiency. If problems could be predicted and the most appropriate way to deal with them predetermined, corrective procedures could be programmed into a machine or computer. But this is impossible, and the time taken in trying would witness a host of changes in machinery and products, adding to the effort's futility. Instead, workers must acquire the know-how to handle problems and changes. This underpins efficiency.

This, however, entails a superb knowledge of machinery and production processes. Identifying and rectifying the cause of a defect demands such knowledge. It is so important that I call it intellectual skill. To acquire it, workers must experience the full range of a workshop's principal jobs. In Japan, even production workers thus possess know-how approaching that of engineers'. Greater demands for intellectual skills are placed on white-collar workers, but what is distinctive about Japan is that these skills also exist among blue-collar workers. This is why compensation, employment, and dismissal for Japan's blue-collar workforce approximates that of the white-collar workforce.

The difference between intellectual skills and human capital theory is the nature of the skills and their incorporation into and formation through on-the-job training (OJT). Years of experience and schooling are generally used as proxies for the level of skill in quantitative analysis, but in this book I emphasize that skill levels vary depending more on how OJT is conducted. Furthermore, once skill formation is explained the process can be adapted to and developed in other countries.

Long-term competition is vital in forming intellectual skills. Many people say that Japan is not a competitive society. In fact, intense competition surrounds the upgrading of skills in Japan. Psychological theories on corporate commitment do not explain this. Corporate commitment is of no help in dealing with problems. Problems call for technical know-how, the formation of which is difficult without a deliberate promotional policy. Raising skill levels takes time, necessitating long-term competition and incentives, such as unbiased evaluations of skill improvements and commensurate pay.

Long-term competition and incentives are not apparent unless looked for. Intellectual skills are intangible, and the long-term competition needed to develop them obscures the connections between achievement, evaluation, and rewards. I try to define these relationships in chapters 5 and 11. Because intellectual skills are a type of software or technology, it is eminently possible for other countries to introduce them provided the necessary conditions are in place (chapter 10).

Chapter 1 indicates that there are, contrary to popular opinion, a variety of workers in Japanese workplaces. There are workers in small and medium-sized companies, female workers, and older workers. These groups form the majority of the workforce, and prevailing views about them defy the facts. The dual-structure argument maintains that workers in small and medium-sized companies are sacrificed to the interests of large enterprises, that their wages are low, and that there are large wage differentials according to company size. It is also said that few Japanese women, long confined to the household, join the workforce. Both assertions contradict observations.

Size-based wage differentials do not appear to be especially large in Japan. This is not definitive because quality statistics like Japan's are not sufficiently available for other countries. Intellectual skills, moreover, are present in small and medium-sized companies, although to a lesser extent than in large corporations. They are the basis of contributions by workers from the majority workforce groups to the nation's overall industrial productivity. Without them and the substantial proportions of these groups, would it be possible to increase Japan's competitiveness? The proportion of Japanese women who work outside agriculture, where it has always been high, has long been higher than in Western Europe and North America. Proportions in those regions, however, have increased rapidly over the past 15 years, catching up with and even exceeding Japan's (chapters 8 and 9).

In the last chapter, I present a theory that attempts to explain the trend behind Japan's overtaking other industrialized countries in some respects. It is a version of the latecomer theory that assumes that some as of yet undetermined country will take the lead in the next stage of development (chapter 14).

The concepts that I have set down in this book and the means by which they were derived differ significantly from the usual approach of labor economics. The key concept is skill, particularly intellectual skill. The word *skill,* of course, has been widely used, but few attempts have been made to analyze skill.

Furthermore, this and many of the book's other concepts result from actual observations of practices in Japanese workshops. Statistics and other references were also used, but the literature does not provide statistics for the key concept of skill. This concept can only be studied through patient observation of workers' mobility and performance at the workplace. This is the foundation of this book. Amid the popularity of econometric analysis, my analysis relies on old-fashioned methods.

I am deeply indebted to all those who made this analysis possible—the many people on the shop floor who took the trouble to explain things clearly to an outside observer. Because comparison is essential to an understanding of one's own country, I applied the same methods in other countries. My gratitude thus extends beyond the shop floors of Japan to people in workshops in many countries, particularly in the United States, Thailand, and Malaysia. I thank them for their cooperation.

I am very pleased to have this book translated and published as part of the Long-Term Credit Bank of Japan's LTCB International Library Selection. My sincere thanks to Uehara Takeshi of the LTCB International Library Foundation. My sincere gratitude also to the translator, Jean C. Hoff, of Simul International, for taking charge of such a troublesome translation and to the Simul staff members who undertook the whole process from researching, editing, and proofreading to publication with such fine teamwork. Because I use concepts and terminology that differ from the conventional in texts in other countries, the translation must have been particularly difficult. A personal check of each of the translated and edited chapters, however, revealed a job well done. Again, my thanks.

I also thank all the young scholars and friends—particularly Professor Inoki Takenori, of Osaka University, and Professor Muramatsu Kuramitsu, of Nanzan University—who over the years have made many discerning comments on the original Japanese edition of this book and who have guided my research in so many ways. Finally, I thank Yamashita Kenkichi, of Toyo Keizai Shinposha, for taking such care in publishing the Japanese edition.

Chapter 1 Various Worker Groups

THE SELF-EMPLOYED AND EMPLOYEES

Gainful Employment

It is sometimes mistakenly believed that most Japanese workers work under long-term employment and seniority wage systems. But, as is true everywhere, a variety of worker groups exist within Japan.

An important distinction must be made between the self-employed and employees. Working conditions are quite different, even for workers doing the same job, depending on whether workers are self-employed or salaried employees. In statistical parlance, this distinction is called employment status. Employers make up a third category, but they constitute a very small minority of the labor force and will not be discussed here.

What percentage of the total does each of our two categories account for? To find out, we must clarify how many people in Japan are gainfully employed. These figures are seldom recorded, and when they are no explanation of how they were calculated is offered. Answering the question, therefore, will be no easy task. We must delve into basic data.

The most reliable data for postwar Japan are provided by the National Census and the Basic Survey of Employment Structure, both compiled by the Statistics Bureau of the Management and Coordination Agency. A national census is a country's basic statistical survey. For the time being, we will look for the numbers we need in Japan's 1985 National Census. The National Census divides Japan's gainfully employed workers into the following groups:

Labor Force	60,390,000	
Employed	58,360,000	100.0%
Self-Employed	14,360,000	24.6%
Farm & Forestry	4,710,000	8.1%
Nonagricultural	9,670,000	16.5%
Employees	41,300,000	70.8%
Employers	2,690,000	4.6%
Unemployed	2,030,000	3.5%
Not in the Labor Force	34,410,000	

The census first classifies the 94.97 million people in Japan who are 15 years of age or over by whether they are in the "labor force" or "not in the labor force." Those in the labor force are the "employed" and the "unemployed" who are looking for jobs. Those not in the labor force include students, housewives, the elderly, and others who are neither employed nor seeking employment.

Establishing who is in the labor force is somewhat troublesome. The method is to ask people using questionnaires and to make a decision based on their responses. But people can be asked about their activities in two ways: either for a specific period or in general. The former approach is known as the actual situation method, while the latter is the usual situation method.

Japan's National Census uses the actual situation method. For the last week of September, it classifies all those who answer "yes" to the question "Did you work?" during that week as "employed." Work is defined as "a paying job," which "includes part-time work, side jobs, and helping out in a store or on a farm." Even those who worked "at all" during that one week are considered "employed."

As a result, the census counts as employed those people who normally do not work but who happen to work even slightly during that one week. This approach inevitably results in an overestimate of the working population. To counter this, the Basic

Survey of Employment Structure adopts the usual situation method, which asks whether someone usually works. Inevitably, this method estimates the size of the labor force to be smaller than does the actual situation method. According to the 1985 census, 63.6 percent of Japanese aged 15 or over belonged to the workforce. Two years later, in 1987, when one would expect the figure to have grown, the Basic Survey of Employment Structure revealed that the number had instead declined to 62.2 percent. The variation between these two methods is greatest in the case of women and the elderly. International comparisons of the percentages of women and the elderly who work must take this into account.[1]

Nonetheless, these two sources of basic data are invaluable and help illuminate factors in addition to those discussed. The Basic Survey of Employment Structure collates more important facts. Information on workplace size and on income, for example, is available only in the Basic Survey. This degree of detail is possible because the Basic Survey entails having statisticians ask questions directly at each household of a sampling on a scale of 1:100. The National Census tends to avoid questions that may infringe on privacy and so cannot probe as deeply. On the other hand, any study of trends that predate World War II is dependent on the National Census, which has been carried out every five years since 1920. The National Census is also the source to turn to for information on every city, town, and village in Japan. Because it is a survey of the entire population, it collects and classifies extremely detailed statistics for each part of Japan.

Self-employment

The figures cited earlier indicate that of the gainfully employed nearly a quarter were self-employed while 70 percent were employees. The existence of large-scale self-employment has long been regarded as a sign of late economic development. In all countries prior to modernization, the self-employed, especially farmers, accounted for most of the gainfully occupied, but their numbers were thought to decrease with economic development, as many farmers become employees.

The trends depicted in figure 1-1 suggest that this was not the case in Japan. True, the percentage of employees has increased rapidly, and the number of self-employed in farming and forestry has precipitously declined, but there has been no decrease in the number of self-employed in nonagricultural areas; in absolute terms, their numbers are clearly rising, while the relative importance of nonagricultural self-employed has leveled off. According to the figures given previously, self-employed farm and forestry workers were a mere 8 percent of the gainfully employed in 1985, whereas nonagricultural self-employed, at 17 percent, already accounted for most self-employed. What is the reason for this? Is Japan alone in having so many nonagricultural self-employed?

Figure 1-2 gives an international comparison of self-employment rates. Please note that the figures for Japan differ from those given earlier because only the owners of businesses are included. The self-employed in any country consist of business owners and

Fig. 1-1. Self-Employment and Employee Rates for Japan (1920–85)

Sources: National Census. Figures for 1920 and 1930, however, are from Ishizaki's estimates based on the National Census (Showa Dojinkai, ed., *Koyo to Shitsugyo* (Employment and Unemployment), p. 40).

Notes: 1. For 1920 and 1930, the category "self-employed in farming and forestry" has been substituted for the employed in farming and forestry. The difference between the two categories is thought to be insignificant for the agricultural sector.

2. For statistical purposes, "employees" includes "executives."

3. The number of gainfully employed workers for each year is set at 100.

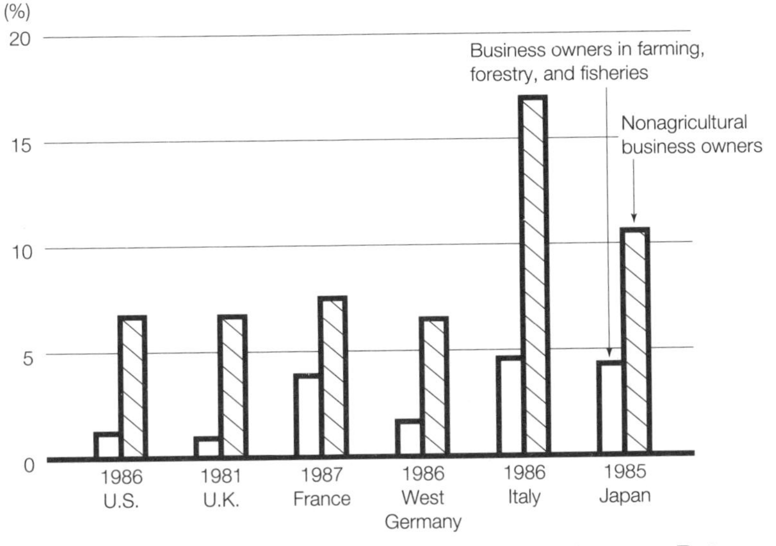

Fig. 1-2. International Comparison of Self-Employment Rates

Source: International Labor Organization (ILO), *Yearbook of Labor Statistics 1987, 1989–90.*
Note: Because the treatment of "unpaid family workers" varies greatly from one country to the next, the figures given here are only for business owners.

the unpaid family members who work for them. The definition of a business owner is obvious worldwide; however, unpaid family workers are defined differently from country to country. Some countries include all family workers except those who work only a few hours (less than 15 hours, for example) a week; others don't count them at all. This is a problem for researchers attempting international comparisons. For that reason, this discussion is limited to business owners.

Compared with the United States, the United Kingdom, and West Germany, Japan has a large number of self-employed. It is similar in this respect, however, to France and Italy. It has nearly the same percentage of self-employed in farming, forestry, and fisheries as France and Italy, but though the rate of nonagricultural self-employed is only somewhat higher in Japan than in France it is considerably less than in Italy. Why Japan belongs with France and Italy and not with the United States and the United Kingdom in this regard should be examined at some future date, but it would be hazardous to conclude that Japan is different simply on the basis of a comparison with the United States and the United Kingdom.

Self-employment is virtually unexplored territory, perhaps because self-employment has long been regarded as a sign of late economic development. The remarkable rate of business start-ups and failures, however, is one small but fascinating aspect of self-employment. The statistics for Japan, especially since World War II, are superb. Every three years, the Statistical Survey of Business Establishments—a sort of national census of establishments—collects data on the total number of business establishments and on those that began operating during the preceding three years. From it, we can estimate the number of establishments that have gone out of business. In the 1980s, the failure rate was between 20 and 25 percent over a three-year period; the start-up rate was also around 25 percent. Generally speaking, most companies that last three years remain in business for a long time; thus, we can see how many new companies go out of business and how many others spring up. Where do these new companies come from, and where do the people who worked for those that fail go? The Basic Survey of Employment Structure, which compares employment at the time of the survey with figures from the previous year, indicates that new businesses are started by employees who quit small and medium-sized companies and that these people go back to work for small and medium-sized businesses when their own companies fail.[2]

There are many indicators of the competitiveness of Japanese industrial society, but this movement is considered its basis. Fierce competition exists not only among workers at large firms but also among employees of small and midsize companies. Many who work in smaller companies attempt to become their own bosses. If they succeed, they gradually increase the size of their companies to become themselves managers of small and medium-sized businesses. Those who fail go back to work for small and medium-sized companies. This sort of social ferment underlies the competitiveness of Japanese industrial society.

Employees

Japan's largest bloc of gainfully employed workers consists of salaried people and other wage earners subdivided into several different groups. These differences are reflected in the wages each group earns. Figure 1-3 shows wages by age for various groups. It has been compiled from the extremely detailed Statistical Survey of Wage Structure and the Wage Survey in Construction and Transportation Industries, which examines the wages of unskilled labor. The usual practice is to refer solely to the Statistical Survey of Wage Structure, but it surveys only workers employed in a company for two months or more. Even in Japan many workers frequently move from one firm to another, so we have to combine the findings of the two surveys.

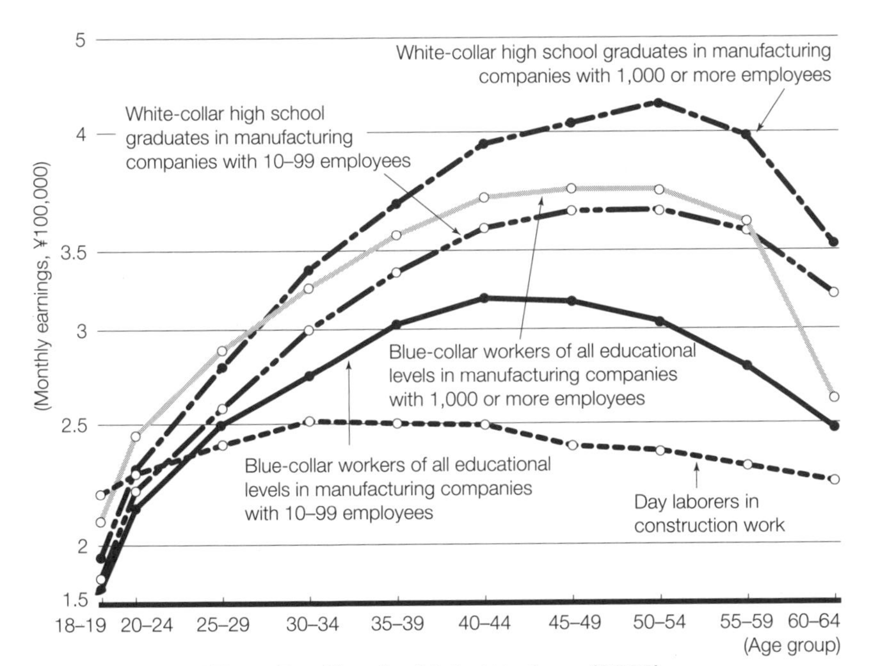

Fig. 1-3. Age-Wage Profiles for Male Workers (1986)

Sources: For white-collar and blue-collar workers, Ministry of Labor, *1987-nen Chingin Kozo Kihon Chosa* (Statistical Survey of Wage Structure, 1987); for construction day laborers, Ministry of Labor, *Okugai Rodosha Shokushubetsu Chingin Jittai Chosa* (Wage Survey in Construction and Transportation Industries), 1963. For the former, the survey period was July 1986; for the latter, August 1986.

Note: Monthly wages for construction day laborers are found by multiplying the average daily wage by the average number of workdays in a month.

If the age-wage profiles for production workers at large corporations are tentatively called seniority wages, we must distinguish among at least three groups. The first is a seniority wage group, which includes blue-collar workers at large firms and white-collar workers at companies of all sizes. This group's white-collar high school graduates, even in companies with from 10 to 99 employees, show a wage curve similar to that for production workers at large companies. The second group has a horizontal, even downward, wage curve for workers past their mid-30s: experienced blue-collar workers at small and medium-sized companies. And the third group—unskilled workers—shows wages with little or no variation for all ages. Construction day laborers epitomize unskilled workers. Female workers, too, belong to one of these three groups, despite their various wage levels.

The relative importance of these groups is impossible to estimate precisely. Perhaps 40 percent belong to the seniority wage group, and most of the rest to the second group. No statistics are available, so this is only an estimate based on general assumptions. Taking those listed as "regular employees" in the most recent Basic Survey of Employment Structure, a seniority wage group for the following was assumed: the total number of men and women in (1) "professional occupations" and in (2) "managerial positions"; the number of men in (3) "clerical positions" and in (4) "retail and sales"; and (5) 23 percent of the regular male employees in all other occupational categories. The 23 percent represents employees in companies with more than 500 employees to the total employees of all sizes of companies. This is, of course, a rough estimate. A seniority wage group exists for women in "clerical positions," too, but it is assumed to be small. And the size of the unskilled worker group is hard to estimate. In particular, we do not know how many recent part-time workers belong in this category.

Since little is known of the composition of these groups, it is even more difficult to discuss changes in them. Findings indicate, however, that reality differs somewhat from what is thought to be true. In accordance with popular belief, the percentage of workers at large companies has diminished. The Basic Survey of

Employment Structure indicates that the proportion of workers employed by companies in the private sector with 1,000 employees or more declined between 1968 and 1987, from 23.5 percent of all employees to 18.4 percent. However, the proportion of white-collar workers increased significantly, causing the seniority curve to rise in companies of all sizes. The influence, therefore, of the seniority wage group appears large.

AN UNLIMITED SUPPLY OF LABOR

The Lewis Model

The greatest shift in Japan, as elsewhere, has been that from self-employment in farming and forestry to employee status. The country's largest source of labor has long been farmers and their unpaid family workers. In the early stages of industrialization, the majority of a country's population lives in farming villages. Despite a developing country's rapid construction of factories in its cities, the labor supply from the surplus population in agricultural communities is seemingly inexhaustible, making development appear hopeless. However, when development reaches a certain level the labor supply peaks, and the situation changes. Economic development policies differ depending on which stage a country is at. How can a country's stage of development be determined? In his classic essay, Arthur W. Lewis has created a brilliant model that is extremely important and elegantly simple.[3] Because the economic development of industrializing countries is an important issue for Japan, the Lewis model requires discussion.

A labor surplus model may seem irrelevant to present-day Japan, but it was long argued that Japan's vast farming population generated surplus labor conditions that lowered wages and distorted Japan's economic development. This argument dominated Marxist and neoclassical economic circles.

The Lewis model uses wage differentials. Finding economic indicators of whether or not a surplus labor supply exists is not easy. In Japan, the ratio of job offers to job seekers is available, but such complicated indicators are unlikely in developing countries. Nations that could compile such reliable statistics would no longer be classed as developing. Statistics on wages, on the other hand, because they are expressed in monetary terms, are available. The Lewis model states that in the early stages of economic development, when there is a labor surplus, the gap between wages paid to skilled and unskilled workers widens over the long term but shrinks when the surplus in farming villages disappears.

The seemingly inexhaustible supply of workers who account for most of the population in the early stages of economic development are unskilled and live in agricultural communities where the supply of land is limited. The construction of even a few factories in the cities creates a demand for labor that these workers fill. There is, however, a shortage of skilled workers. Occupational training centers either do not exist or are rare, and only a few people have the time or money to attend school. Skilled workers, at any rate, best learn their skills through factory experience, but few factories exist. Consequently, wages for skilled workers rise sharply, and wage differentials between skilled and unskilled workers widen over time. This is the stage of an unlimited supply of labor.

This reservoir of workers in the farming villages, however, cannot last forever. If the economy continues to develop, unskilled workers eventually fall in short supply, driving their wages up. The supply, meanwhile, of skilled workers rises sharply as more people go to school and as more occupational training centers and factories are built. As a result, wage differentials between the two groups begin to shrink, and the developing country enters the stage of a limited supply of labor. The juncture between these two stages is called the turning point, and economic development policies differ depending on which stage a country is in. This simple model has been used for many years to analyze economic development in developing countries.

The Lewis Model's Applicability to Japan

A fierce debate rages over the applicability of the Lewis model to Japan. Pioneering the debate were two American scholars, John Fei and Gustav Ranis, who saw World War I as the turning point and who regarded the period preceding it as the unlimited supply of labor stage.[4]

Two different counterarguments were published at roughly the same time by Minami Ryoshin[5] and Taira Koji.[6] Minami set the turning point at around 1960, and this became the view of Marxist and neoclassical economists. Taira asserted that Japan never experienced an unlimited supply of labor during its modernization in the Meiji period (1868–1912) and was from the outset at the same limited supply of labor stage as the West. About 10 years later, Yasuba Yasukichi argued that there had been two turning points, one around 1900, another around 1960.[7]

All these views have the same origin: the Lewis model. Judged, though, on the accuracy of their data, Fei and Ranis's view is inferior, while the other views rely on first-rate sources yet come to different conclusions. Minami's data are probably the most accurate. He was a member of Hitotsubashi University's Institute of Economic Research, which was collating and analyzing long-term economic statistics for Japan, and he made full use of this material. Taira also uses superb data, but he was limited to what had been published.

This book supports Taira's view. Minami could not explain one extremely important long-term trend in Japan—throughout the twentieth century, real wages increase at a far higher rate than in Western countries where reliable data exist. This was revealed in the superb work of Umemura Mataji, which resulted from the statistics kept after World War II.[8] If conditions in Japan had been those of a developing country until around 1960 and there had been a labor surplus, no matter how much the demand for labor grew a sufficient supply would still exist. Real wages, therefore, would be unlikely to grow at the same rates as in North America and Europe, never mind exceed them. To Minami, the rise in real wages merely indicated an increase in the cost of living at the subsistence level, which has caught up with price increases. But why would an increase in the cost of eking out an existence in Japan exceed the rates of increase for real wages in North America and Europe, which had limited supplies of labor? The situation is better understood by positing a faster rate of economic development in Japan than in the West. That the increase in the rate of growth in real wages was sharper than in North America and Europe reflects this.[9]

World War II, moreover, had enormous impact on Japan. Almost all its factories were razed, leaving many workers unemployed. The repatriation of Japanese from abroad combined to create a huge surplus population. To regard this surplus as existing since before the war is to overlook the impact of the war and the extent of Japan's prewar economic development. Such a view underpins the Japan-is-different argument: The fact that a late-developing country could achieve high-level growth must mean that it has an extremely different system and is not a fair competitor. This view probably forms the background of the Japan–U.S. Structural Impediments Initiative.

Yasuba, who believed in a turning point around 1900, uses indicators other than wage differentials but comes to a conclusion similar to Taira's. He also recognizes the impact of the shock caused by Japan's defeat in World War II. Yet, no matter how great that impact may have been is it reasonable to depict Japan as once more a developing country after the war?

Chapter 2 Examining the Seniority Wage Legend

THE COMMONLY ACCEPTED VIEWS

Seniority Wage Theory I

Of the groups of workers discussed in chapter 1, let us consider those who work for large companies, beginning with wages. A firmly held belief about wages is the seniority wage theory, which is so widely accepted that no one knows who advanced it or how it was defined. Two versions prevail.

The first version defines seniority wages as wages (a) that rise in accordance with age and length of service; (b) that are not paid by the job; and (c) that are unique to Japan. This assumes that seniority wages in Japan differ from wages in the West, which are thought to be job determined and unrelated to age and length of service.

This version emphasizes the late development of the Japanese economy. The vast surplus population in farming villages and the prolonged unlimited supply of labor resulted in extremely low wages. Paying workers by job made it difficult for them to make a living, interfering with their ability to do their jobs. Wages thus were paid according to age to offset the cost of living, making seniority wages a kind of cost of living guarantee. The expectation is that when the unlimited supply of labor stage ends and a limited supply of labor stage begins, wages will be paid by the job, and the seniority wage system will disappear. However, even amid a labor shortage Japan's seniority wage curve did not break down.

Seniority Wage Theory II

The second version of the seniority wage theory rejects the proposition that wages are not paid by the job. Wages, it maintains, correspond with age and length of service only because the skills needed to perform certain jobs increase with age and length of service.

This version, too, draws on the late development of Japan's economy. The focus, though, is on machinery. Japan imported advanced machinery from the more developed West and had to train operators to use it, mostly on-site by the large companies that had imported the machinery. Workers thus were trained while gaining in-house corporate experience. Skills roughly corresponded to length of service and age. The proposition that this system is unique to Japan remains unchanged.

This argument was advanced by Ujihara Shojiro and other Marxist economists, but it shares much with neoclassical economic views.[1] Analyses of the Japanese economy present it as a difference of opinion independent and, indeed, regardless of economic schools.

The second version assumes that when Japan has modernized and caught up with Western technology, seniority wages will collapse because the need to develop skills within companies will diminish. Again, however, the seniority wage curve shows no signs of breaking down, despite the rapid improvement of Japan's technology.

Recent Reassessments

Whereas these versions of the seniority wage theory emphasize Japan's late development, another view, which emerged in the wake of the first oil crisis in the early 1970s, stressed Japan's spectacular economic achievements. It is perhaps best expressed in a 1977 OECD report.[2]

After the first oil crisis, the Japanese economy was far better off than Western economies in terms of prices, unemployment, and growth rates. This was true despite the crisis's severer impact on Japan than on Europe and North America. The OECD report reasons that this is because Japanese companies guarantee their employees their livelihoods through a system of seniority wages and permanent employment. In response, employees work hard. This system, it argues, underpins Japan's success.

Do people work hard because their livelihoods are guaranteed? No doubt praiseworthy individuals exist, but so do other, less admirable people. If jobs are guaranteed whether people work or not, many cease to work. This is probably what gave rise to the necessity of a Japanese worker mentality that attaches special importance to the group.[3] The most important group is the company; therefore, this view argues, if the company cares about its employees the employees reciprocate with hard work.

This assessment of seniority wages contrasts sharply with the two earlier versions, but the framework remains. The definition is close to that of the first version; only the assessment differs. But when the assessment changes, other changes easily ensue. The Japan-is-different argument, which appeared at the time of the Japan-U.S. Structural Impediments Initiative, must be regarded as one example of this tendency.

THE WAGE PROFILE AND WAGE SCALE

Two General Concepts

To examine whether wages in Japan and the West are seniority based or not, we must define seniority wages precisely. Otherwise, it is impossible to determine if seniority wages exist. A definition entails distinguishing between the general concepts of wage profile and wage scale.

The wage profile refers to the wage curve achieved by graphing age along a horizontal axis and wages along a vertical axis. A seniority wage curve that moves up in almost a straight diagonal is one example of the variety of wage curves that can be plotted. Wages for Japan's unskilled workers plot almost horizontally, while, although not indicated in figure 1-3, wages rise sharply for carpenters as they pass through their apprenticeship and level off once a carpenter becomes a full-fledged craftsman.

The wage scale calculates wages for workers or jobs utilizing age, length of service, type of job, or job grade. Wages are classed, respectively, as pay for age, pay for service, pay for job, and pay for job grade.

The wage profile and the wage scale are frequently confused. Pay for age or pay for service are mistakenly thought to result in a seniority wage curve in a wage profile. Imagine, however, a pay-for-job system, commonly considered the opposite of seniority wages. The pay for job A is ¥100,000; for job B, ¥130,000; for job C, ¥160,000; and for job D, ¥190,000. Add to this a practice that is widespread among large companies in the United States—the seniority system, whereby workers advance on the basis of length of service (see chapter 4). If we plot length of service along the horizontal axis, it forms a seniority wage curve. Even if we replace length of service with age, the wage spread increases, but the general trend toward a seniority curve remains. Thus, even pay for job may have a seniority wage curve, and even pay for age may sometimes move in more or less a straight line. We should not jump to the conclusion that because of pay for job there cannot also be seniority wages in the profile.[4]

Of these two general concepts, the wage profile is the more important. Because a worker's livelihood depends on it—it determines ranking in the workplace and company—it deserves further attention. What is more, the statistical data necessary for international comparisons are available only for age-wage profiles. This does not mean, however, that the wage scale should be ignored.[5]

The Wage Scale

The wage scale for Japan is thought to be determined by age or length of service, but this is not the case. Examples of pay for age or pay for length of service accounting for the majority of basic wages in Japan do not exist. In a few cases, they are a small part of wages—around 10 percent.

No statistics are available for international comparisons, so observations must suffice. An almost perfect pay-for-age system that made up the greater part of basic wages once existed in large British banks (today, this is more a pay-for-job-grade system). A basic salary scale was determined for each age, beginning at age 17. Three salary schedules were drawn up: for male office workers, for female office workers, and for non-office workers. The basic, publicly dislcosed salary schedule by age for male office workers ended in workers' early 30s. Not only was the basic salary for each executive position different, salaries increased while workers stayed in the same position. For non-office workers and women, few of whom gained managerial positions, pay raises by age continued until their 40s. A basic salary by age did not mean, however, an absence of merit ratings. When an employee's performance was especially good, an addition was made to the basic salary. Basic salary scales also varied slightly from bank to bank.[6]

No such example of pay for age can found for Japan. And Australian banks in the early 1980s offer the only perfect example of a pay-for-length-of-service system. Except for assistant branch managers or higher, a basic salary was established in a salary schedule for each year of service. This is now a job-grade pay system.[7]

In large Japanese corporations, wages are usually based on a yearly increment system applicable to blue-collar and white-collar workers. Length of service has some influence, but pay increases vary depending on two additional factors. First, 5 to 10 job grades exist. Salary increases differ even for workers with the same length of service depending on their grade. Managerial positions, too, have job grades on which pay raises depend. Second, pay raises differ even for workers with the same job grade depending on merit ratings. An assessment by a superior affects the amount of increase. High assessments correspond to high raises. The yearly increment system, the job-grade system, and merit ratings are believed unique to Japan and are regarded as important features of Japan's seniority wage system.

Yearly increment systems for blue-collar workers are rare in the United States, the United Kingdom, and West Germany, even in large companies. And if companies have labor unions, merit ratings are seldom sanctioned. An exception is France, where about one-sixth of the basic wage pays for length of service. Commonly, basic pay does not go up, at least for workers doing the same job, except when increases are negotiated by the union. Even so, wages do rise somewhat over the long run to reflect worker promotions. In the United States and the United Kingdom, seniority systems have been established whereby workers move up to the job immediately above strictly according to length of service. Sometimes the wages result in seniority wage profiles, but without determining the way promotions are made the real situation defies understanding.

The situation for white-collar workers is completely different. Statistics are again unavailable, so this discussion, too, stems solely from observation. In general, the three criteria—yearly increments, job-grade systems, and merit ratings—appear widely accepted for white-collar workers. The difference between the West and Japan lies in the time span for yearly increments—shorter, around 5 to 10 years after a worker has been at the same job in the West, against a longer period, say 15 years, in Japan. To regard this as a qualitative difference prevents an appreciation of the close resemblance of wage curves. Job-grade systems and merit ratings, meanwhile, are thought to be widespread among white-collar workers.[8] Yet, studies of salary rating methods for white-collar workers are so rare that conclusive remarks must be reserved.

AN INTERNATIONAL COMPARISON OF AGE-WAGE PROFILES

The Nature of the Data

It has long been concluded that the wage curve is seniority based in Japan but not in the West. This assumes that good-quality statistics for wages by age exist in Europe and North America as well as in Japan. With minor exceptions, however, statistics were not available in Western Europe until the mid-1970s. Thus, there was no way of knowing whether a seniority wage curve was uniquely Japanese before that time.

Wage-by-age statistics, albeit rough, did exist before the 1970s. They were painstakingly tested not by proponents of the seniority wage theory but by its critics. Monumental among these efforts was the work of Umemura Mataji.[9] During the late 1930s and early 1940s, the U.S. government compiled statistics on annual income by age as basic data for setting up a public pension system. Because annual income includes income other than wages and is affected by unemployment, it is insufficient evidence of age-wage profiles. Umemura was the first to analyze the U.S. data and to point out that there was no major difference in the age-wage profiles for Japan and the United States. He later compared Japan and Europe, using Western European family expenditure surveys. Although Umemura's work overall is not definitive because of the rough quality of the data, few researchers, sadly, recognize the significance of his efforts.

In the mid-1970s, when reliable statistics on wage structure rivaling those in postwar Japan were compiled in Western Europe, it became possible to compare age-wage profiles with a degree of accuracy. The statistics were published in a European Community (EC) survey: the *Structure of Earnings in Industry*. Unlike the United Nations, the Organization of Economic Cooperation and Development (OECD), and other international organizations, the EC has authority to collect taxes, albeit on a small scale. It therefore compiles valuable statistics that its member countries do not compile. The *Structure of Earnings in Industry* is one of its surveys. It has been compiled every six years since 1966, but the best is the 1972 survey.

The 1972 data are particularly good in three respects. All three result in the EC survey sharing much in common with Japan's more detailed Statistical Survey of Wage Structure. International comparisons rarely offer such similar data.

1. The data are from establishments' ledgers. This is elementary, but nonetheless important. Contrast asking individual workers to respond to questionnaires. Who can remember one's wage exactly? The origin and process by which data has been gathered is crucial.
2. The data are good because they are based on a sampling, not a universal survey. Universal surveys are flawed because many cases, especially the smallest, tend to be missed and because, to deal with the abundance of cases, the survey encompasses

fewer items. The EC survey and Japan's Statistical Survey of Wage Structure are sampling surveys based on large sampling rates of around 1:10.

3. Very small workplaces are eliminated from the samplings. This appears contradictory, but the excessive start-ups and failures of very small businesses make it difficult to establish the working population.

In analyzing the available data, it is important to use what in historical studies is known as data criticism. This avoids the danger of finding numbers in a database to fit any supposition instead of using numbers to test a supposition. Common sense, moreover, must be the rule.

A Comparison between the EC and Japan

Figures 2-1 and 2-2 are based on the data discussed above. The manufacturing industry has been chosen because the EC survey covers secondary industries. Minor discrepancies arise from the EC's survey of establishments with 10 workers or more and the Japanese survey of companies with 10 workers or more. This would be fatal in a comparison of service industries but poses no problem for manufacturing. The seniority wage curve is expressed using 100 for the average wages of men in their early 20s. These figures do not indicate pay levels, and it should not be concluded that wages in Japan are far higher than in Western Europe. Three observations can be made from these figures.

1. Figure 2-1 confirms popular conceptions about wages for production workers. Wages for blue-collar workers in Western Europe rise steeply for young workers but level off or rise only 10 to 15 percent after workers reach their mid-20s. Blue-collar wages at large and even at small and medium-sized companies in Japan are more clearly seniority based than in Western Europe. Trends are consistent in all surveyed European countries, so Italy, the Netherlands, and Belgium are omitted from figure 2-1 for simplicity.

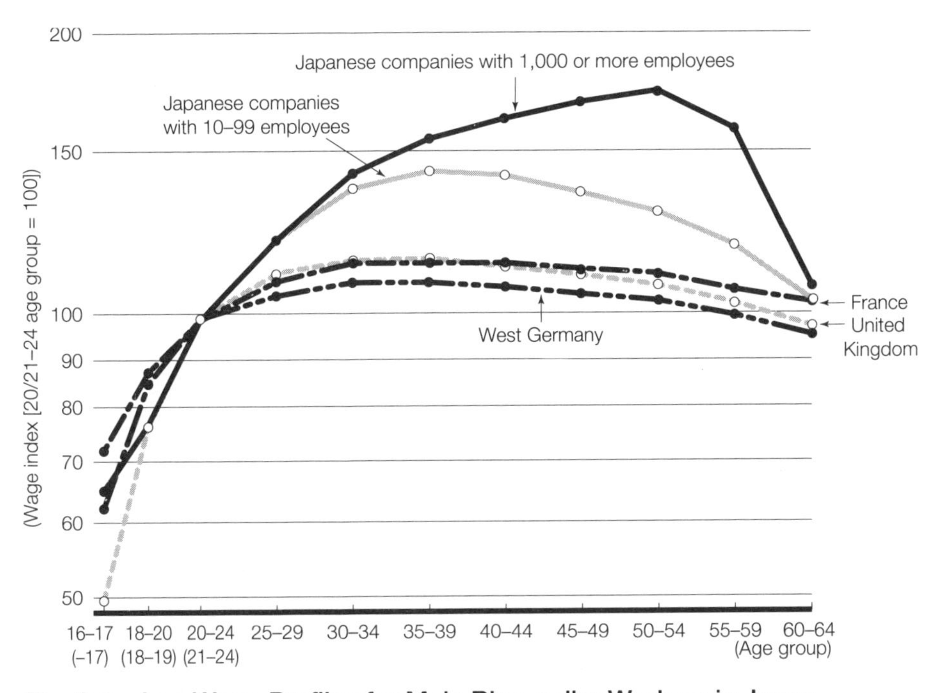

Fig. 2-1. Age-Wage Profiles for Male Blue-collar Workers in Japan and the EC

Sources: Japan, Ministry of Labor, *1976-nen Chingin Kozo Kihon Tokei Chosa* (Statistical Survey of Wage Structure for the Year 1976); EC, *Structure of Earnings in Industry for the Year 1972*, 13 vols., 1975–76; U.K., Department of Employment, *New Earnings Survey*, 1975.

Notes: 1. Distributions are for all industries in the case of the United Kingdom and for manufacturing industries in the case of all other countries.
2. Companies with 10 or more employees in the case of Japan; establishments with 10 or more employees in the case of the EC; companies of all sizes in the case of the United Kingdom.
3. Ages given in parentheses are the age groups for Japan.

2. Older workers in Japan experience a far greater drop in pay than their Western European counterparts. Wages at large Japanese companies decline precipitously after age 50. At small and medium-sized companies, the drop is less steep, but wages start falling while workers are in their 40s. Is this because there is a seniority curve for Japanese wages, or is there some other reason? Figure 2-2, which shows white-collar wages, provides a clue. These findings belie the popular belief that Japanese companies generously protect their middle-aged and older workers through a seniority wage system.

3. The white-collar wages in figure 2-2 reveal an important fact, also contrary to conventional wisdom. Salaries for Western European white-collar workers, including those at small and medium-sized companies, show a seniority curve similiar to, even slightly higher than, the one for blue-collar workers at large Japanese companies according to Japan's seniority wage curve, which for ease of comparison has been copied from figure 2-1. The curves for Western Europe are seniority based; those for the Netherlands, Italy, and France are slightly steeper than that for blue-collar workers at large Japanese companies. Although the curve for West Germany is slightly

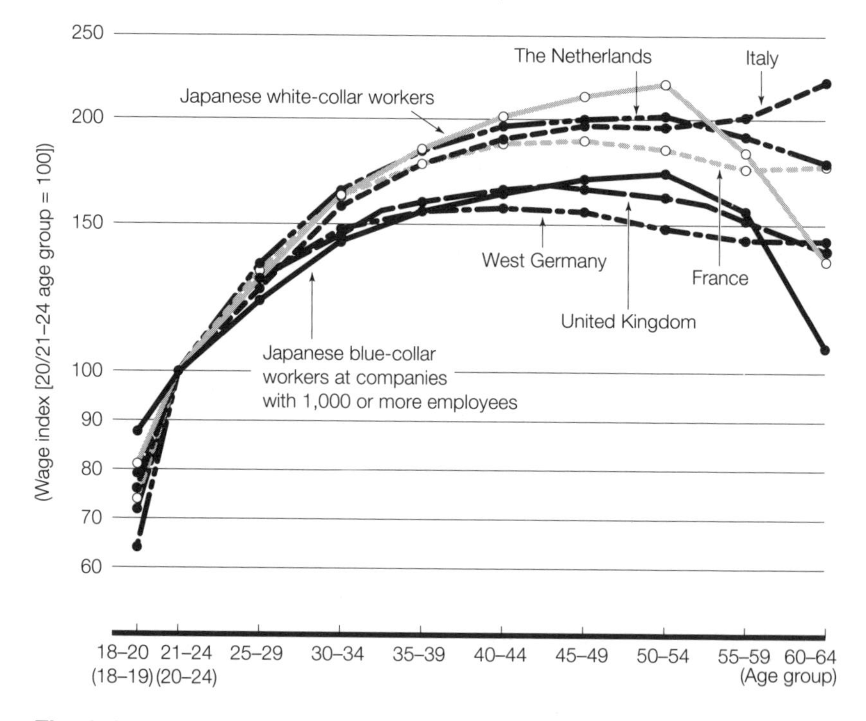

Fig. 2-2. Age-Wage Profiles for Male White-collar Workers in Japan and the EC

Sources: Japan, Ministry of Labor, *1976-nen Chingin Kozo Kihon Tokei Chosa* (Statistical Survey of Wage Structure for the Year 1976); EC, *Structure of Earnings in Industry for the Year 1972*, 13 vols., 1975–76; U.K., Department of Employment, *New Earnings Survey*, 1975.

Notes: 1. Distributions are for all industries in the case of the United Kingdom and for manufacturing industries in the case of all other countries.

2. Companies with 10 or more employees in the case of Japan; establishments with 10 or more employees in the case of the EC; companies of all sizes in the case of the United Kingdom.

3. Ages given in parentheses are the age cohorts for Japan.

> less steep, the peak is 57 percent higher than for white-collar workers in their early 20s, markedly different from the 10 to 15 percent increase for blue-collar workers.[10]

The seniority curve for white-collar workers in Japan could well be called the white-collar wage curve. The wage curve for these workers is higher than the other curves, but not significantly so from those for Italy and the Netherlands. Japan's peak is 120 percent higher than the base level, compared with 100 percent for the Netherlands. Seniority-based profiles are therefore not a distinctive feature of Japanese wages because white-collar workers in Western Europe also have seniority-based profiles. What does seem distinctively Japanese is that the pay of some blue-collar workers in Japan equals that of white-collar workers in Western Europe—for the white collarization of blue-collar workers at large Japanese companies. The content of this white collarization is the main theme of this book. Determining that content requires careful analysis.

Comparing Japanese and U.K. wages by age and length of service, as in figure 2-3, is one way of analyzing Japan's white collarization. The EC-Japan comparison confines itself to observations about wages by age. Although the EC survey studied length of service, it did not tabulate it by age. Fortunately, the United Kingdom collects data on wages by age and length of service. The U.K. data used are from a time when the United Kingdom was not yet part of the EC survey team and conducted its own study. The classifications are less precise than those for Japan, so only the observations in figure 2-3 are possible. Those observations, however, support our previous findings, even when length of service is included.

A Japan-U.S. Comparison

The quality of the data for the United States is not as high as it is for Japan and the EC. Part of the U.S. population census taken since World War II has involved asking various sampling ratios of Americans about their annual incomes for the preceding year. The 1980 and 1960 statistics are the best. But even then the shortcom-

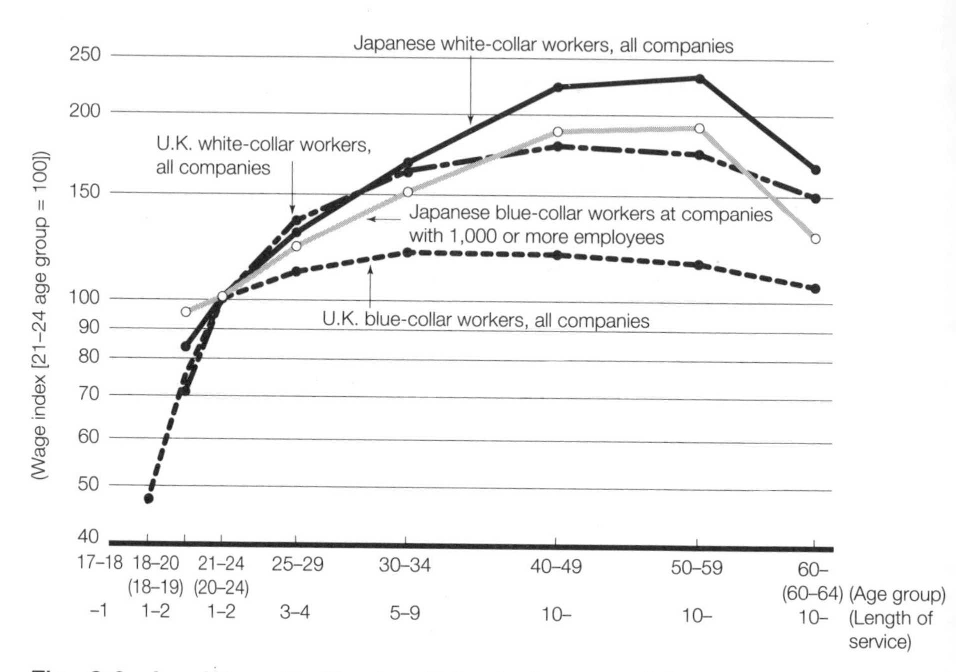

Fig. 2-3. Age-Wage Profiles for Males in Japan and the U.K.

Sources: Japan, Ministry of Labor, *1976-nen Chingin Kozo Kihon Tokei Chosa* (Statistical Survey of Wage Structure for the Year 1976); U.K., Department of Employment, *New Earnings Survey*, 1975.

Notes: 1. Distributions are for all industries in the case of the U.K. and for manufacturing industries in the case of Japan. For Japan, no distinction is made between white-collar and blue-collar workers if we take all industries.

2. Ages given in parentheses are the age groups for Japan.

ings are many. First, since annual income, investment earnings, and sources of earnings other than wages and salaries are included obscure pay profiles arise. Second, any period of unemployment during the year would significantly affect pay profiles, especially for young workers, whose unemployment rates are higher than other age groups. Third, and most importantly, the U.S. census questions individuals in their homes, it does not cull data from documents at their places of work. Despite these shortcomings, this data is valuable for the large sampling it affords.[11]

Figure 2-4 compares age-wage profiles of Japanese and American males by education. U.S. figures are annual income, and Japanese figures are monthly wage earnings. All figures are for 1979. Small differences in distribution by education makes such a comparison feasible. The 25–34 age group—its wage level indicated as 100—is the basis of comparison, not the youngest age group. This avoids the effect of high unemployment among young Americans on the U.S. figures; their annual incomes are likely to underestimate the pay levels of the employed.

Figure 2-4 indicates a characteristic shared by both countries: the higher the education, the steeper the pay profiles. Yet, wage differentials by education are greater in the United States than in Japan. This counters the widely held view that education largely determines social status in Japan.

The first finding in the EC-Japan comparison is that wage profiles for Japanese blue-collar workers are steeper than for their EC counterparts. Although this does not apply fully for the U.S.-Japan comparison, conclusive remarks must be reserved because of insufficient data. In addition, another study, which utilized data from even smaller samples, indicated that the curve is somewhat gentler in the United States than in Japan, such that an educated guess places the United States somewhere between Japan and the EC but closer to Japan in this regard[12]. The second finding in the EC-Japan comparison—the drop in wages for older Japanese

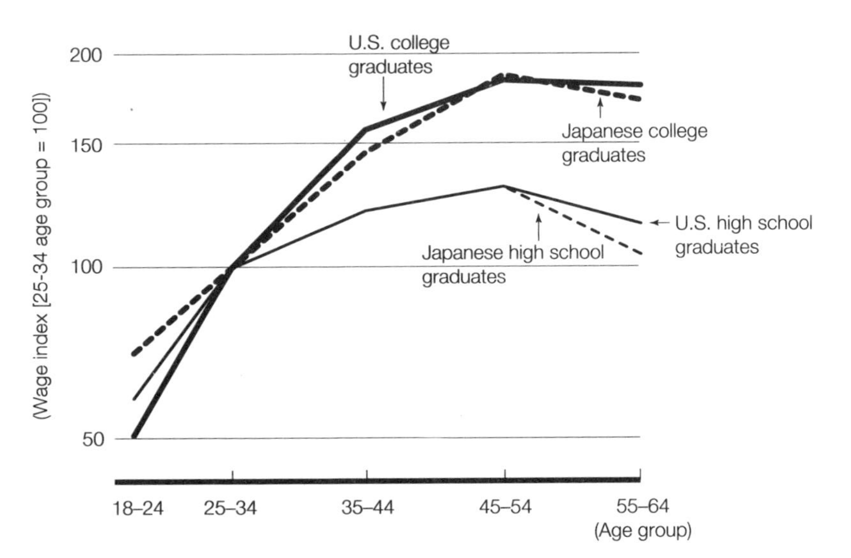

Fig. 2-4. Age-Wage Profiles for Males in Japan and the U.S. (1979)

Sources: Japan, Ministry of Labor, *1979-nen Chingin Kozo Kihon Tokei Chosa* (Statistical Survey of Wage Structure for the Year 1979); U.S., Census of Population, 1980 PC 80-I-DI-A, table 296.

workers—is confirmed in the U.S.-Japan comparison. The drop appears smaller only because the age classification is broader. The third finding, that the pay profiles for white-collar workers are similar in Japan and the EC, holds true for Japan and the United States. The profiles for college graduates, most of whom seem to be white-collar workers, are no different in the two countries.

Conclusions

First, white-collar workers have seniority pay profiles; this is true in Japan, Western Europe, and the United States. Second, a seniority pay profile is not a Japanese feature; seniority pay profiles also exist for white-collar workers in Western Europe. What is distinctive about Japan is the white collarization of blue-collar workers at large companies—some blue-collar workers in Japan earn the same wages as white-collar workers in Western Europe. Third, American blue-collar workers fall somewhere between their counterparts in Japan and Western Europe.

Of these three conclusions, the first has the greatest impact. The share of white-collar workers is steadily increasing worldwide. Thus, wages with a seniority-based curve are also likely to increase. The task of this book is to examine the reasons for this trend.

These three conclusions are each strong counterarguments to prevailing theories. Can late economic development, the technological imports of a late-developing country, or a unique mentality such as group centeredness be used to explain seniority wages for white-collar workers in Western Europe and the United States? The first version of the seniority wage theory, which depicts seniority wages as a kind of cost of living guarantee, runs into problems explaining why seniority wages are more prevalent among highly paid white-collar workers.[13] According to this version, seniority wages should apply to lower-paid workers who have a hard time making ends meet. But in the United States, Japan, and Western Europe, the higher the wages and the education, the steeper the seniority curve.

What factors contribute to the creation of a seniority wage curve? To explore this question, we must analyze length of service, the subject of the next chapter.

Chapter 3 Examining the Permanent Employment Theory

This chapter compares the rate of job attachment among Japanese workers with the rates for Western Europe and the United States. First, it explores the reasons for the white collarization of workers at large Japanese firms, reflected in, among other things, wages. Conventional economics says skill is a major factor in determining wages. No satisfactory method for directly measuring skill exists, however, so some other indicator is needed. The most common way of acquiring skills is on-the-job experience, either within a single company or within several. Good statistics are unavailable for the latter, but experience at one company is measurable by length of service, for which enough good data exist for an international comparison.

Second, this chapter examines the so-called permanent employment theory. It is said that Japan's system is rare in other countries, that it sustains the Japanese economy, and that its mainstay is permanent employment. Textbook permanent employment, however, does not exist in Japan, which has a system of mandatory retirement and even dismissals. The real issue is the extent of long-term employment in Japan compared with other countries. This requires comparisons of numerical data. Fortunately, the EC's *Structure of Earnings in Industry* survey compiles reliable statistics on length of service in Western Europe. To compare job attachment rates, however, what immediately comes to mind are job separation rates.

JOB SEPARATION RATES

Examination by Age

The job separation rate for the United States in 1981 was a high 43 percent. In Japan, it was 16 percent.[1] Japan's low rate is thought to be so removed from the optimal allocation of resources that it inhibits workers from seeking suitable jobs. The assumption that job turnover in the United States indicates an optimal allocation of resources lies behind this thinking. The U.S. mobility rate, though, may be higher than optimal. Japan's 16 percent figure is not low; at that rate, half the workforce quits every three years.

Such conventional thinking is seldom challenged, chiefly because of the view that Japan's workforce is excessively stable. The assumption is that Japanese workers rarely leave their companies; they continue working even at jobs they find unsuitable. This, it is said, deviates from the economic postulate of an optimal allocation of resources. But is the assumption true? In the United States and Japan, looking for the right job occurs while a worker is young. Job separation rates, therefore, must be studied by age.

Statistics on separation rates by age, however, appear to exist only in Japan. Almost every year since 1964, the Japanese government has compiled statistics in its Survey of Employment Mobility (*Koyo Doko Chosa*). Questionnaires are sent out to 15,000 establishments of five persons or more, and 120,000 recruits and 140,000 workers who have left their jobs (figures for 1988) are selected and asked about their situations.

Figure 3-1 relies on the 1970 Survey of Employment Mobility because that survey offers the best data. Subsequent surveys ceased compiling statistics by age, company size, and sex, statistics that are vital to job separation analysis. Figure 3-1 tells a story alien to popular belief.

1. Among full-time male workers at large companies, considered exemplary components of the permanent employment system, the annual job separation rate exceeds 20 percent until workers reach their mid-20s. At 20 percent, all of a company's pre-mid-20s employees would be replaced in five years' time.

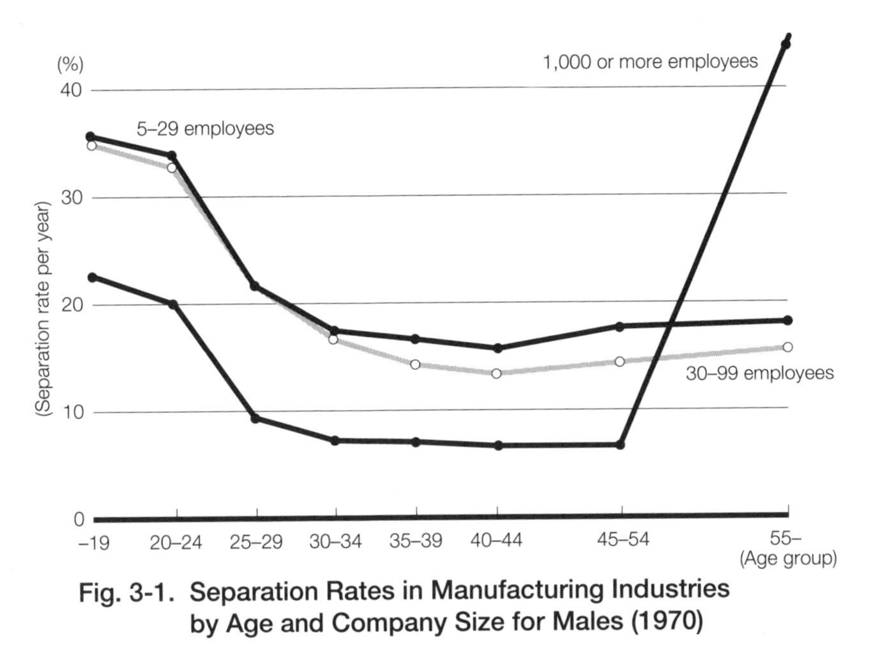

Fig. 3-1. Separation Rates in Manufacturing Industries by Age and Company Size for Males (1970)

Source: Ministry of Labor, *Koyo Doko Chosa* (Survey of Employment Mobility).

All the employees aren't actually replaced, of course, because the rate also includes workers who change jobs more than once. But this makes it impossible to assume that job attachment is so high as to preclude Japanese workers from looking for the right job.[2] Lacking data, we can only guess that the job separation rate among young Americans is higher than among young Japanese. There is no guarantee, however, that America's is the optimal level. Turnover may be too high. Moreover, it indicates that in the United States the burden of layoffs is borne by the youngest workers.

2. After workers reach their mid-20s, separation rates drop to 6 or 7 percent. This is the maximum degree of job attachment in Japan. Workers who quit are not the exception.
3. In large companies, the annual separation rate for workers in their mid-50s and older reaches 45 percent under the mandatory retirement system. Older workers move to other companies when they reach retirement age and as they approach it.

4. Separation rates at small and medium-sized companies are higher than at large firms, as is commonly believed. The rates are 30 to 35 percent for workers below the age of 25, before dropping to around 15 percent. Employees in their mid-20s and older at small and medium-sized companies have more job attachment than young employees at large firms, and separation rates for older workers do not shoot up the way they do at big companies. The retirement system at small and medium-sized companies differs from that at large firms and does not inevitably result in separation. Individual cases reveal that mandatory retirement is not always enforced.

Striking differences exist, therefore, in separation rates depending on worker age and company size. Thus the danger of assumptions. The main reason for these differences can be surmised. The chief factors behind decisions to leave jobs are the costs and benefits involved. The costs of changing jobs are related to the nature and level of a worker's job skills and the expense of moving. The cost to young people of moving is less than for older people. Even the cost of changing jobs is minor because their skill levels are lower. These factors probably account for the high job separation rates among young people worldwide. Likewise, the bigger the company the more its older workers with high skills and the greater their loss if they change occupations; in many cases, a change in companies means a change in job type. Moreover, the larger the company the more likely it is that a part of the workers' skills is specific to the company, again increasing the costs of leaving. These factors are thought to account for the great differences in job separation rates related to worker age and company size.

Fluctuations in the Job Separation Rate

Job separation rates also vary with the passage of time. Change can be cyclical or long term. The separation rate rises in a period of economic prosperity and falls during a recession. Because most job separations are the result of workers quitting of their own volition, they mainly occur when the economy is booming and workers find it easier to find new jobs. Dismissals, though, affect few people amid a strong economy. During a recession, the situation is reversed. Yet, dismissals constitute only a small part of job separations and have little impact on job separation rates. Long-term change results from new ways of thinking or the development of new and different systems. An extension in the payout period for unemployment benefits, for example, permits workers more time to find new jobs.

The mobility rate among Japanese workers is thought to be rapidly rising. The Survey of Employment Mobility, however, indicates that this is a misconception. Although it is true that the job separation rate rose for companies of all sizes in the latter half of the 1980s, it is far from the levels reached in the mid-1970s (figure 3-2). By age group, the separation rate since the late 1970s diminishes somewhat, but this is not indicated in the figure. If the present economic boom and labor shortage continue, the separation rate may approach the levels seen in the early 1970s.

What accounts for the widespread belief that Japan's mobility rate is sharply rising is that most people believe Japan to be a perfect model of permanent employment and jump to conclusions when they see even a few people changing jobs. This misconception again underscores the importance of examining assumptions using reliable data.

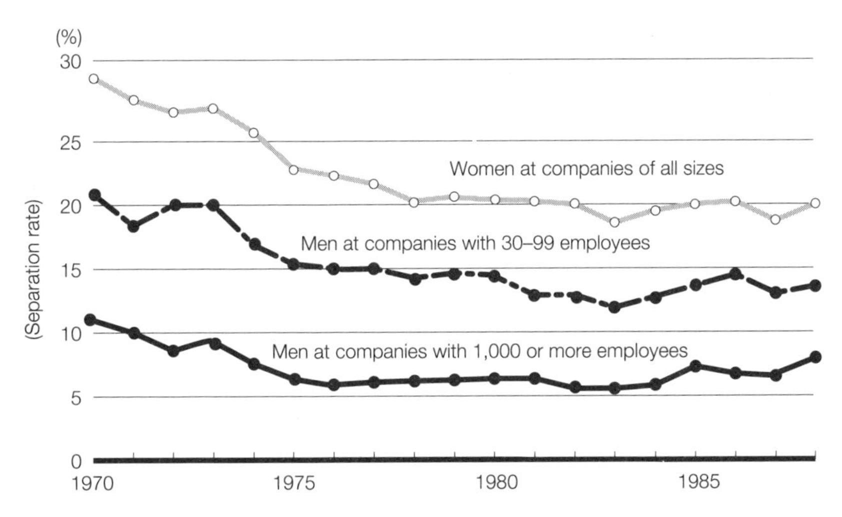

Fig. 3-2. Changes in Separation Rates for All Ages (1970–1988)

Source: Ministry of Labor, *Koyo Doko Chosa* (Survey of Employment Mobility).

INTERNATIONAL COMPARISONS OF JOB TENURE

An EC-Japan Comparison

To compare international rates of job attachment, we must examine workers' length of service; a high separation rate might be the result only of a few mobile individuals changing companies many times while most remain at their jobs. The EC's 1972 *Structure of Earnings in Industry* survey provides reliable statistics on length of service in Western Europe. The EC's statistics, however, are not cross-referenced by age as they are in Japan, but better publicly available statistics may not appear for some time. Figure 3-3 makes use of the *Structure of Earnings in Industry* and its

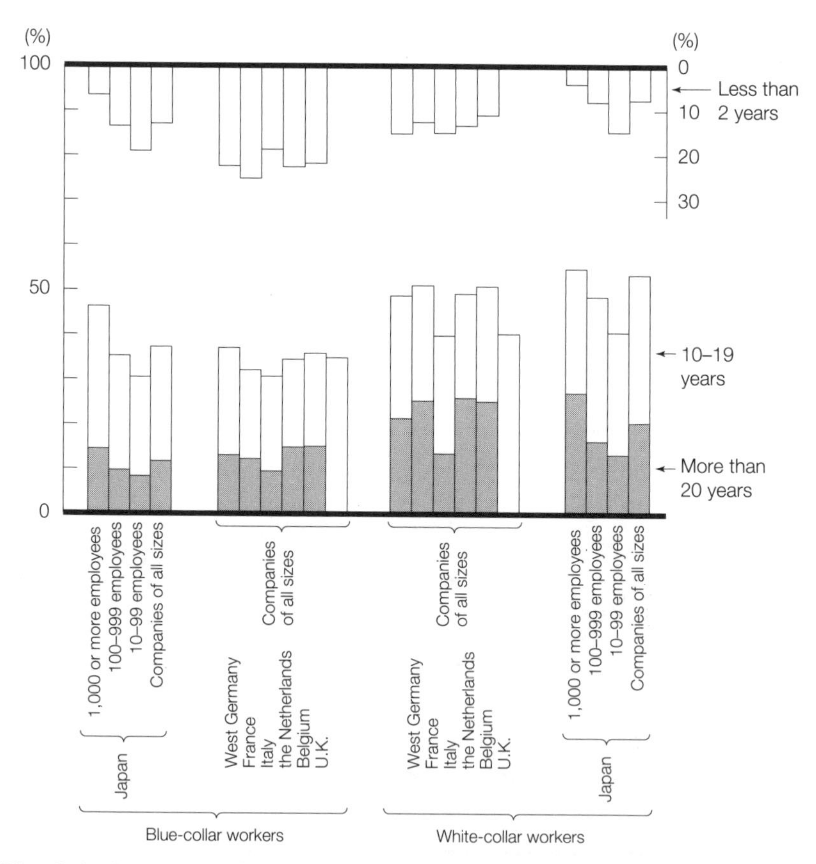

Fig. 3-3. Length of Service among Males in the Manufacturing Industries in Japan and the EC (1972 and 1976)

Sources: Japan, Ministry of Labor, *1976-nen Chingin Kozo Kihon Tokei Chosa* (Statistical Survey of Wage Structure for the Year 1976); EC, *Structure of Earnings in Industry for the Year 1972*, 13 vols., 1975–76; U.K., Department of Employment, *New Earnings Survey*, 1975.

Japanese equivalent, the Statistical Survey of Wage Structure, to compare the EC and Japan. Three things are revealed:

1. Western Europe has a larger group of mobile workers than Japan. Workers with less than two years at their present employment account for slightly more than 12 percent of Japanese blue-collar workers at companies of all sizes, compared with more than 20 percent in Germany, France, the Netherlands, and Belgium. Italy alone falls below the 20 percent mark, but at 18 percent its rate is still higher than Japan's. The same is true for white-collar workers. Thus, we seem to have found a source for the popular view about permanent employment in Japan.
2. Western Europe, however, also has a high proportion of stable workers. Its job attachment rate is about the same as Japan's, even slightly higher. Indeed, the percentages for workers with 20 or more years of service are higher than Japan's in all Western European countries except Italy. Slightly more than 12 percent of workers in Japanese companies of all sizes have 20 or more years of continuous service; percentages for West Germany, France, the Netherlands, and Belgium are higher. The United Kingdom is not included in the 1972 EC survey, and its independent survey does not encompass workers with 20 or more years of service. But that does not mean that no such workers exist there. Although we may not be able to isolate a U.K. group with 20 or more years on the job, the figures for those with 10 or more years of service are not much different from those for other Western European countries or for the averages for all companies in Japan.
3. The white collarization of blue-collar workers at large Japanese companies is confirmed. The focus is on large companies because they are thought to be the locus classicus for permanent employment in Japan. Unfortunately, the EC survey does not classify data by company size, making for an odd comparison between large firms in Japan and the average for all companies in Western Europe.

The proportion of blue-collar workers at large Japanese companies with 10 or more years of service is 47 percent, exceeding proportions for production workers at companies of all sizes in Western Europe. This appears to be the source of the belief in permanent employment at large Japanese companies. But compare this figure with those for white-collar workers in figure 3-3. It has no equal—including for white-collar workers at small and medium-sized companies—in all of Western Europe except the United Kingdom and Italy. In West Germany, 49 percent, and, in France, 50 percent of white-collar workers have 10 or more years of service. Consider workers with 20 or more years of service, and the job attachment rate for blue-collar workers at large Japanese companies falls short of that for white-collar workers at companies of all sizes in Western Europe. Here, too, we detect the white collarization of blue-collar workers at large Japanese companies.

A survey conducted by the EC in 1978 makes it possible to directly compare length of service with 1972 EC findings. Another survey, of service industries, was made in 1974. Figure 3-4 uses

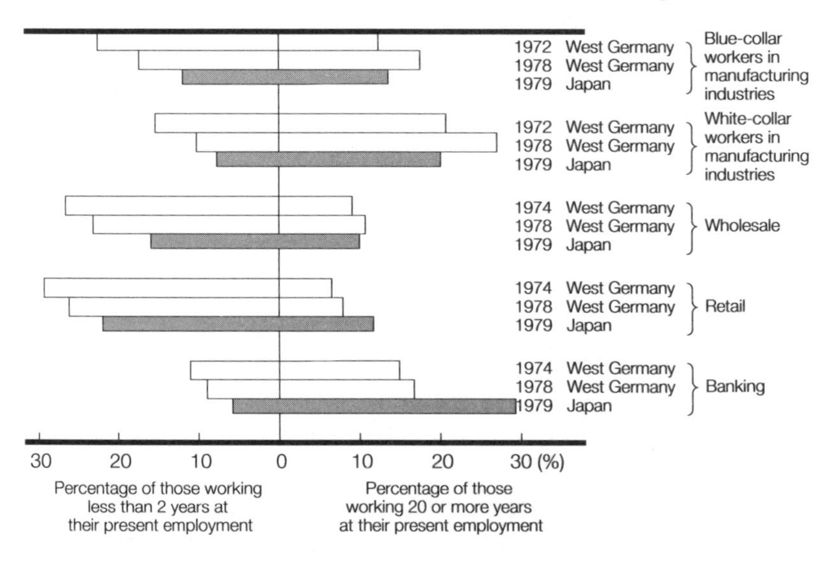

Fig. 3-4. Length of Service in Japan and West Germany among Males (percentage of those with short- and long-term job tenure, 1972, 1974, 1978, and 1979)

Sources: EC, *Structure of Earnings in Industry, 1972, 1974, 1978;* Japan, Ministry of Labor, *1979-nen Chingin Kozo Kihon Tokei Chosa* (Statistical Survey of Wage Structure for the Year 1979).

these surveys to show subsequent changes in Western Europe. Growth in EC membership provides data for many more countries, but West Germany's are cited, as it is representative.

Figure 3-4 shows that job attachment is advanced in West Germany in manufacturing and service industries. The aging population may have some influence, but statistics on length of service by age are unavailable so we cannot confirm this. In manufacturing, West Germany has a higher percentage of white- and blue-collar workers with long-term job tenure than Japan. Only in banking does Japan have greater job attachment.

These are, however, only observations on the length of service for all age groups. The average age of the population was older in Western Europe than in Japan and might have affected the comparison. We cannot confirm this for all EC countries, but statistics that cross-reference length of service with age are available for the United Kingdom.

Figure 3-5 shows that workers in the 18 to 20 age group in the United Kingdom stay with jobs longer than their Japanese counterparts. This does not mean true job attachment, however; it merely indicates that U.K. youths finish school and start work earlier. Consonant with popular belief, older Japanese workers show greater job attachment. The gap narrows, however, until the attachment rate is virtually the same for workers in their 50s then reverses for those in their 60s. Roughly the same can be said for white-collar workers, who are not included in figure 3.5.[3] In figure 3-4, the United Kingdom and Italy have the lowest job attachment rates in Western Europe. Even so, their job attachment rates for middle-aged and older workers is the same as, or exceeds, that of Japan. Such findings show the dangers of regarding Japan as unique.

A Japan-U.S. Comparison

Reliable statistics on length of service are available for the United States, but a direct comparison with other nation's data is difficult because the nature of the U.S. data differs. The U.S. *Job Tenure Survey* gathers data not from establishments but through questionnaires of households nationwide. Individuals are not apt to err,

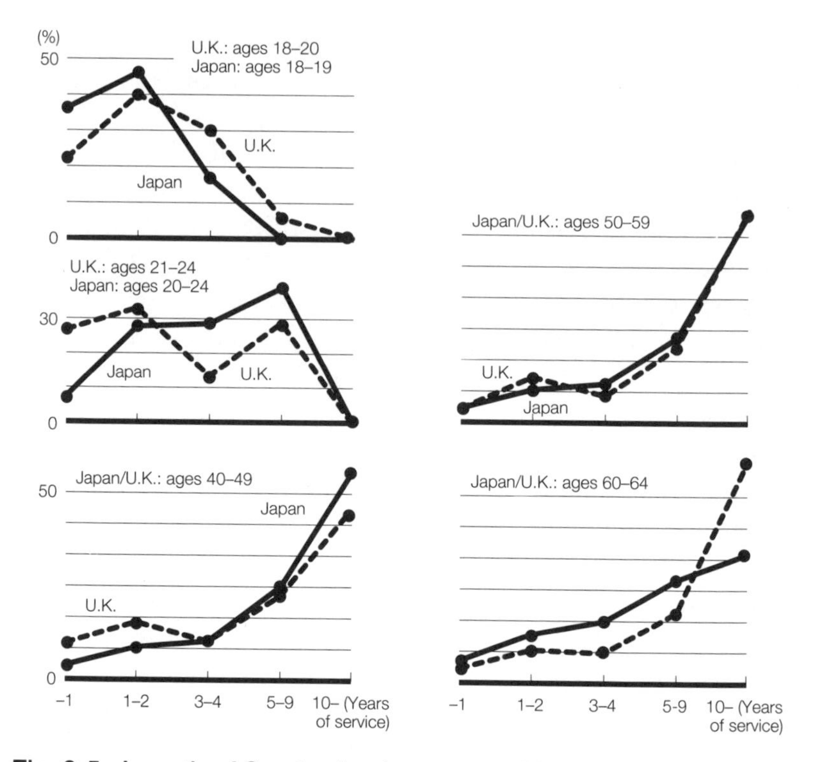

Fig. 3-5. Length of Service by Age among Males in Japan and the U.K. (1975 and 1976; cf. *Understanding Industrial Relations*, pp. 64–65)

Sources: Japan, Ministry of Labor, *1976-nen Chingin Kozo Kihon Tokei Chosa* (Statistical Survey of Wage Structure for the Year 1976); U.K., Department of Employment, *New Earnings Survey*, 1975.
Note: Percentages for the U.K. are for all industries; those for Japan are for manufacturing industries only. When classifying white-collar and blue-collar workers, Japan does not cover all industries.

as with wages, in recalling how long they have worked. The U.S. sample, moreover, is good. This basic, large-scale survey is part of the monthly *Current Population Survey*, which examines official unemployment figures. The *Job Tenure Survey* has been carried out at irregular intervals since 1951, but because of differences in classifications the figure in part based on it, figure 3-6, begins with the 1962 survey. From time to time, this survey asks, How long have you been working for your present company?

In comparing statistics of this nature, it is difficult to use Japan's annual Statistical Survey of Wage Structure. For one thing, the size of the companies surveyed is different. The U.S. *Job Tenure Survey* includes small, single-person companies, whereas Japan's survey targets companies with 10 or more employees. The way the data are gathered also differs: information is from households in one case, from establishments in the other. A direct comparison of qualitatively different material would be unreliable. Only data of similar quality should be compared. The Labor Force Survey (*Rodoryoku Chosa*) is Japan's equivalent of the U.S. *Current Population Survey*, but it never asks about length of service. Japan's Basic Survey of Employment Structure, however, which, like the U.S. *Job Tenure Survey*, is aimed at households, asked about length of service in 1962 and almost every three years since 1974. These two surveys are compared in figure 3-6.

Figure 3-6 shows trends since the 1970s that support the commonly accepted view about long-term employment in Japan and the United States. This does not mean, however, that that view is correct. Quite the contrary, misunderstandings can make facts appear to agree with opinion. In this case, the first misunderstanding concerns the 1960s. The number of mobile workers in the United States in the 1960s was higher than in Japan, but so was the number of immobile workers. Although fewer than 10 percent of all Japanese workers remained less than a year at their jobs, true to popular belief the percentage for American workers was much higher—nearly 25 percent. On the other hand, slightly more American than Japanese workers had 15 or more years of service at one company. These results resemble those for Japan and Western Europe.

The second misunderstanding concerns changes since the 1960s. It is thought that mobility has greatly increased in Japan. However, figure 3-6 and our earlier examination show that, in fact, job attachment has grown, turning opinion into fact. According to figure 3-6, the trend toward job attachment in the United States has leveled off or shifted slightly toward mobility. Trends by age group, however, although not included in figure 3-6, suggest virtually no change in the job attachment rate in the United States, whereas in Japan the rate has greatly increased.

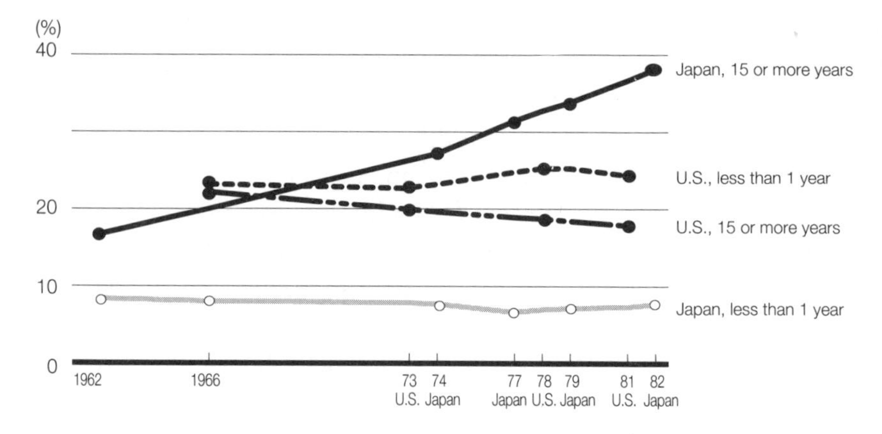

Fig. 3-6. Length of Service in Japan and the U.S. among Males

Sources: U.S., *Job Tenure Survey*; Japan, *Shugyo Kozo Kihon Chosa* (Basic Survey of Employment Structure).
Notes: 1. Figures for the United States are for the gainfully employed; those for Japan are for employees. Because the percentage of self-employed is extremely small in the United States, the use of these figures has a very slight impact on the results.
2. The *Job Tenure Survey* was also conducted in the United States in 1951, 1963, and 1968, but because the categories vary slightly we have chosen the years given above. The survey seems to have been discontinued after 1981. It was published as a Special Labor Force Report, and the main points were included in the Department of Labor's *Monthly Labor Review*.
3. Prior to 1982, the length of service figures in Japan's Basic Survey of Employment Structure are only available for the above dates. It has been continuously compiled since 1982.

Researchers in the United States and Western Europe are becoming aware of the existence of workers who remain in the same companies over the course of their careers. Economics generally pays no attention to these workers because it assumes that all workers will move to companies that offer better pay or working conditions. Fortunately, a few scholars are paying attention, including Robert Hall, author of the 1982 article "The Importance of Lifetime Jobs in the United States."[4] Similar research on OECD member countries has also been published.[5] This research, however, confines itself to indicating the existence of long-term job tenure and does not explore the reasons for it. These reasons are examined separately in several theoretical studies, which are dealt with in chapter 6.

Both Western Europe and North America have large groups of workers with long-term job tenure; long-term employment is not a Japan-specific phenomenon. That conclusion flies in the face of the facts. All countries have mobile and immobile workers, and Western Europe has more of both than Japan. Japan is distinctive in neither the existence of workers with long terms of continuous employment nor the high percentage of such workers. Far more important is that job attachment among blue-collar workers at large Japanese companies equals that for European white-collar workers. This, too, confirms Japan's white collarization.

To discover the nature of this phenomenon and the reasons for it requires delving deeper into the nature of long-term service. We must follow a worker through recruitment, deployment, training, promotion, reassignment, and all the other work-related experiences over a long-term career.

Chapter 4 The Careers of Workers at Large Companies

WORKERS AT LARGE AMERICAN COMPANIES

Source Material

A career is an individual's total work experience. Careers begin with hiring and include deployment, training, promotion, transfer, quitting, and layoff. This chapter first examines careers at large U.S. companies. Without a general idea about careers elsewhere, we risk assuming that Japan's situation is culturally distinct. Conventional wisdom in Japan mistakenly assumes that careers elsewhere are as described in economics texts. In fact, studies that reveal the truth about careers are rare.

The United States is our example because it falls between Japan and Western Europe. As in Japan, workers employed long term at one firm exist in North America and Western Europe. The wage curve for Western European blue-collar workers, however, differs dramatically from that in Japan. American blue-collar wages are midway between those in Japan and Western Europe and appear to have a seniority curve close to Japan's.

Two sources provide U.S. data: U.S. court decisions and interviews.[1] Investigating careers is made difficult by a scarcity of written material. Ultimately, one must speak directly with people. Interviews, though, are not always reliable. Careers are often dependent on unrecorded and obscure shop floor practices; interview findings must be verified with written records.

Fortunately, court decisions first published in the early 1970s under the Civil Rights Act of 1964 occasionally throw light on careers. African Americans initiated a series of lawsuits under

Article 7 of the act, which prohibits discrimination in employment. Lawsuits take time and money, and many Americans supported the cause by working without pay. Suits were filed against almost all stock exchange–listed companies and their unions, and around 1970 the first court decisions appeared.

Promotion—a move to a higher paying job—is most sensitive to discrimination. To determine if discrimination existed, the courts examined promotions among white workers. Some of the decisions thus provide invaluable career documentation—the most detailed from a large steel company. Careers at that company, however, are not representative of careers at all large U.S. firms. Careers manifest themselves in many ways. Although we will touch briefly on careers in other industries, for a more detailed account please refer to the author's 1977 book.[2]

The Labor Pool

A career begins with entry into an occupation as a new recruit. Japanese believe that an American worker enters a company equipped with skills acquired through training at another company or outside the workplace and that U.S. wages are determined by skill. Is this in fact the case?

Blue-collar workers at large U.S. steel companies are hired to do the lowest-grade shop floor jobs, regardless of skills acquired elsewhere. In workplace jargon, they are the labor pool: a grouping of unskilled workers whose jobs are the lowest paying.

U.S. steel companies are famous for having job classification plans since roughly the 1940s. Japanese are wrong to think that such plans imply a pay scale for each job. If that were true, then any wage in Japan determined by job even for low-paid, unskilled workers would also be a job classification plan. Job classification plans at U.S. steel companies are a method of classifying the countless jobs within a big company according to degree of difficulty and of then dividing them into job grades.

At the steel firm cited in the early 1970s' court decisions, jobs were divided into 33 grades. Wages for the top grade were 74 percent higher than for the lowest. Because this classification plan only goes as far as group leaders and does not include foremen, wages rise considerably. (This book defines those in positions of authority who also operate equipment as group leaders and their immediate superiors—supervisors at the lowest level of management who no longer operate equipment—as foremen. These definitions are important in an international comparison.) A classification of 33 job grades up to group leader is an elaborate subdivision to which the periodic increment wage system does not apply. The 3 or 4 lowest grades constitute the labor pool.

Wages for the 33 job grades were determined companywide, but job grade classifications were decided at each establishment. Wages for jobs were not, as is commonly believed in Japan, the same throughout the industry.

Understanding the labor pool is the key to understanding the labor market and industrial relations in America.

1. The pool is an employee's port of entry. Years of experience at another company and skill levels notwithstanding, a steelworker who changes jobs starts out at the new company doing jobs in the pool. No evaluation of skills or assignment to a highly paid job occurs. How firm this practice is can be understood by considering promotion procedures. In Japan, large companies have career conversion coefficients to measure skills acquired at other companies. Identical experience is rated at 80 to 100 percent, different experience is rated at anywhere from 60 to 80 percent, and so forth, but this system is not found at large U.S. steel companies with labor unions. Good jobs go to longer-term factory employees.
2. The pool does low-grade work, such as loading and unloading iron ore and other raw materials.
3. Pool workers receive the lowest pay.
4. The pool bears the brunt of layoffs. In large, unionized U.S. companies, workers are laid off in reverse order to their length of service. A one-fourth decline, for example, in demand for heavy metal sheets means that one in four workers at each job in the sheet rolling shop becomes redundant. If four groups work three shifts, four people must be dismissed, but not necessarily one person from each job. Of the four people assigned

to the highest-paid jobs, the worker with less seniority moves to the job immediately below. Two workers thus become redundant at the second-level job. Of the four workers doing that job, the two with less seniority move down to the third-level job. In this way, workers with the least seniority in a workshop are forced out. They are not laid off; they return to the labor pool, and recently employed workers in the pool are laid off. Pools, moreover, exist for each division: iron making, steelmaking, rolling, etc. Above each pool are 10 or more workshops. If workers become redundant in any workshop, the procedure for laying off pool members is followed. This means the pool is jointly shared. This is the seniority system, a practice confined mostly to the United Kingdom and the United States.

5. Working in the pool is a hard life. Pool members, however, are company employees and union members. In this regard they differ from workers who do similar jobs at large steel companies in Japan. In Japan, such jobs are generally done by workers recently hired by a so-called related firm that, albeit independently owned, undertakes part of a large company's operations. These workers are neither employees of the large company nor members of its labor union. They are members of the related firm and its union and of an industrial union that also includes workers of the large company, such as the Japanese Federation of Iron and Steel Workers' Unions (Tekko Roren). In the United States, pool workers are hired directly by the company. As a result of the power of American unions, pool jobs are listed individually in a local agreement so that management cannot expand the scope of the pool's tasks.

   If American unions are so powerful, why don't they abolish the pool? Simply because the pool is thought to be necessary to protect veteran union members. When markets change and demand shrinks, layoffs are unavoidable. American unions place the burden of layoffs on younger workers to protect workers who have paid their union dues over the years.

6. Pool members are promoted to better jobs if they wait long enough, and promotion is not possible without working in the pool. When a vacancy opens in a workshop above the pool, a pool member moves into the workshop. Never is someone new hired from outside.

   This arrangement is also common in the United Kingdom, as is made clear in Kikuchi Kozo and Ishida Mitsuo's study of the British steel industry.[3] Understanding labor-management relations in the West, specifically in the United States, requires familiarity with the labor pool.

Promotion

For jobs above grade 4, each workshop has a progression line—a job ranking system—up which workers move step by step. Some lines are long, more than 30 grades; some are short, only 7 or 8.

This reflects the broader hiring of large U.S. companies compared with their counterparts in Japan. In Japan, core workers (*honko*)—regular full-time employees—are usually involved only in the operation of key workshops of key divisions. Other jobs are left to workers from related firms. Large Japanese companies, therefore, directly hire fewer employees than comparably sized U.S. firms. A progression line in a U.S. workshop equivalent to a key Japanese workshop with regular workers may have 30 job grades and wage differentials as great as in Japan. U.S. workshops equivalent to Japanese workshops with workers from related firms have shallower progression lines and smaller wage increments.

In the United States, progression lines differ between even plants and companies in the same industry. Decisions about which jobs to include in which line are left to the discretion of each plant. This accounts partly for enterprise-specific skills, a topic for later discussion.

For people working on shop floors, promotion to upper-grade jobs is extremely important. Lacking periodic pay raises, they have no other way of increasing their salaries. But what are the promotion procedures? In the United States, agreements between unions and companies are very detailed, not industrywide, mostly at companies or plants. They usually contain the clause: "Ability to perform the work and fitness being relatively equal, seniority shall govern." This appears to confirm the view in Japan that in the West ability comes first, followed by fitness and then seniority.

Interview-based case studies indicate otherwise. Of four people assigned to jobs below a vacancy on a progression line, the person with as little as one day of seniority is almost automatically promoted. The court decisions mentioned earlier substantiate this: "Under the contract, seniority [i.e., length of service] is the determining factor only where ability to perform the work and relative fitness of the competing employees are relatively equal. In practice, most vacancies are filled in accordance with the seniority factor."

Promotion occurs strictly in order of seniority within the progression line. This is called strict seniority, something the author has never seen in Japan, with its loose sense of seniority. Strict seniority is firmly established in the United States; regardless of experience, a new hire is not assigned a high position on the progression line.

The seniority system has two results. First, the system is so powerful that even when wages are determined by jobs they show a splendid seniority-based curve. Second, careers are narrower in the United States than in Japan. Since a progression line is confined to a single workshop, it is difficult for a worker to move to another shop. At best, a senior worker among candidates for a job in another workshop could move to the lowest-ranking job in that other shop. The considerable loss involved is unlikely to encourage a change of jobs. Promotion from the pool is limited to vacancies in positions at the lowest rung of a progression line. Narrowness of career is a crucial point in a comparison between the United States and Japan.

Dismissal

Given the U.S. system, job changes happen when a worker is still young. Though statistics on job changes by age are unavailable in the United States, this seems a reasonable surmise. Changing jobs is not the only reason for leaving a company, of course; a worker may also be dismissed. Dismissal is an important topic dealt with fully in a later chapter. Here, we will take a glance at dismissal procedures using a case study.

Workers are dismissed in reverse order of seniority—last in, first out—beginning with those in the labor pool. Unions do not interfere because rehiring is in order of seniority. When economic conditions improve and the company resumes hiring, preference goes to dismissed workers. Dismissals are thus termed layoffs in the United States. In Japan, layoffs are often interpreted as temporary dismissal or temporary release, but reality differs. Although rehiring in the United States is based on seniority when it happens, there is no guarantee that it will happen. If economic conditions do not improve, the worker remains laid off. A layoff, therefore, must be considered a dismissal.[4]

When rehiring based on length of service, suppose, for example, that 10 workers have been laid off and that only 5 will be rehired. Of the 10, the 5 with the longest service records are told to apply to the personnel department by a certain date if they wish to be rehired. Most workers do; company benefits, pensions, and promotions are dependent on length of service. Seniority rights in rehiring do not continue down the job ladder indefinitely. Generally, priority is given to workers who have worked for the company for a certain number of years. For a worker with long years of service, rehiring is practically guaranteed before mandatory retirement generally at age 70 according to the Mandatory Retirement Act of 1978, though many workers retire with pensions before 70.

General Practices in the United States

The discussion above is confined to the practices at large U.S. steel companies. Although some aspects are unique to the process industry, the main points are shared by all industries.

1. That skill formation is based on long-term experience is a common point. Skill formation through work is referred to as OJT—on-the-job training. Japanese believe that American workers acquire skills by moving from company to company

or by studying at training centers outside companies. This requires discussion.

Skill formation takes various forms depending on the industry. Industries can be roughly divided into two types: the process industry and the machine industry. Process industries like steel have a labor pool, above which extend progression lines. Machine industries have neither a labor pool nor progression lines, their wage scale is divided into ranks, with several jobs per rank. The similarity between the two industries is that workers advance to higher-paying jobs on the basis of length of service.

2. The importance of length of service and seniority rights is striking. These features are unique to the United States and the United Kingdom. The vast differences within Europe and North America must be understood, as must how at variance with reality is the common perception that it is only Japan that values length of service.

STARTING A CAREER

Many Japanese Workers Change Jobs

In Japan, the prevailing view is that new employees are primarily recent graduates but that this trend is breaking down. It is also believed that new employees are not hired for their skills or ability to do a particular job but are asked to show common sense and basic competency in the Japanese language. Is this in fact true?

Figure 4-1 was compiled from Japan's Survey of Employment Mobility. Each year, this survey asks a large sampling of entry-level workers about their careers. It notes what percentage of the new recruits for the year are recent graduates and what percentage are workers from other companies.

Figure 4-1 shows that, contrary to popular belief, even among male workers at large companies job changers outnumber recent graduates and are an overwhelming majority at small and medium-sized companies. Careful examination of the data, however, shows the percentage of recent graduates at large companies rises slightly. The reasons for this are somewhat complicated.

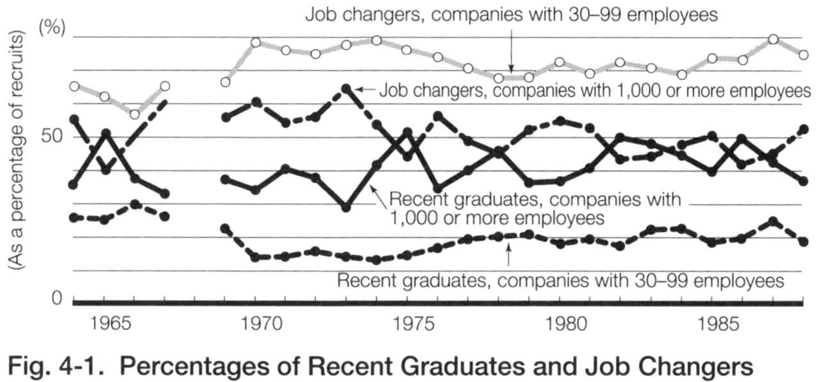

Fig. 4-1. Percentages of Recent Graduates and Job Changers among Male Recruits

Source: Ministry of Labor, *Koyo Doko Chosa* (Survey of Employment Mobility).

The target group for the Survey of Employment Mobility is regular workers (*joyo rodosha*). This appears suitable for the purpose. In fact, because the target workers of this study are seniority wage earners at large companies it is instructive to consider regular workers. The regular workers category in this and other government surveys, though, is for statistical purposes and is, therefore, defined more broadly than would normally be the case. For statistical purposes, the target group includes both those who are employed, with no stipulations of length of time, and those who have worked more than 18 days in the two-month period prior to the survey date. As a result, the group includes not only regular company workers but also some temporary or casual workers. These two categories are described in the Survey of Employment Mobility as "regular workers that are nominally regular" and "regular workers that are nominally temporary or casual workers." No distinction is made between new graduates and job changers. Guessing from the percentages for each category, new graduates and job changers each probably account for roughly half those hired as regular full-time employees. No conspicuous time-series trends can be confirmed. Compared with the 1970s, the number of job changers cannot be said to have increased recently.

Trainees and Temporary Workers

Observations of hiring practices indicate that the data in figure 4-1 are accurate. Unfortunately, written documentation describing such practices is scarce, so this discussion relies on interviews the author conducted during the late 1950s and early 1960s in the Tokyo-Yokohama industrial belt. At that time, the majority of those hired by large companies were job changers. Two hiring routes existed: for trainees, a very select group of recent graduates, and for temporary workers, the vast majority.

Trainees were selected from among promising junior high school graduates through grueling entrance examinations, then trained over three to four years. Training comprised ordinary high school subjects for most of the workday until the final year, when trainees' work responsibilities increased and they entered the workshop. These workers were the heart of the workshop and the main source of foremen and labor union leaders.

This was the route aspired to by young people who desired to learn but who were from families that were financially unable to give them an advanced education. Capable and intelligent, these young workers rebelled against the bureaucratic system in large companies that promoted only advanced degree holders to management positions in the head office. Many became able union leaders. Until the 1970s, most union leaders in well-established companies are thought to have emerged from the trainee system. Today, the supply of such people has dried up, and Japanese unions have a hard time developing leaders. Only a small number of recruits, however, became trainees. Most were hired as temporary workers.

It is wrong to regard the temporary worker system as a form of temporary employment. It was, instead, a kind of recruitment process. Companies selected core employees from among temporary workers. Consequently, large firms received numerous applications from young people, including workers at small and medium-sized companies and recent high school graduates. Anyone fulfilling the sole requirement of being in their early 20s could apply. Getting hired was not difficult, and the recruit immediately started work in the workshop. Foremen judged recruits' work and recommended who could take the examination to become a core employee. Those not accepted as core employees within two or three years of hiring either went back to work for small and medium-sized companies or became temporary workers at other large companies. The number of people involved suggests that this was the major route to becoming a core employee. Many foremen emerged from this system.

From management's perspective, there is no more efficient method of hiring than this. Crucial to hiring is information about the quality of potential employees. The best way to determine if a worker is inclined to absenteeism or is diligent and serious is observation over an extended period, not a two- or three-hour interview. The temporary worker system allows the company to observe a worker over a period of one or two years.

This advantageous system was abandoned because of Japan's labor shortage. Even large companies were unable to attract temporary workers. Between the end of the 1960s and the beginning of the 1970s, the temporary worker system became a probationary employment system.[5] When the labor shortage disappeared after the energy crisis, the temporary worker system was not revived. Instead, part-time workers increased dramatically.

Formerly, therefore, young Japanese workers had a fair degree of mobility. The temporary worker system, which encouraged mobility, disappeared, however, amid an extreme shortage of labor, and another system took its place. Conventional wisdom overlooks this in its belief that workers used to be permanently attached to their jobs and then all at once became mobile.

Moreover, this discussion applied only to blue-collar workers. No distinction is made in figure 4-1, but it is reasonable to surmise that even white-collar workers were not always immobile. College graduates at large companies probably were, but the percentage of college graduates among white-collar workers was less previously than now, and some of the high school graduates then correspond to college graduates today. Considering only college graduates, it is natural that today's workers are more mobile.

The employee selection process requires the following observation. A look at careers in large U.S. steel companies showed that recruits were not expected to have prior skills in steelmaking. Skills were acquired on-the-job, and not only for one job. Workers were to master a whole series of jobs in a progression line. The same is true in a Japanese company. Thus, there is something wrong with hiring on the basis of ability to do a particular job. What needs scrutiny is the potential employee's ability to acquire skills. A person's basic competency in such areas as language skills is probably an important indicator of this. The situation in Japan thus may not be so bad.

BROAD OJT

Non-Mass-Production Workshops

Japan is thought unique in relying on on-the-job training (OJT). Yet, OJT is also common in large U.S. steel companies. As in Japan, the training U.S. steelworkers receive before entering a company's workshop is brief. Japanese trainees once had long periods—three to four years—of off-the-job training, but that system has disappeared. Today, a young worker hired with virtually no job knowledge receives about one or two weeks of off-the-job training before assignment to a workshop. This training usually entails a general introduction to the company and the products it makes. Longer training periods of up to a year can be found, but are limited to specific workshops, such as maintenance. Most blue-collar workers enter workshops without skills and depend on shop OJT for skill formation. What kind of OJT do they receive? What sort of skills are formed? How does Japan's system differ from the United States'?

A workshop—defined here as a group of workers and a foreman—usually has from 15 to 30 workstations at which workers acquire experience. Workstation rotation can be regular, with workers spending equal time at each position; irregular; or confined to select stations. Rotation, moreover, is distinguished as (a) broad in scope; (b) at least superficially egalitarian; and (c) based on shop floor practices. Note the following examples.[6]

The switchboard assembly division of a heavy electric machinery plant with 1,500 employees provides examples of non-mass-production workshops. The company's switchboards are custom-made in three sizes—small, medium, and large—one assembly workshop per size. Examination reveals that each shop produces its switchboards in varying sizes and specifications. The medium-sized switchboard shop, for example, has 30 or so workers divided into seven groups, each comprising experienced and inexperienced workers, each responsible for a size and specification. Once a year, the groups are disbanded, and workers are reassigned to other groups. Over seven years, workers experience assembling all types of medium-sized switchboards.

A large percentage of these workers, moreover, trade places with workers in the workshops that make large and small switchboards. Consequently, over the long term many workers can assemble almost all the company's switchboards. Broad experience proves valuable when workers must go abroad to adjust switchboards installed overseas.

Workshops in the Process Industry

An example of a workshop from the process industry is a fermentation workshop. This survey was conducted in the early 1980s when a decline in workers had reduced the shop to a mere 10 men. They were divided into five 2-man groups. Four groups worked in three shifts in the control room, regulating fermentation in the mammoth tanks. The fifth group maintained the equipment. Twice during the day shift, morning and afternoon, it inspected the equipment, immediately repairing defects.

Every two months, the five groups changed assignments. Workers eventually undertook every job, exemplifying egalitarian rotation. Whereas many of the maintenance jobs would in other countries be done by maintenance specialists, the Japanese plant, which also had maintenance workers, utilized the broad experience of fermentation workshop employees when malfunctions were not too serious. The workshop had done no hiring for several years, so its workers were veterans. Presumably, the training of newcomers would occur as part of a 2-man team.

A look at a large Japanese steel mill contrasts with the earlier U.S. example. The blast furnace charging workshop in the

Japanese mill has 10 workstations where 10 or so workers spend a half day each, moving equally among all 10 positions in, apparently, another example of egalitarian rotation. The group leader oversees operations and sometimes substitutes for an absent worker. This is unlike the U.S. steel mill, where jobs are seniority based, although there is little difference between the two countries in the difficulty of the jobs. New workers are also assigned to the rotation, something that, at a glance, seems unfeasible. However, a new worker is looked after by an experienced worker assigned to a workstation next to the new worker's to provide instruction on the new worker's workstation tasks. Experienced workers thus undertake two jobs, three including instruction. This would be impossible if workers were paid by the job. Who would undertake such responsibility without pay? If Japanese blue-collar workers did not receive incremental pay increases and did not get merit ratings for training newcomers, this system could not be implemented.

Breadth of scope manifests itself as follows. The Japanese mill has three blast furnaces overseen by a group each. Every year, several members of each group trade places. Blast furnaces are so enormous that even large companies cannot build more than one at a time. Subsequent furnaces, therefore, vary in size and degree of mechanization, automation, and computerization. By moving to different furnaces, workers gain experience with all the mills' equipment. Skills acquired at one blast furnace are applicable at others, but job rotation facilitates a broader scope of skills. And when the groups responsible for the three blast furnaces trade places in their entirety, workers experience close to 40 different job assignments. Statistics are unavailable, but this experience is probably wider than at similar workshops in the United States.[7]

A dependence on workshop practices is revealed insofar as worker rotation has no basis in an agreement between management and labor union. Rotation is neither negotiated by either side nor does it seem to be a management decision. Some interviewed union members say that the decision is the foreman's and group leaders'; others say that it is based on discussions within work-

Table 4-1 Rotation Practices within a Workshop

	Yawata	Hikari	Hirohata	Sakai	Nagoya	Kimitsu	Kamaishi	Muroran
Blast furnace charging	—[e]		○	—	◎[a]	○[b]	◎	◎
Sintering	×[d]		○	—	△[c]	○	◎	◎
Coke oven operations	×		△		◎		△	◎
Converter operations	△	○	—	△	◎	—	○	△
Steel pouring	△		◎	△	◎	—	×	○
Reheating furnace, hot strip mill	△		△	△	△	△		○
Hot strip finishing mill	△		○	△	△	○		◎
Plate finishing mill			○		◎			
Crane operations			—	◎		—	◎	—
Cold strip mill operations	×		×		△	△		
Pipe mill operation		△						
Galvanizing	×		△		△			
Boiler engine room	△	△	○	△	◎	—	—	—
Instrumental analysis		△		—		△	—	—
Locomotive operation	○		○		◎		○	—

Source: Koike Kazuo, *Shokuba no Rodokumiai to Sanka—Roshikankei no Nichibei Hikaku* (A Comparative Study of Industrial Relations on the Shop Floor in the United States and Japan) (Tokyo: Toyo Keizai Shinposha, 1977), p.178.

[a]Regular rotation to all positions in the workshop.

[b]Rotation to all positions in the workshop on an irregular basis.

[c]Partial rotation.

[d]No rotation.

[e]No reference to rotation.

shops. In either case, it is a workshop practice. The only published documentation, see table 4-1, corroborates this.

Table 4-1, is not another case study. It is a survey of shop floor job assignments conducted by labor unions to align job classification plans at two large steel companies that had merged. The survey covers 79 workshops of 15 occupational groups in the companies' eight plants. Each workshop was asked whether it had (a) complete and regular rotation; (b) complete rotation covering all jobs in the workshop; (c) partial rotation; or (d) no rotation. Of the companies' seven blast furnace charging workshops, three have regular rotation and two have complete rotation, proving that the findings of the previous case study are unexceptional. Of 79 workshops, 31 have regular or complete rotation, further indicating that the case study findings, though not those of the majority, are unexceptional. Most notable is the diversity of response. Within the same establishment, practices differ by shop. It cannot be said that each establishment has its own policy on job rotation. Nor can it be said that technology is the determining factor; rotation practices differ from mill to mill, even for the same occupations. Nonetheless, this does not contradict the view that job rotation is determined by workshop practices.

Mass-Production Workshops

Automobile assembly is obvious mass production. The first example from two companies is an assembly line workshop with 20 to 30 positions. Approximately every three months, workers change positions. A job matrix lists worker's names and the jobs they have experienced. The number of positions a worker masters rises with length of service. In the second example, rotation is irregular. Group leaders are those with experience in most of the major jobs. Here, too, rotation plays an important role. Seasonal and contract workers also work on this plant's assembly line. What distinguishes them from core employees is rotation practices. Core employees experience most of the job assignments; seasonal workers do not rotate. Core employees can trade places at will; contract workers cannot.

Japan's rotation practices take many forms but share the following characteristics:

1. Rotation is broad in scope. It encompasses the major jobs in individual workshops and occasionally extends to related workshops. This is broader than in the United States, where workers remain in a single workshop or part of it. Core workers in Japanese car plants are equivalent to relief or utility workers in U.S. car plants. Make no mistake, however: Japanese workers move only between closely related workshops, not to any workshop at all as is often claimed. Were the latter true, a worker would be unable to make use of acquired skills. A Japanese worker only moves where acquired skills can be applied and enriched. Movement elsewhere is disadvantageous and a subject of intense union negotiation regarding job transfers.

2. Job assignment is on a more or less egalitarian basis. Japan is often said to value seniority, but comparisons with the United States reveal otherwise. In that country, job assignments are clearly more seniority based.
3. The range and methods of job rotation depend on workshop practices and not on clear management policy. They seem, instead, to be based on the autonomy of the workshop.

Transfer

In addition to promotions, a career may involve such disadvantageous moves as a transfer. Transfers are disadvantageous whether they occur within a plant to a workshop that does different work or to another plant, which may also require a change in residence. Statistics are available only for the latter, but despite the absence of percentages it is known that for production workers transfer within companies is more common.[8]

The disadvantage of a transfer to an unrelated workshop within a plant is that workers can no longer use acquired skills. They must develop new and different skills. This can be devastating. In Japan, such transfers nevertheless occur not because Japanese labor unions are especially weak, but, rather, to prevent dismissals. When business expands in one division and declines in another, workers are transferred from the latter to the former to avoid dismissals amid a need for workers elsewhere in the firm.

That transferred workers cannot use their acquired skills and must, instead, cultivate new skills is a loss not only for the workers but also for the company. To minimize the loss, in most cases the transfer is limited to three to six months. This is referred to as a temporary transfer (*oen*). During a recession, temporary transfer is insufficient to avoid dismissals.

Permanent transfers, for which labor unions negotiate terms in great detail, also occur. Conditions for retraining in new workshops and for wage guarantees are minutely prescribed. All companies guarantee for a certain period of time the wages of employees who are transferred, but unions press to lengthen the period of the guarantee and to maintain, say for three years, the salary and merit ratings that workers had in their former workshops.

Japanese blue-collar wages are based on merit ratings. Workers who move to new workshops for which they possess no skills inevitably receive low ratings. Salaries may hold under temporary guarantees, but they decline when merit ratings occur after the period expires. Unions, therefore, insist that salaries be guaranteed for longer periods.

What is not clear in Japan is who is subject to transfer. Japan does not have America's seniority system, which places the burden on workers with the shortest length of service. Other than this, Japanese labor unions do a good job of negotiating, especially amid the intensity of negotiating interplant transfers, which entail the disadvantages of a change of occupation and, possibly, of residence.

After the energy crisis, transfers, especially of white-collar workers, are thought to have been excessive in Japan. Transfers occurred inside companies and within groups of companies without much regard for the work involved. This latter practice, known as transfers within groups of companies, apparently arose because Japanese white-collar workers are not thought to have many professional skills.[9] In chapter 11, however, we determine that most white-collar workers in Japan do have professional expertise. Transfers must keep this expertise in mind or the resultant loss to company and employee will be excessive.

Other stages in a career are dismissal and retirement; they will be addressed in another chapter. This chapter draws attention to the formation of job skills and to the importance of on-the-job training in this process. But what is the nature of the skills formed? A summation of the comparison of on-the-job training in the United States and Japan provides a clue.

Summing-up

Popular perception suggests that skill formation in Japan occurs in the company during lengthy on-the-job training, whereas in the United States workers receive formal training outside the company and move from firm to firm in a kind of training-based meritocracy. Were this true, then the result—a meritocracy being bested by a deviant skill formation system—is strange. The Japan-is-different argument agrees with popular perception.

A comparison of careers at large companies in the two countries defies popular belief. Workers' skills in both countries derive from lengthy, in-house on-the-job training. No training center in either nation teaches workers to operate blast furnaces or assemble automobiles. No substitute exists for first-hand experience in a workshop. The two countries differ, however, in breadth of experience. Japanese workers broaden their experience by moving among related workshops. American workers experience the major positions in only a single workshop or part of it. What is the significance of this difference? What effect has it on skills? The next chapter addresses these questions.

Chapter 5 Intellectual Skills

DEALING WITH CHANGES AND PROBLEMS

Usual and Unusual Operations

What sort of skills result from broader work experience than in the United States? The answer: intellectual skills, skills that account for the efficiency of the Japanese workplace.[1]

Workshop jobs include usual and unusual operations. Work on a mass-production assembly line does not appear to be dependent on skills and seems entirely repetitive. Only speed seems to affect efficiency. This, however, is usual operation. Observe the line closely, and you see frequent changes and problems. Dealing with these situations constitutes unusual operations.

Change occurs in five areas: product mix, output, new products, production methods, and workforce composition. It is most frequent in product mix, output, and workforce composition.

Changes to product mix are easily observed. Operations on a production line may seem repetitive, but in as little as half a day a wide variety of products flow down a line. Include minor variations, and this can amount to dozens of product types. A varied product mix results from diversifying consumer demand. A production line per product is too costly, so workers on a single line must make a variety of products in different quantities on any given day to meet demand.

To accommodate diverse products, workers must replace tools and jigs in a process that alters the previous setup. Skills, not mere speed, are required. Skillful setup results in defect-free products and speeds production by avoiding slowdowns due to defective products. Skills affect efficiency.

The ability to do most of the jobs in the workshop is also important in handling changes in product mix. On an automobile assembly line, procedures differ depending on whether four-door or two-door models of even the same car predominate. Workers with limited experience can maintain line speed with two-door models, but when four-door cars increase in number they must yield certain jobs to experienced workers. Experienced workers capable of many jobs are essential.

Versatility is necessary, too, when output changes. Output can be increased by speeding up the assembly line. But this entails veteran workers, who can do a variety of jobs, taking over certain jobs from less-experienced workers.

Changes in workforce composition also call for versatile veterans. Workers take holidays and call in sick. Others must do their jobs. The more workers capable of a variety of jobs, the lower the costs. Shifts in the proportion of experienced to inexperienced workers likewise demand experience. Large Japanese companies have many inexperienced workers at the beginning of their fiscal years, but not at year-end. An abundance of veteran workers who can teach new employees boosts efficiency. Knowing a job sufficiently to teach others is thus a valuable skill.

Production methods, meanwhile, are surprisingly subject to change. The automobile industry remodels cars every four years. Manufacturers must therefore reorganize parts of their production lines. New products necessitate new production methods. An ability to improve and fine-tune production methods is extremely important. A new line calls for new tools and jigs—designed by specialists. But their suitability is unproven until line workers start using the new equipment. Having veteran workers who can suggest improvements raises efficiency. This is among the most sophisticated forms of dealing with change, attainable only if workers have a thorough knowledge of production methods and related machinery. Only the unusual operation of problem solving exceeds this level of sophistication.

Dealing with Problems

All workshops confront problems—mechanical failures, defective products, the list is endless. Advances in quality control notwithstanding, defective products—the most obvious problem—are always a possibility. Three steps deal with defective products:

Step 1. Detect defective products immediately. This contributes to efficiency by eliminating waste and by cutting down on later work.

Step 2. Diagnose the cause of the defect. This most important step increases efficiency by preventing recurrences. It entails, however, on-the-spot, mid-operation diagnosis, not laboratory tests of equipment. If machine operators lack aptitude for such diagnosis, their machines will continue to produce defective products. Stopping machines is untenable because it halts production. In either case, the impact on efficiency is enormous.

Step 3. Fix the cause of the defect. Efficiency is greatly enhanced if production workers can make most repairs themselves without recourse to maintenance personnel. Major repairs, though, are left to specialists.

The first step is impossible if workers lack experience with unusual operations. And the two crucial subsequent steps require a knowledge of production and production machinery. Defects and malfunctions occur when something goes wrong with the machinery. Diagnosing and fixing the cause is difficult without this knowledge. Quality control (QC) circles often claim to identify causes solely through statistical inference. This might work once or twice, but not indefinitely unless members of the QC circle have a basic knowledge of machinery. Unlike QC, diagnostic and repair work is an everyday job. People are often so dazzled by the reputation of QC circles that they overlook important but lower-profile everyday skills.

These are rightly called intellectual skills. A knowledge of production and production machinery has much in common with the expertise of engineers. The efficiency of the Japanese workplace is founded on intellectual skills— large Japanese companies are highly efficient because many of their production workers possess intellectual skills. All theories about company loyalty aside, efficiency has a technological basis.

This explains white collarization and why the wage curve for blue-collar production workers at large Japanese companies is as seniority based as for white-collar workers in Western Europe. The wage curves are similar because the basic skills expected of Japanese blue-collar workers are similar to those of white-collar workers. A look at how these intellectual skills are formed will clarify this.

SEPARATED SYSTEMS VERSUS INTEGRATED SYSTEMS

Is Standardization Efficient?

Why are production workers required to possess such complicated skills? Can unusual operations be standardized? If not, why not employ engineers and other specialists to deal with unusual operations?

Standardization would be inefficient. First, problems vary greatly. Were standard and optimum responses to be developed for each variation, their number would defy practical use. Second, standardized responses that might be practical would be oversimplified and less efficient than a worker with intellectual skills. In a fermentation workshop in a food chemistry plant, regulating many factors, such as temperature and amount of oxygen, is vital to fermentation. Excess oxygen causes bacteria to multiply and impedes fermentation, as does insufficient oxygen, which causes bacteria to die. A standardized response involves setting limits on oxygen and adjusting the amount if the limits are breached. In a Japanese workshop, it is more efficient to rely on workers with intellectual skills to make subtle adjustments.

Dealing with unusual operations involves investigating methods of raising efficiency under uncertain conditions. Amid uncertainty, it is impossible to predict all problems, standardize ways of dealing with them, and record everything in a manual. It is more efficient to rely on workers' intellectual skills, provided the cost of forming these skills is not too great, something considered in the third section of this chapter.

The Superiority of the Integrated System

If standardization is difficult, why not simply employ engineers and other specialists to deal with unusual operations instead of asking blue-collar workers to acquire intellectual skills? Two divisions of labor must be considered. One is a separated system that delegates usual operations to production workers and unusual operations to engineers and others with high-level qualifications. The other is an integrated system that puts production workers in charge of both operations, although not all the unusual operations. Which of these two divisions of labor is better?

Provided one condition is fulfilled, the integrated system is thought to be more efficient for the following reasons:

1. More workers are available to deal with problems.
2. The workers who can deal with problems are on the spot. With the separated system, an engineer must be called in when something appears to be or does go wrong. And, lacking the skills to identify problems, line workers may miss many defects. The alternative—hiring an engineer to constantly inspect the line—raises personnel costs significantly.
3. The separated system requires only repetitive work and lacks challenge for production workers. Boredom leads to many defects being overlooked.

The precondition for the integrated system is that production workers have sufficient education and aptitude to acquire intellectual skills without too much cost. It is reasonable to surmise that the minimum requirement would be around a ninth-grade education based on the experience in Japan during the 1960s. That was about the level of the core groups in the workplace that were responsible for achieving that period's high-level growth rate. Although the incoming "flow" were high school graduates with 12 years of schooling, most of the "stock" were junior high school graduates with 9 years of schooling. Beyond this precondition, the important elements that remain are the policies of management and labor organizations in promoting intellectual skills.

Observations reveal that most large Japanese corporations use the integrated system. The separated system is common in small and medium-sized companies.[2] Since most Japanese work for smaller firms, the integrated system cannot be ascribed to Japanese culture.

METHODS OF FORMING INTELLECTUAL SKILLS

Three Methods

The core method of learning intellectual skills is broad on-the-job training: acquiring experience in a couple of closely related workshops to get a better understanding of the flow of production and the mechanisms to achieve it.

The first of the two supplementary methods for this purpose is also OJT, specifically worker participation in maintenance operations. Initially, workers observe maintenance personnel conduct repairs before gradually helping. Later, they undertake the repairs. This is the best way to learn the structure of the machinery.

The second supplementary method involves off-the-job training (off-JT) courses. OJT insufficiently develops intellectual skills; brief courses of two or three days to a week to allow for internalizing experiences are important. Table 5-1 shows that these courses are taken mostly by the currently employed. Longer courses seem to be for supervisors and managers.

The aim of internalizing experience necessitates that off-JT courses emphasize theory. Machinists, for example, might study such variables as cutting speed and angle in relation to the materials to learn optimal speed. These theoretical concepts are basic to machining. They increase ability to recognize the causes of malfunctions and other problems. A course for workers in a continuous, automated, electronically controlled machine processing line workshop would include the theory of machining and the elementary principles of hydraulic pressure, air pressure, and electronics underlying their line machinery. Trouble with hydraulic or

Table 5-1 Length of Off-JT Courses (distribution by course hours, %)

	Total	Less than 9	10–49	50–99	100–199	200–499	More than 500 hours
New recruits	100.0	9.5	49.5	20.2	9.3	7.3	4.2
Recent graduates	100.0	6.7	47.9	22.5	10.0	8.1	4.8
Mid-career job changes	100.0	23.9	58.2	8.5	5.7	2.8	0.9
Currently employed	100.0	20.8	63.0	8.2	4.5	2.2	1.3
Company size							
1,000 or more employees	100.0	10.3	58.2	14.0	8.2	6.0	3.3
500–999	100.0	16.2	58.9	14.2	5.7	3.0	2.0
100–499	100.0	21.9	59.5	10.0	4.3	3.0	1.3
30–99	100.0	30.4	54.6	7.1	4.0	1.8	2.1

Source: Japan, Ministry of Labor, Human Resources Development Bureau, *Jigyonai Kunren Jittai Chosa* (Survey of Internal Training Programs), 1982.

air pressure affects the line, so workers need background to locate problems and effect repairs.

Contrary to the usual argument, a shortcoming of human resource development at large Japanese companies is the lack of theoretical courses. Japan's special feature, it is said, has been its exclusive reliance on OJT, but with an increasingly mobile workforce off-JT is gaining importance. The central role of OJT, which is by no means unique to Japan, has not been undermined. OJT, though, could be made more effective through short, theoretical off-JT courses, an area that remains undeveloped.

To date, the preparatory course for the National Trade Test has filled the gap. In 1958, the Japanese government created a skill testing system based on the Meister system in West Germany, believing that European methods were best. Today's National Trade Test goes beyond its original plan. The number of candidates for the examination has grown from 30,000 to around 150,000. These figures may seem low, but the trades covered represent only a part of industry, and candidates only take the test once or twice in their careers, so the diffusion rate is quite high.[3] The test appraises practical skills and theoretical work, and passing the latter is said to be very difficult. The preparation for the theory test, however, is important in forming intellectual skills.[4]

Further development of a theoretical course would be advantageous.

Incentive Methods—the Job Matrix

The three methods described are alone insufficient to develop a worker's intellectual skills. An incentive program is essential. Only a fair assessment of skill development and fair compensation for it is required. For intellectual skills, however, this is surprisingly difficult to achieve.

Two factors complicate assessment: the long-term and the cumulative nature of intellectual skills. Intellectual skills take a long time to develop and are constantly being upgraded. Minus these two factors, evaluation would be simple and based on current job—someone doing a difficult job would receive a high rating and a high salary. The two factors cited, however, ensure that some workers have higher skills than others at the same job.

There are two reasons for this. The first is a worker's ability to handle unusual operations. Among workers doing the same job, the ability to deal with change and problems varies. If differences are not properly evaluated, why take the time and effort to acquire intellectual skills?

The other reason is previous experience. Job content for same-job production workers varies depending on workers' previous experience. Workers experienced in most of the jobs in the workshop contribute greatly to efficiency because they fill in for absent workers and teach newcomers. If this experience is not evaluated, why learn to do different jobs? If workers are simply paid according to current job, then no effort has been made to assess their experience.

Assessment ultimately depends on the judgment of a veteran worker. A worker's skill in dealing with changes or problems cannot simply be measured in output, as with repetitive work; evaluation must be by a veteran worker well versed in the job—the foreman. This, however, opens evaluation to subjective opinion and possible bias. Bias on a foreman's part can shift emphasis from skills so that workers do not make the effort to upgrade them. To minimize bias, Japanese workplaces use a job matrix.

A job matrix, as in tables 5-2 and 5-3, consists of two charts showing workers' experience. A chart indicating breadth of experience lists the positions workers have experienced and indicates skill levels—whether a worker can do the job alone, teach it to others, and so forth. A chart citing depth of experience lists a workshop's main unusual operations and shows which operation each worker is able to handle and how well. The foreman makes evaluations and drafts the charts, so subjectivity remains. But the charts are sometimes posted in the workshop, so the foreman's judgments must withstand the scrutiny of workers who work

Table 5-2 Job Matrix 1: Breadth of Experience

	Usual operations			
	Job 1	Job 2	Job 3	Job 4
Abe	c	c	b	—
Ito	c	c	b	a
Ube	b	b	b	a
Eto	a	a	b	a
:				
:				

a. Can fill in when reqular operator is absent.
b. Can do the job alone.
c. Can teach others.

Table 5-3 Job Matrix 2: Dealing with Changes and Problems

	Unusual operations			
	Change 1	Change 2	Problem 1	Problem 2
Abe	c	—	c	—
Ito	—	c	b	b
Ube	b	b	b	a
Eto	a	b	b	a
:				
:				

a. Can fill in when regular operator is absent.
b. Can do the job alone.
c. Can teach others.

together every day. This minimizes bias. The charts are revised every three months, for example, to reflect improvements in skills.

The job matrix is an important factor in determining compensation. Pay raises depend on annual increments in the main components of pay and on promotion to a higher job grade, both of which are influenced by the job matrix. The job matrix does not directly determine pay raises and promotions, it is only one important component of merit ratings, and any raise or promotion must be consistent with it. Although there may be discrepancies between the work done and the compensation received in the short term, over the long run the two even out.

Japan's white collarization of wages is therefore explainable in terms of the nature of the skills deemed necessary to do the job. Because intellectual skills take a long time to develop, incentive is needed to encourage long terms of service at one company. The seniority wage curve fills this requirement. In the short term, a pay-for-job system hinders skill formation. Compensation plans must include a periodic increment system and merit ratings to assess individual skill development. Japanese blue-collar workers possess intellectual skills and are paid on a wage curve resembling that of white-collar workers. Consequently, the wage gap between blue-collar and white-collar workers in Japan is smaller than in other developed countries.

THE FUTURE OF INTELLECTUAL SKILLS

Automated, Electronic Workshops

What is the future for all-important intellectual skills? Will advances in automation and computerization render them irrelevant? Or will they become more important? Observe a fully electronic, automated machine processing workshop surveyed in summer 1986.[5]

The workshop, which machines small parts, belongs to a large automobile parts maker with nearly 10,000 employees. Its 15 workers work under a single foreman and are divided into two groups. One group, of seven men and a group leader, is responsible for three production lines, one of which is our example. The line contains 13 machine tools arranged in a U-shape and interconnected so that processing is completely automated. Materials are supplied automatically at one end of the line to the first machine, then transferred to subsequent machines by robots. When processing is completed, the product emerges at the other end of the line. The work is so thoroughly automated that there appears nothing left for human beings to do?

One worker per shift is in charge of operating the line. The job entails unusual operations. Their degree of sophistication has increased dramatically. Less-difficult operations, such as changes in product mix, account for only a small part of the job, as only four parts are made. Little time is needed for setup changes—10 minutes and 40 to 50 minutes.

Dealing with changes to the production line is crucial. Because, for example, parts also change when automakers alter their models once every four years, many production lines for parts must be replaced, with new tools and jigs designed by engineers for making the new parts. When line workers operate the equipment, they often find that it is inefficient. If skilled, they can improve the equipment and contribute to operational efficiency. Dealing with production line changes has become an increasingly important part of a worker's job, as shifts in production methods are not confined to a single major change every four years. Minor changes are frequent.

Dealing with Problems Predominates

Among unusual operations, dealing with problems predominates. In the fully electronic, automated machine processing workshop, a machine stoppage caused by a small problem is termed a brief stop; they happen frequently. The line could turn out 120 parts an hour, but brief stops reduce output to between 85 and 100 parts. And this is achieved only because a skilled worker fixes small problems immediately. Otherwise, the affected machine stands idle, and output tails off. Operators handle these stoppages themselves because waiting for repair specialists means further downtime.

Workers require a high level of knowledge and skill to effect repairs because of the sophistication of the equipment. The 13 machines are interconnected, so line workers must deal with conveyors, with hydraulic and air pressure devices used in automation, and with electronic parts. Previously, workers had to understand the structure of the machinery. Now, they must know various other things as well, such that intellectual skills have assumed even greater significance.

Generally speaking, the more standardized a process is the easier it is for a machine to do. Computerization and automation have made it possible to transfer usual operations to machines, but not unusual operations. Heightened mechanical sophistication and fewer usual operations mean that a growing proportion of the work done by human beings consists of unusual operations. The skills to deal with unusual operations have a huge impact on efficiency. Thus, with advances in computerization intellectual skills will grow in importance.

Chapter 6 Current Theories

THE HUMAN CAPITAL THEORY

Enterprise-Specific Skills

A seniority wage curve and job attachment rate like those in Japan exist in Europe and North America, primarily among white-collar workers. In fact, contrary to textbook theories and classical economics, stable groups of workers occur across a range of not just white-collar occupations. The assumption was that workers would always move on when offered even slightly better conditions and that companies would seek workers willing to settle for even slightly less pay. This presupposed a mobile labor force and pay-by-job wages. Continuity of employment and a seniority wage curve were considered impediments to competition, and were thought exclusive to Japan.

The same phenomena, however, exist in the West. Amid the free market environment especially in the United States, theories developed to account for their presence. The oldest and most cogent is the human capital theory.

Gary Becker's 1964 book is the standard on this theory.[1] An essay by Walter Oi appeared at roughly the same time, but Becker provides the most representative formulation of the theory.[2] What follows is based on his book.

The *capital* in human capital theory refers to skills and is meant to indicate that, as with economic capital, it is possible to invest in and derive profit from skills. The investment is in education or training. A university student pays tuition and cannot work while attending classes. The salary a student forfeits during this period in place of tuition is an investment called the opportunity cost in economics; it is later recouped in high wages.

The investment in on-the-job training is harder to understand, yet should be understood because this form of training predominates. The trainee, unlike the student, works during OJT, so the costs are lower but just as real, even for easy jobs. They amount to decreased efficiency and defective products caused by inexperienced workers. If, moreover, the training salary is ¥50,000 and that of an unskilled worker is ¥100,000, the opportunity cost is ¥50,000, or the difference between the two wages. After training, the worker must recoup these costs, with interest.

Figure 6-1 gives the return on investment as ¥60,000, of which ¥10,000 is interest. This is reasonable assuming that the skills are general skills applicable anywhere. The ¥160,000 post-training salary should correspond with the worker's skill levels. If it does not, the worker will leave or be hired by another company, and no reason will remain to dwell on the investment term and cost or the return on investment.

The first important point about this theory is its long-term perspective and emphasis on return on investment over time, which relates to its second important point: enterprise-specific skills. Skills are either general skills applicable at any company or specific skills applicable at one company. For example, companies A and B make the same widgets using the same machinery. In seven hours, a worker at company A can make 100 widgets but only 85

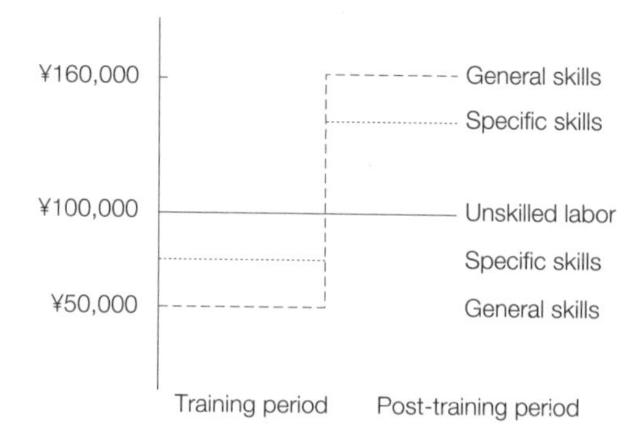

Fig. 6-1. Human Capital Model

at company B. In this instance, general skills account for 85 percent of productivity; specific skills for 15 percent.

Specific skills include an understanding of the idiosyncrasies of the machinery and the other members of one's work group.[3] Every machine has its quirks, and efficiency depends on workers' knowledge of them. Efficiency also depends on workers' understanding of co-workers' personalities and ability to interact effectively. Exclusively specific skills, however, do not exist, although it is easy to mistakenly assume that they do. No statistical evidence is available, but an educated guess would have specific skills amount to around 10 to 20 percent of the skills needed to do a job. This is based on the wage differentials for similar jobs between companies in the same industry.[4]

Sharing Training Costs—Long-Term Correspondence

Enterprise-specific skills encourage long-term relationships because worker and company share the costs of training. To acquire general skills, training costs and salary in the previous example were set at ¥50,000. The worker thus pays the full cost of training. Suppose, though, that the company paid the difference between the wage and the cost of training and that the training salary was ¥80,000. The company would have to recoup its ¥30,000 share of training costs after the training period. The worker's post-training salary would be ¥130,000, not, as previously, ¥160,000. The worker, however, has ¥160,000 worth of skills and the prospect of being hired by another company for ¥160,000. Companies have workers bear the full expense of training for general skills on the premise that a worker with general skills may quit at any time.

Enterprise-specific skills, however, are another matter. Training costs are commonly shared by worker and company. If the company assumes the entire cost and pays, say, a salary of ¥100,000 in both the training and post-training periods, incentive for a worker to acquire complex skills is removed. If, on the other hand, the worker assumes all the costs, the worker faces the prospect of being unable to recoup the investment given the possibility of losing the job if the company goes bankrupt amid rampant market competition. This is why worker and company share the costs.[5]

When both sides share the training costs, the expectation is that employment will be for the long term. If workers quit or are fired during training, neither they nor the company can recover their investment. From this is deduced the essential feature of this theory—the need for long-term correspondence between salary and skills. Most arguments say that these have to match at all times, but with enterprise-specific skills it is enough if they agree over the long term.

This framework accounts for the seniority wage curve. Salaries are low during training, but high thereafter. The preceding discussion assumes only two periods of time when, in fact, OJT continues for much longer. This not only explains the seniority wage curve, it also accounts for white-collar wages—the fact that highly paid blue-collar workers receive seniority-based pay. Contrast this with the theory of cost of living guarantees. This latter theory fails to explain why in the same country a highly paid group of workers receives seniority wages and lower-paid workers do not. Given the emphasis on cost of living guarantees, seniority wages ought to be paid to workers with low salaries who are barely making ends meet. In reality, the situation is just the opposite. The human capital theory offers a brilliant construct for explaining this phenomenon.

Nevertheless, problems remain. What exactly is the nature of these important, specific skills? Why are they developed and where? And why does a seniority wage curve occur in some places but not in others?

INTERNAL LABOR MARKETS

The History of the Discovery of Internal Labor Markets

The theory of internal labor markets delves into the nature of specific skills and clarifies the reasons for job attachment. Labor allocation and pricing occur in labor markets classed as internal because these processes take place mostly within companies. An internal labor market is where a worker acquires experience within a company and is promoted to more difficult jobs. It refers to the situation, for example, in U.S. steel companies described in chapter 4 and in large Japanese corporations.

Despite classical economics' assumption that only an external, mobile labor market exists, internal labor markets are not a recent concept. References to them were made at the end of the nineteenth century, but it was not until after World War II that they began to attract attention.

The earliest mention is in *Industrial Democracy,* the classic study of labor issues by Sidney and Beatrice Webb, published in 1897.[6] U.K. workshops in the nineteenth century were textbook cases. Apprentices became craftsmen in their mid-20s and saw their salaries level off and remain unchanged. Only skilled workers who had apprenticed could operate difficult machines; unskilled workers were rarely promoted. Conditions had begun to change somewhat by the end of the century, when the Webbs noted a trend to promote workers who had not apprenticed. But even today, wages in a U.K. workshop practically level off after workers reach their mid-20s, and promotion within the workshop affects only a limited few. Nonetheless, a trend toward internal promotion, though shallow, continues to be noted.

This trend is stronger in the United States, where industrial development occurred later than in the United Kingdom. But the first references to it do not appear until the 1950s. In his 1954 article, Clark Kerr pointed out that the American labor market had a division of labor within each company and that promotions to high-paid jobs went not to outsiders but to company employees who entered the company doing low-paying jobs. He called this trend toward an internal division of labor the balkanization of labor markets and used the term port of entry to describe entry-level employment.[7]

A few years later, labor expert Professor John Dunlop, of Harvard University, pointed out that when a balkanization of labor markets occurs a closely linked group of jobs exists within the company in what he called a job cluster.[8] Although he did not specify what this job cluster was, it seems to correspond to the group of jobs linked together in a progression line.

Today, the standard work on internal labor markets is the 1971 book by Dunlop's students Peter Doeringer and Michael Piore.[9]

Internal Labor Markets

Unlike earlier researchers, whose general observations and hypotheses were based on only a few case studies, Doeringer and Piore studied more than 70 companies and for the first time defined internal labor markets.

1. The allocation and pricing of labor occurs chiefly within the company. This involves a job ladder and internal promotions. Continuous employment and an upward slope to the right of the wage curve are natural, as observed in the earlier examination of U.S. and Japanese workshop practices.
2. Although workers remain with the company, mechanisms exist to allow the company to adjust to changes in external conditions. When demand contracts, the company dismisses workers at the bottom of the job ladder. When demand rises, it promotes existing workers up the job ladder and recruits from outside the company to fill the lowest-level jobs. Doeringer and Piore showed that internal labor markets are not rigid and inflexible, but instead respond efficiently to changes in the economic environment.
3. Doeringer and Piore cite three reasons for the development of internal labor markets: skill specificity, on-the-job training, and customary practices.

The importance of OJT was confirmed through Japanese case studies. But sometimes internal labor markets do not develop even with OJT. Apprentices, for example, acquire skills through OJT in a craftsman's workshop but then form an extremely mobile labor market. Similarly, Japanese case studies suggest that internal labor markets can develop even without such customary practices as the seniority system found in U.S. steel companies. Seniority affects the formation of internal labor markets but does not cause internal labor markets to develop.

Ultimately, the most important factor is specific skills. The internal labor market theory defines skills in much the same way as the human capital theory—despite contrary claims by the authors—but also includes a definition of specific skills. Doeringer and Piore define specific skills as an understanding of the idiosyncrasies of machinery and of the personalities of co-workers, a now widely accepted definition.

Here, an enormous problem arises. Undeniably, even among identical equipment individual machines exhibit quirks, and efficiency depends on workers' understanding of them. Similarly, whereas some operations are done individually, when teamwork is involved efficiency depends on how well workers understand each other. Machines and people with idiosyncrasies are universal. Thus, internal labor markets—if they are so efficient—should be universal: found in all periods, in all industries, and in all companies. Internal labor markets, though, have only really existed since World War I ended, earlier references notwithstanding, and even then seem limited chiefly to large Japanese and U.S. corporations. The preceding, therefore, must be too general to explain internal labor markets. The questions remain: What is the true nature of specific skills and the real cause of internal labor markets? Before tackling these questions, some other theories must be introduced.

EXPLAINING JOB ATTACHMENT

Transaction Cost Theory

Several other theories that attempt to explain job attachment deserve attention, including Oliver Williamson's theory of transaction cost economics.[10] His ideas on labor can be summarized as three assumptions, beginning with bounded rationality. Neither employers nor employees know everything; complete information is unavailable. Since the world is an uncertain and complex place, bounded rationality—meaning that it is impossible to tell immediately a worker's skill level or diligence—is a reasonable assumption. Williamson's second assumption is opportunism. Provided they can get away with it, individuals will behave in ways that benefit themselves and will even cheat. This, too, is a realistic appraisal. Opportunism, however, is not a factor in simple operations where the output of individual workers is discernable. This is where Williamson's third assumption, the concept of specific assets, comes in. Specific assets are synonymous with specific skills, and their presence makes who is doing what work very relevant in that they leave room for opportunism.

These three assumptions make an internal labor market rational and efficient. Bounded rationality implies that it is impossible to know at the time of hiring whether a person is right for the job. Potential for promotion up the job ladder, however, clarifies the worker's suitability. Compare this with hiring directly from the external market to fill the higher-ranking jobs on the job ladder. The transaction costs of hiring someone without knowing whether that person is right for the job are greatly reduced by an internal labor market, hence transaction cost economics, a result of which is long-term employment.

Williamson's theory is convincing because it covers a wide area, beginning with industrial structure. Its relevance is undeniable, but it is still slightly unsatisfactory because it does not account for the way skills evolve. It confines itself to a negative explanation—the savings on transaction costs—and overlooks the positive reasons for an internal labor market: the possibility of cultivating skills over a long period of time.

Another theory—the efficiency wage theory—assumes the existence of opportunism.[11] It argues in favor of paying long-term employees more than their skills merit, for given the opportunity employees will cheat. If employees with long years of service receive higher salaries than their skills merit, the loss is great if their deception is revealed. The worker will have to leave and work elsewhere for less pay. The cost thus is enough to prevent opportunism. Although this theory presupposes long-term service, it disregards the cumulative development of skills and can only explain why the wage curve is slightly higher than the skills involved merit.

Implicit Contract Theory

The implicit contract theory, which had its origin in articles by Martin Neil Baily and Costas Azariadis, too, is noteworthy.[12] An implicit contract is an unwritten understanding observed by employers and employees. Both accept that the employer will not dismiss employees or reduce their salaries during a recession and that the employee will not simply quit.

The essence of the theory emanates from the risk-averse behavior of workers. Risk refers to the fact that no one can predict upswings or downturns in the economy. Employees are risk averse because they accept employers' tacit promises not to reduce salaries significantly or to cut jobs even during economic downturns. On the other hand, employers will not raise salaries when business is booming. The opposite—enjoying profits when business is good and accepting losses when business is bad—is called risk taking. Because employees are responsible for their families' livelihoods, it is only natural to assume that they will forgo the possibility of large assests and be risk averse. This theory thus tries to explain job attachment.

The theory has two sources. The first was an attempt to explain Keynes' hypothesis of the downward rigidity of money wages. Keynes assumed that one cause of recessions was that money wages did not go down during an economic downturn. His tentative reasoning was workers' money illusion, whereby nothing bad could happen as long as their wages did not decline. The implicit contract theory tried to explain the money illusion concept, but it also had a second, more important motive. It attempted to draw inferences about wages and employment under conditions of economic uncertainty.

Although this theory and the reasons for it are considerable achievements, it, too, is limited. In explaining long-term employment, it is convoluted and overlooks the cumulative evolution of skills.

CONSTRUCTING A CAREER

Career Formation

What are enterprise-specific skills, and how are they formed? Explanations considered thus far attribute their origin to the operating characteristics of machinery and the personalities of co-workers and have been so general as to suggest that internal labor markets are universal and long-standing when, in fact, they were found primarily in large firms after World War I. Is it not more conceivable to think of enterprise-specific skills emerging while constructing a career—defined as a series of jobs through which a worker develops skills? Although they probably only account for about 10 to 20 percent of a worker's skills, enterprise-specific skills are nevertheless sufficient to form an internal labor market.

Career formation demands two conditions: high-level skills and employment with long-term prospects. An examination of the former must ask why OJT is preferable to off-JT and discuss career formation.

OJT is preferable for its lower costs and tailored training and because of the indefinable nature of some skills. It is less costly than off-JT because skill formation occurs while the trainee works. With off-JT, acquiring skills takes a long time, while everything, including living expenses, is a cost. OJT costs, though lower, do nonetheless exist. They include reduced efficiency resulting from assigning inexperienced workers to unfamiliar jobs. A recruit assigned to a job requiring skill would be clueless, and the costs infinitely greater than with off-JT.

This is where a discussion of career formation comes in. New workers are not assigned to difficult jobs. They are first given the easiest jobs. When experience with those jobs is gained, costs decline. As workers progress through a cluster of related jobs, from easy to more difficult, costs diminish significantly. This is career formation.

OJT is also preferable because it is tailored. The instructor shows the trainee how to make a sample widget, and the trainee emulates the operation as the instructor observes. The instructor comments and corrects before returning to work. The trainee operates unsupervised and shows the result to the instructor. In time, the trainee asks for assistance only when something is difficult to understand. The time and nature of OJT instruction depends on the trainee's progress. The advantage is its one-on-one nature. With off-JT, a professional, full-time teacher instructs a class of 20 to 30 students. The classroom method, moreover, teaches generic operations on generic machinery, such that students learn operations that they may never use. OJT involves operation of a machine in the workshop with a clear objective and where the trainees knows immediately whether success has been achieved. It, therefore, is the more efficient method.

The indefinable nature of skills, making their verbal communication difficult, is a third reason that OJT is preferable. This is what is known as tacit knowledge.[13] There is no way to acquire it except from those who possesses it. And that is what OJT is all about.

The Nature of Enterprise-Specific Skills

Examining career formation illuminates an important characteristic—its internalization in a company. A career develops primarily within a company and to some extent is specific to that company.

A career may, of course, develop as a worker moves from firm to firm. But the cost of OJT makes it more probable that a career develops within one company, after the worker concludes an initial firm-to-firm search for a suitable place. Earlier, it was said that an efficient way of reducing costs is to have workers gain experience of a cluster of related jobs. The development of a career within one company has the advantage in this respect because it is easy to arrange a cluster of related jobs within one company and because a great deal of cost-reducing overlap between jobs can be assured.

If careers were formed by moving from one company to another, some way of ensuring that changing jobs did not entail overmuch loss would be needed. Skill levels and career stages would have to be obvious. A practical way of measurement would be a career path in which very little overlap occurs between jobs, since overlap makes it hard to define skill levels. This, however, would raise the cost of skill acquisition because it is through overlap that costs are reduced. Career formation, therefore, tends to occur within a single company.

A career, moreover, tends to be enterprise specific. Jobs in different companies may be the same, but how career paths are formed differs at each firm. In a company with many veteran workers, the career path may be broad. Where inexperienced workers predominate, the career path might be narrower. Some job ladders have many rungs; others, few. These differences define enterprise-specific skills. A career forms because of the labor mix, company policies, and the business environment—product changes, technological developments, and decisions to boost production even at the expense of workers. Such factors are present every day but are no guarantee that career formation for the same jobs in another company would be the same.

Enterprise-specific skills can also be affected by the content of individual jobs. Suppose that two rival companies have the same equipment and operate it in exactly the same way, with, say, 10 work units. There would still be no guarantee that each job would be identical. If a company had many experienced workers, 3 might be able to handle the 10 units, whereas 10 might be needed at a company with few veterans. This is another form of enterprise-specific skill development. Although based on observations of workshops and unsupported by sufficient statistical evidence, it seems that the way a career is formed reveals the importance of enterprise-specific skills.

Likewise, although no statistics are available enterprise-specific skills are thought to constitute about 10 to 20 percent of a worker's skills. In industries with labor unions, wage differentials for similar work at same-industry companies are thought to be around that rate.[14]

Conditions

The formation of enterprise-specific skills does not occur everywhere. Two conditions are necessary: high-level skills, to ensure differences in costs no matter their method of development, and long-term prospects. It takes a long time to build a career, and corporate failures may affect confidence to invest in careers. Workers require large companies with stable markets, so this condition does not hold for small companies or for craft skills like carpentry. The technology involved, however, does not matter. In Japan, internal labor markets are generally distributed among large companies of all industries, where they only appeared after World War I.

Internal labor markets became noticeable in the West after World War I, and do not seem to have existed during industrialization in the nineteenth century. They are not, however, found in all industries; internal labor markets for blue-collar workers exist only in some industries. Moreover, their rate of diffusion among countries differs considerably. They do not exist as widely among large companies in Europe and North America as in Japan. An exploration of what caused these differences occurs in the final chapter. It is sufficient here to note that internal labor markets became evident at a particular point in time and primarily in large companies.

Chapter 7 Adjustment to Change: Dismissal and Unemployment

EMPLOYMENT ADJUSTMENT

Employment Elasticity to Production

Economies are in a constant state of flux, either expanding or contracting. How do companies adjust, not only to changing economic environments but also to market competition? A company that cannot compete must dismiss workers or face bankruptcy and the necessity of dismissing its entire workforce. When enterprise-specific skills are involved, dismissal raises complicated problems. Moving to another company even within the same industry entails a loss for the worker. The dismissal of workers with enterprise-specific skills is a serious issue worldwide, but especially in Japan, which is said to have permanent employment. Would such a system mean that Japanese companies never resort to personnel cutbacks or that Japan lacks market competition? If so, how has Japan achieved such high levels of efficiency? Does the Japan-is-different argument agree with the facts?

It is inconceivable that dismissals do not occur in Japan. However, this needs confirmation and not merely an inquiry into their presence or absence. What is required is the ratio between actual dismissals and necessary dismissals. Statistics showing necessary dismissals are unlikely. And statistics of actual dismissals are rare even in Japan, where statistics abound. Instead, the elasticity of employment to output is used. This is expressed as the rate of decrease in employment ÷ the rate of decrease in output.

Elasticity is thus the rate of change in one factor compared with the rate of change in another. In this instance, necessary dismissals are expressed by the rate of decrease in output, and actual dismissals are represented by the rate of decrease in employment.

Production in Japan clearly declined for a year following the energy crisis of the 1970s. That period therefore provides the required comparisons. The first of two sets of measurements comes from Shimada Haruo.[1] Shimada compared the rate of decrease in employment with the rate of decrease in output for each quarter in Japan and in the West. Shinozuka Eiko, on the other hand, used a more sophisticated method involving production functions.[2] The results were identical: only the United States showed great elasticity; ratios for Japan and Europe were smaller than the U.S. ratio.

Elasticity approaches one if the necessary number of people are dismissed immediately. In the United States, elasticity approached one after six months. Elasticity in Western Europe and Japan never reached one. A trend practiced by all countries—adjusting employment by limiting working hours rather than employees—took place far more frequently in Western Europe and Japan.

The reason for this is what is known as the theory of labor hoarding. Once workers, especially those with specific skills, are dismissed costs are involved in rehiring when the demand for labor expands. Recruiting, screening, and training workers cost money. In a short recession, keeping workers on while limiting their hours is more economical.[3]

But this does not explain why the elasticity of employment is so much greater in the United States than in Japan and most of Western Europe. This requires consideration of the facts behind the statistics, namely, U.S. employment adjustment practices. If, in Japan's case, only large companies are looked at instead of the economy as a whole elasticity might be much smaller than in Western Europe, the said effect of permanent employment. Elasticity of employment, however, is not easy to measure by company size; output by company size is unavailable. Output in monetary terms is available, but no wholesale price index by company size exists. Since fluctuations in product prices vary between large, small, and medium-sized companies, elasticity cannot be measured. It is necessary, therefore, to forgo statistics and observe employment adjustment practices.

The Cost of Dismissals

Observing employment adjustment practices demands in-depth scrutiny to penetrate complex practices. When production fluctuates, the most extreme measure of employment adjustment is dismissal. But even dismissals involve costs. The extent of the costs depends on the number of people dismissed and, significantly, on who is dismissed. The dismissal costs of two companies who dismiss the same number of people vary widely depending on who is let go. Costs also vary depending on the perspective—the company's, the dismissed worker's, or the national economy's. From the perspective of the national economy, these costs include the following:

1. Loss from the disuse of skills. The person dismissed may not immediately find another job, as the dismissal has occurred during a recession. This loss entailed stems from the worker's inability to use skills while unemployed. The higher the skills and the longer the period of unemployment, the greater the loss. When enterprise-specific skills are involved, unemployment is prolonged because such skills restrict the worker's job marketability.
2. Loss from the waste or underuse of skills. The worker's skills may go to waste at a new job to which they do not apply. The higher and the more enterprise specific the skills, the greater the loss.
3. Loss from labor disputes. Because of the gravity of dismissal for the worker involved, the propriety of procedures often causes disputes, leading to a strike and, subsequently, to a loss. Avoiding this calls for placing the burden of layoffs on those whose dismissal entails the smallest costs and for doing so according to clear-cut rules.

The costs of dismissal rise particularly when a worker with enterprise-specific skills is involved. Even when specificity is as low as 10 percent, the loss is great because the skills are high. Employment adjustment that avoids such dismissals is needed.

The most observable method is to shorten working hours or, rather, to reduce operations. There are, however, two problems. From the company's perspective, the costs for machinery and equipment remain fixed amid reduced operations, so that unit costs rise. This discourages companies from reducing operations. From the worker's perspective, a reduction in operations means decreased income for all employees. They demand a method whereby some workers are dismissed but compensated with unemployment benefits to thereby minimize the difficulties for employees overall. Failing that, reducing operating hours is untenable from the worker's perspective.

Internal transfer is a method of employment adjustment that keeps workers on staff. Large companies may have several divisions, each making different products. When production declines in one division, surplus labor is transferred to other divisions in need of workers instead of being dismissed. This is a practice of contemporary Japanese companies that is also found in other countries.[4]

Although good for avoiding dismissals, it is not without problems. Internal transfers are limited as to the number of people involved. Tradeoffs, too, are a problem. The weaker the relationships between divisions, the greater the ability to transfer employees internally because production declines in one division do not drag unrelated divisions down; production is sufficient in unrelated divisions to accommodate surplus workers. However, if divisions are unrelated the skills involved will be so different as to make transferred workers inefficient. These problems affect internal transfer and, as with all the problems mentioned, must be taken into consideration when examining employment adjustment practices.

Employment Adjustment in the United States

To study employment adjustment practices in Japan, a firsthand look at practices in the West is helpful. Otherwise, there is a risk of assuming that practices in Western Europe and North America are as described in textbooks, allowing the conclusion that Japan is unique. The United States, which emphasizes seniority, and West

Germany, which emphasizes legal prescriptions, exemplify Western practices.

Japanese believe that U.S. companies dismiss workers as soon as the necessity arises. In U.S. companies with labor unions this is not necessarily the case. Labor contracts generally state that management can lay off workers only when the workload has fallen to less than 32 hours a week for more than four consecutive weeks. Given that the prescribed working hours are 40 hours a week plus overtime, this is roughly equivalent to saying that layoffs are possible only after production has been reduced about one-fourth.

Once that situation is reached, however, management can lay off workers without further input from labor unions. This differs vastly from union practices in Japan and Western Europe, where no dismissal occurs without negotiating with labor unions. U.S. practices differ because there the choice of who will be laid off is predetermined. Despite the presence of labor unions, American managers reduce operating hours very seldom. Work reductions longer than a month are found in only a few industries, such as the garment industry. American companies thus place little importance on reductions in operations as a means of employment adjustment.

The same is true of internal transfers, though they do occur. In the United States, transfers happen when workers with five or more years of service bump workers with less seniority in related workshops. Transfers within an automobile plant division can be widespread. Even so, far less use is made of internal transfers than in Japan, where transfers occur even to unrelated workshops.

An earlier examination of a U.S. steel plant revealed dismissal practices based on the principle of last in, first out, or reverse the order of seniority in number of years of continuous workshop or divisional service. For blue-collar workers in Japan, too, there is little difference between continuous service in the company and in a division because workers tend to stay in the same division of the same plant. This minimizes loss from the disuse of skills. Cutbacks begin with workers with the shortest service, and rehiring with those with the longest service. A level of seniority thus makes possible a shorter period of unemployment in the event of a layoff.

And because the possibility of being rehired by the same workshop is strong, there is little chance that skills will go to waste.

In addition, disputes do not occur over who will be laid off because this is strictly determined in reverse order of hiring. That is why strikes rarely arise over layoffs in the United States despite that country's strong labor unions. The issue most likely to cause problems with cutbacks is not the number of workers to be laid off. A strike is a union's only recourse against layoffs. But unions know the futility of even a long strike over numbers. Strikes have limited effectiveness amid recessions severe enough to cause layoffs. A strike amid excess inventory actually works to management's advantage by reducing inventory and thus is far less effective than in prosperous times.

Employment adjustment practices in the United States entail fewer costs and less social tension than elsewhere in proportion to the number of people involved. The argument that in the United States anyone can be dismissed at any time, impeding efficiency, ignores the issue of who is being laid off.

Employment Adjustment in West Germany

In West Germany, the preferred practice is to reduce operating hours. For workers paid hourly wages, this results in diminished income, 60 percent of which is compensated by social insurance. Transfers within large firms also occur frequently according to case studies done after the energy crisis.[5]

The *Kündigungsschutzgesetz* (the law concerning dismissals) contains important provisions on dismissal procedures. They require that negotiations take place between management and corporations' employees' organizations on such matters as how many workers will be let go and their selection. In West Germany and most Western European countries, as discussed in chapter 12, a de facto labor union exists within companies in the form of an employees' organization. It comprises everyone regardless of occupation, including all white-collar workers under the rank of section chief. These organizations arose in response to the law on workers' participation in management. They are not legally labor unions, so their expenses are paid by the companies, but they function like labor unions. German studies and the author's interviews indicate that negotiations do occur between management and employees' organizations on the terms of dismissal.

The provisions of the law extend even to which workers will be let go. The law prescribes that social considerations (*soziale gesichtspunkte*) be observed.[6] Consequently, those dismissed are unmarried workers, married but childless workers, and others least seriously inconvenienced. And care is taken to protect employees over 50 years of age who have worked more than 10 years for the same company. Case studies show that the law is carefully observed. Although West German employees with long years of service are not as protected from layoffs as U.S. workers, they are better protected than their Japanese counterparts.

Losses from the disuse or waste of skills thus are not as low in West Germany as in the United States but are much lower than in Japan. However, because West German dismissal selection is vague—its order of workers not automatically determined as with the American seniority system—losses from disputes ought to be high. In fact, strikes are rare in West Germany, so this is not the case.

Around the end of the 1970s, a new trend emerged in West Germany—the voluntary redundancy system. An excellent study has been done of its application to blue-collar workers at large companies, and observations have been made about its use among white-collar workers.[7] This system sees retirement benefits and company pensions paid earlier than usual to workers in their late 50s and early 60s with a financial inducement to apply for redundancy. It is similar to the voluntary redundancy system in Japan and is gradually becoming the main means of reducing employment at large West German companies. Because it involves dismissing workers with long years of service, however, it increases the costs of dismissal.

The practice of voluntary redundancy also seems widespread among older workers in the United Kingdom. Among blue-collar workers, dismissals in reverse order of seniority used to be as strong a practice there as in the United States, such that the seniority system was thought to be Anglo-Saxon. But the voluntary redundancy system in effect for white-collar workers appears to have caught on for blue-collar workers at large companies.[8] The methods of dismissal in Western Europe seem to be approaching those in Japan.

DISMISSALS IN JAPAN

Employment Adjustment Procedures

It is assumed that unless their viability is endangered large Japanese companies do not dismiss workers. If true, they apply internal methods almost exclusively to deal with fluctuations in production. This doubtful possibility calls for an examination of the extent to which internal methods actually are implemented.

In West Germany, companies cut back on operations amid hard times, and workers make up the difference in pay through subsidies from employment insurance. Japan's system differs slightly in that the subsidy in Japan is for partial shutdowns rather than for reduced operating hours. The employment adjustment subsidy was established in 1974 and later integrated with subsidies for training programs and intercompany personnel loans. It is an employment adjustment arrangement that promotes shutdowns by paying a sum equivalent to two-thirds of the shutdown allowance (one-half in the case of large firms) for up to 200 days as a way of preventing employee layoffs when production declines. It originated as a way of making it possible for money collected for unemployment insurance to be used for other purposes. In the days of extreme labor shortages before the oil crisis, unemployment had declined to such an extent that a substantial reserve fund had accumulated. No sooner was the system in place than the energy crisis occurred, and the reserve was put to good use.

Internal transfers are so common that they are thought a Japanese specialty. Table 7-1 is based on a survey of employment adjustment practices amid the reduced production after the first oil crisis. Between January 1975 and June 1978, it tallied the workers transferred to other plants or loaned to other companies and who voluntarily applied for redundancy or were subjected to designated dismissal. The information was then cross-classified by

Table 7-1 Transfers, Intercompany Personnel Loans, and Dismissals in the Manufacturing Industries (1975–78)

	Workers Transferred or Loaned		
	Number	Ratio to total personnel cutbacks[a] (%)	Ratio to dismissals[b] (%)
Companies of all sizes	616,795	13.7	88.2
1,000 or more employees	432,280	32.3	337.0
300–999 employees	97,425	15.7	97.0
100–299 employees	54,238	6.9	45.6
30–99	23,777	2.8	15.8
5–29	9,075	1.0	5.0

Source: Ministry of Labor, *Koyo Hendo Sogo Chosa* (Comprehensive Survey of Employment Fluctuations), 1979.

[a]"Total personnel cutbacks" refers to the decrease in the number of workers between January 1975 and June 1978.

[b]"Dismissals" refers to voluntary redundancy and designated dismissals.

company size. This is the most detailed statistical study on personnel cutbacks ever done.[9]

According to table 7-1, transfers within companies or corporate groups were common primarily among large firms; confirming popular perceptions. As expected, they contributed greatly to reducing dismissals. In companies with more than 1,000 employees, more than three times as many workers were transferred to other plants or loaned to other companies than were let go. Some transfers may simply have been reassignments of personnel rather than instances of employment adjustment. The survey, however, refers only to transfers between plants and does not include moves within plants, which may have been more frequent.

Although transfers and intercompany personnel loans are confined to large companies, problems remain when workers end up where their skills do not apply. Personnel loans to other companies extend these problems to corporate groups. The costs of transferring workers thus can be considerable: the worker is saddled with an unfamiliar job and the company with someone of no strategic value. Transfers must take skills into consideration.

Despite efforts to deal with fluctuations in production internally in Japan, dismissals still occur. Competition among companies make them a foregone conclusion. Dismissals nonetheless are depicted as a last resort. But what constitutes a last resort?

Dismissals after Two Years of Deficits

Studies of dismissal practices cannot rely on statistics; observation through case studies is necessary. Fortunately, Japan's Ministry of Labor's Documentary History of the Labor Movement (*Shiryo Rodo Undoshi*), published as a 1,300-page, double-column volume each year since 1945, chronicles strikes and labor-management relations in Japan. It includes the documents of the parties involved in major disputes and is a splendid source for case studies or historical research on Japanese industrial relations that has no equal in any other country.

Its volumes show that dismissal practices in Japan can be classed under two distinct periods: the late 1940s through the 1950s and after the energy crisis in the 1970s. The intervening period of high economic growth saw few cutbacks.

The first period witnessed fierce strikes. Even supposedly weak unions struck for up to six months. Amid the devastation of World War II, no large company could avoid recession, and managements frequently proposed dismissing workers. Initially, they proposed to unions a system of voluntary redundancy. Workers who volunteered would earn an increase in severance pay. Immediate postwar unions, however, were led by Marxists and opposed to dismissals. They rejected voluntary redundancy, compelling managements to designate workers for dismissal and to send them notice, inciting protracted strikes. When strike war chests ran out, a group of union members, fearful for their company's existence, would form a second union, overthrow the first union, and allow management-designated dismissals. Long, bitter strikes occurred at Nikko Muroran, where the union was said to be weak, and at Miike, where it was said to be strong.[10]

In the second period, the energy crisis caused production to plummet 20 percent all at once. Workers had to be let go. This time, the unions accepted voluntary redundancy, and strikes were rare. Some union leaders had experienced the earlier period and knew the toll the unions' uncompromising opposition had taken of workers. They negotiated over voluntary redundancy with the utmost care.

Japanese commonly dispute that dismissals happen all that frequently in Japan. Fortunately, the Comprehensive Survey of Employment Fluctuations provides statistical evidence for this period. Table 7-2 is based on this important, one-time questionnaire survey.

Comparisons with other countries would be helpful, but statistics appear unavailable elsewhere. Large Japanese firms are thus compared with small and medium-sized Japanese firms thought to have high dismissal rates. The table shows that large companies, in fact, have slightly fewer dismissals than small and medium-sized firms. Layoffs occurred at 20 percent of large companies, 26 percent of companies with 30 to 99 employees, and 30 percent of medium-sized companies. Differences exist but are not significant.

At establishments where personnel cutbacks occurred, the ratio of dismissed workers to the total number of employees is smaller at large firms, around 12 percent, and rises in inverse proportion to company size, reaching more than one-third for

Table 7-2 Dismissals by Company Size in the Manufacturing Industry (January 1975–June 1978)

	Establishments with dismissals	Workers dismissed	Workers subjected to voluntary redundancy	Workers subjected to designated dismissal
	Establishments	Total employees surveyed (i.e., in the establishment where the dismissals occurred)	Total personnel cutbacks	Total personnel cutbacks
Companies of all sizes	19.4%	34.8%	12.3%	3.2%
1,000 or more employees	20.3	11.9	8.8	0.8
300–999 employees	30.7	24.3	14.1	2.1
100–299 employees	29.5	28.1	11.3	5.7
30–99	26.1	34.4	14.0	6.1
5–29	16.9	45.2	15.5	4.6

Source: Ministry of Labor, *Koyo Hendo Sogo Chosa* (Comprehensive Survey of Employment Fluctuations), 1979.

companies with 30 to 99 employees. Differences are more noticeable, but even at large companies the percentage of dismissed workers is not so small as to be single digit. Most dismissals were voluntary. Management-designated dismissals were rare at large companies but accounted for a quarter of dismissals at small and medium-sized firms. This is a major size-related difference, and, as discussed in chapter 12, is thought attributable to the presence or absence of a labor union, which are primarily found in large companies.

Under what situations do large companies dismiss workers? The common perception is that dismissals happen only when the viability of a company is endangered. According to a study of the cement industry and the electrical machinery and appliance sector, many large companies with unions resort to dismissals if deficits continue for two years.[11] Another study, of the machine tool industry, confirms this.[12] That is the truth behind Japan's permanent employment myth.

Dismissals Concentrated on Those Whose Loss is Greatest

Dismissal problems are quantitative—how many workers to let go—and qualitative—which ones. In Japan, dismissals focus on quality, on workers who suffer the greatest loss.

Loss from dismissals rises in direct proportion to level of skills, degree of enterprise specificity, and vagueness of rules for designating workers to let go. Statistical measurements of skills are unavailable. Years of service could be used instead, but no statistics exist that cross-classify number of dismissals with length of service. Two statistical surveys, however, cross-classify by age: the Basic Survey of Employment Structure and the Special Survey of the Labor Force (*Rodo Ryoku Tokubetsu Chosa*). Both show similar trends, so only the latter is referred to here. Figure 7-1 shows a clear bias against older workers. Compared with the normal age distribution for employees, there were more dismissals among employees aged 45 and over.

The figures, however, are for all companies. Figures only for large companies reputed to offer permanent employment are preferable but unavailable. The alternative is to make observations

Fig. 7-1. Age Distribution of Dismissed Male Workers (1977 and 1979, cf. *Understanding Industrial Relations,* p. 170)

Source: Management and Coordination Agency, Statistics Bureau, *Special Report of Labor Force Survey*.
Note: "Dismissals" refer to those who "lost their job since 1974" as a result of "dismissal, bankruptcy, etc.," from among those listed as "employees," "unemployed," and "not in the labor force."

on cases in the Documentary History of the Labor Movement.[13] Thirty-six cases of dismissal are recorded between 1953 and 1955, and 84 between 1973 and 1978. Because of differences in detail, however, only 6 cases in the first period and 15 in the second mention which workers were let go. Tables 7-3 and 7-4 summarize these cases.

The reasons for the 6 cases during the first period are not indicated in table 7-3 as those cited by companies at the time of the dismissals. They are thought to be the reasons cited by managements when the unions rejected voluntary redundancy and later used to effect designated dismissals. Because dismissals in the second period (table 7-4) were primarily through voluntary redundancy, references to who left are rare and imprecise. Both tables nonetheless show that dismissed workers were those whose dismissal entailed the greatest loss. The first criterion was that the worker be between 45 and 50 years of age or older, meaning most-

Table 7-3 Criteria for Dismissal in the 1950s (first period, cf. *Understanding Industrial Relations*, p. 172)

	(Aged 45 and older, 50 and older)	5
Absenteeism	Irregular attendance	4
	Long-term absenteeism	4
	Temporary retirement	3
	Ill health	6
Income reasons	Two-income household	3
	Alternative source of income	4
Performance	Unsatisfactory performance	6
	Frequent mistakes	2
	Uncooperative attitude	2
	Rule infractions	2

Table 7-4 Criteria for Dismissal in the 1970s (second period, cf. *Understanding Industrial Relations*, p. 173)

Age, 50 or older	13
Husband and wife working at same company	4
Unsatisfactory performance	3
Absenteeism	1

ly long-service workers. Apart from attendance, the other criteria and rules for dismissal, such as unsatisfactory performance, are so ambiguous that losses from disputes too were probably large.

Japan's situation is therefore the reverse of the United States'. Dismissals in the United States, though they occur more frequently, focus on workers whose dismissal entails the least costs and thus do not heighten social tensions. In Japan, dismissals are the burden of those whose loss is high. Although the numbers are low, dismissals in Japan tend to increase social tensions. West German practices are probably somewhere in between. Contrary to popular Japanese belief, U.S. employment adjustment practices appear superior.

Shock Absorbers

Differences in employment adjustment practices based on company size illuminate another popular belief: the dual-structure argument. This argument claims that large Japanese firms shift the costs of change onto small and medium-sized businesses. Large companies have few dismissals, it claims, because the smaller businesses shoulder that burden. This view of Japanese industrial relations, common in Europe and North America, originated in Japan.

Not enough research has been done on this view, so a hypothesis must suffice. Generally speaking, the tendency to shift the burden of dismissals downward is found in many countries. Methods, however, vary, as do the extent of the shift and the rate of compensation for those who bear the burden, but these three appear common:

1. The U.S.-style labor pool method. The degree to which the burden is shifted to the lowest level is greatest; dismissals concentrate on the pool. However, compensation is greater because promotion is limited to those who start out from the pool.
2. The dual-structure method. Employment in large companies is protected by shifting the burden of dismissals onto small and medium-sized companies, with almost no compensation.
3. The division-of-labor method. Because a division of labor exists between large companies and small and medium-sized companies, which have their own products and labor markets, large companies cannot shift the burden of dismissals onto the latter when demand declines. Each sector must make employment adjustments, for which compensation is small.

Japan appears to employ roughly the third method. Relations between large firms and small and medium-sized companies in contemporary Japan are thought to have three characteristics. The first is a low rate of internal production. Large Japanese companies depend on small and medium-sized companies for much of what they produce. Compare, for example, Toyota and Ford. The number of automobiles each produced domestically was roughly the same in the late 1980s, but Toyota had far fewer employees, at 70,000, against Ford's more than 200,000. Productivity differences may not be all that great, but differences in diversification and rates of internal production are.[14] Ford car seats, for example, are manufactured by a division of Ford, whereas Toyota car seats are made by a medium-sized, Toyota-related company. This appears to confirm the dual-structure argument, but closer inquiry reveals this not to be the case.

The second characteristic is the clear division of labor in the production process. In the case of car seats, Toyota is in no position technologically to do the work of its related company, within a short time. The related company is a specialized parts maker.

The third characteristic is that Japan lacks the U.S.'s seniority system, which values length of service. Amid high internal production at U.S. companies, the seniority system shifts dismissals to the lowest level. Jobs that in Japan are done by workers at a related company are in the United States given to short-service employees who are the first to be dismissed. Jobs done by Toyota employees in Japan are at Ford done by employees with the longest service who, on the whole, are unaffected by cutbacks. Japan's lack of a seniority system prevents companies from shifting dismissals onto workers with the fewest years of service. Rather, the opposite is true.

Large U.S. companies thus have a better system for absorbing the shock of fluctuations in demand than their Japanese counterparts. In Japan, a few dismissals raise social tensions and increase the costs of dealing with change. This is the defect, not the so-called dual-structure system, and it manifests itself in unemployment.

Serious Unemployment

Dismissal practices are revealed through unemployment. Chapter 13 discusses unemployment levels and how to measure them, but it must be pointed out here that Japan's unemployment is severe, contrary to popular perception that unemployment in Japan is rare.

For some unemployed, the situation is especially severe. The indicators for measuring serious unemployment are length of unemployment and age. Most workers are compelled to find jobs, so unemployment is rarely permanent. Unemployment, though, becomes extremely severe when it is difficult to find work. For older, unemployed workers, the cost of living is high. And if they have many years of previous service, their skills are significant. When these skills remain unused during unemployment, the loss is especially great.

Figure 7-2 compares the distribution of unemployment by age group in Japan and the United States. Statistics on the unemployment rate by age also exist, but the levels of employment are so different in the two countries that a direct comparison makes no sense. Distribution by age group is also problematic because allowances must be made for the fact that the age structure for employed workers is not the same in these countries. Only rough observations are possible, but the figure shows clearly that the proportion of males over 45 who have lost their jobs is far higher in Japan than in the United States.

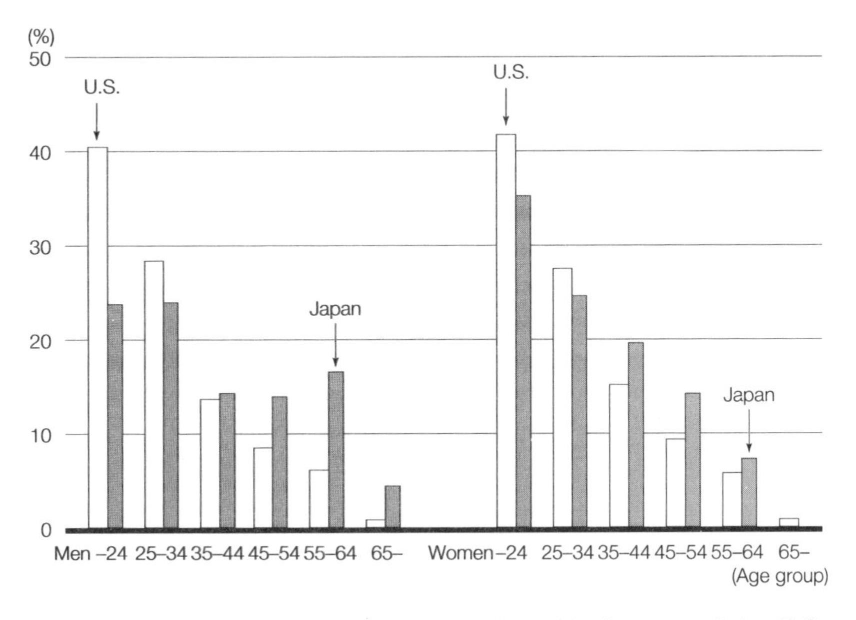

Fig. 7-2. Age Distribution of the Unemployed in Japan and the U.S. (1982)

Sources: U.S., *Handbook of Labor Statistics*, 1983; Japan, *Special Report of Labor Force Survey*, 1982.
Note: The graph shows the percentage distribution by each age group with the total number for all age groups set at 100.

Figure 7-3 compares the duration of unemployment in the United States and Japan. Unemployment lasts far longer in Japan. In the United States, unemployment generally lasts less than five weeks. Japan has higher percentages of unemployment for three to six months and especially for six months or more. Once a Japanese loses his job, it is difficult to find work. This is also reflected in the distribution by age group figure. In both countries, unemployed middle-aged and older workers have more difficulty with reemployment than younger workers. Because these workers are in greater number in Japan, unemployment tends to last longer there.

Japanese like to think that the flexibility of the Japanese labor market makes it better able to respond to change. As seen, however, this is not necessarily so. Certainly, the way it responds to small-scale change is outstanding for the lack of large-scale dismissals. But its response to larger changes is problematic. Dismissals and unemployment may be low in Japan, but because the burden is shifted onto those for whom the costs are high the costs to society rise in proportion to the number of people involved, thereby increasing social tensions. To deal with structur-

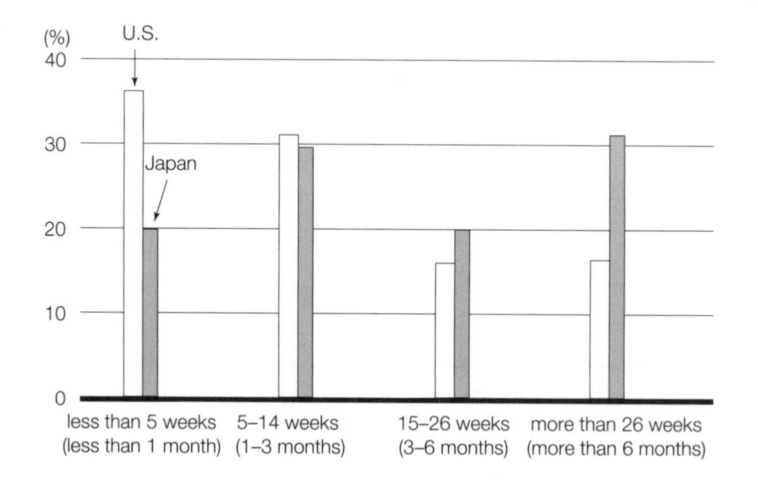

Fig. 7-3. Duration of Unemployment in Japan and the U.S. (1982)

Sources: U.S., *Handbook of Labor Statistics*, 1983; Japan, *Special Report of Labor Force Survey*, 1982.
Note: Unemployment periods given in parenthesis are those for Japan.

al changes in industry or industrial society, society must be prepared to accept a degree of unemployment. Occupational changes resulting from changes in industrial structure, for example, are unavoidable, and large-scale changes in occupation inevitably produce unemployment. It would be difficult to respond to changes in industrial structure without it. Japan's dismissal procedures, contrary to popular belief, are less able to deal with change than those in the United States.

Chapter 8 Workers at Small and Medium-Sized Companies

WAGE DIFFERENTIALS BY COMPANY SIZE

Wage Differentials by Company Size Nonexistent before World War I

Workers employed at large companies constitute a minority in Japan. The majority work for small and medium-sized firms. And according to the Basic Survey of Employment Structure, the percentage of workers at companies with less than 300 employees has increased from 55 percent in 1968 to 61 percent in 1987. Attention must be paid, therefore, to workers at small and medium-sized companies.

Popular belief says that Japanese industry has a dual structure that causes an enormous wage gap by company size. If wages are higher and employment more stable at large companies, this argument goes, it is at the expense of small and medium-sized companies. This is the belief in Japan and abroad. Is it true?

If it were, why do large companies not hire workers from small and medium-sized firms? If they work as efficiently for less pay, surely that is what large companies would do. Why would fiercely competitive large companies pay unnecessarily high salaries? Perhaps the wage gap is not as large as believed.

The dual-structure argument assumes, using sketchy evidence, that size-related wage differentials do not exist in the West. The EC's *Structure of Earnings in Industry*, however, now provides data that addresses the question, Are wage differentials between companies of different sizes unusually large in Japan? Using this better evidence, this section examines the nature of size-related wage differentials.

Japan has published extremely good statistical evidence almost every year since 1954 in its Statistical Survey of Wage Structure. Prior to World War II, no reliable nationwide statistics by company size exist, but there are statistics compiled by the Tokyo, Osaka, and other municipal governments and by industrial groups, such as the spinning industry, and individual large companies. Several detailed studies have made exhaustive use of this material.[1]

This material shows that until roughly World War I, a size-related wage gap did not exist; it only emerged later. If true, this counters some widely held views about Japan. Industrialization, it is said, came late to Japan and did not develop completely. As a result, a huge surplus population built up in farming villages. Once the large companies had taken their pick of workers, they closed their doors, and this huge surplus population flooded into small and medium-sized firms. This, it is claimed, produced the distinctive size-related wage gap not found in Western Europe or North America. If this surplus supply theory is correct, then by all rights the most striking wage differentials by company size should occur in the period before World War I, when the labor surplus was greatest. However, the reverse is true.

Trends after World War II

Japan's Statistical Survey of Wage Structure, published almost every year since 1954, facilitates exploration of wage differentials by company size and what changes they may have undergone. Conditions other than company size, however, must be as similar as possible before attempting a comparison because wages vary greatly even within a company depending on occupations and duties involved.

Male blue-collar workers in typical manufacturing industries, which throughout this period have employed many workers, serve as the sample. Their educational backgrounds, ages, and length of service must be matched across companies of all sizes. In the period under review, the education level for blue-collar workers rose from a junior high school diploma to a high school diploma. However, educational background is merely an aspect of a generation gap for production workers' deployment in the workshop, hence the aggregate will be used.

Age can be considered a proxy indicator for experience in companies of all kinds, and length of service is an indicator for experience within a particular company. Japan's statistics cross-classify wages with age and length of service at roughly 5-year intervals. The problem is how to match age and length of service. One way would be to estimate the effect of all data on age and length of service on wages. This would not be a bad method, but it presupposes that age and length of service in all age and service brackets have the same effect on wages. But a year of employment for a 30-year-old worker with 10 years of continuous service would be quite different than for, say, a 50-year-old worker with only 3 years of service. For the former, it would be a normal case of skills formation by a core blue-collar worker in a production workshop, for the latter an experience at peripheral operations. There is little likelihood of same-level skill formation. Here, wages that reflect skill formation by core production workers are to be observed.

The method adopted is to observe the matching of age and length of service that fills the following conditions: The match must reflect the skills formation of production workers but also must apply to a large number of workers—not most workers because matches for the largest number of workers differ depending on year and company size. Observations have revealed that workers in their early 20s, regardless of company size, change jobs frequently. The age/length of service groups thus are those workers with relatively continuous service from their mid-20s on because these are likely to be precisely the workers who form the important workshop skills.

Figure 8-1 gives a general overview of changes in size-based differentials beginning in 1954 and ending in 1988, with two intervening dates. Because the vertical axis is a logarithmic scale, the intervals between the points on the wage curve represent the size of the differentials. The figure also makes clear the differences

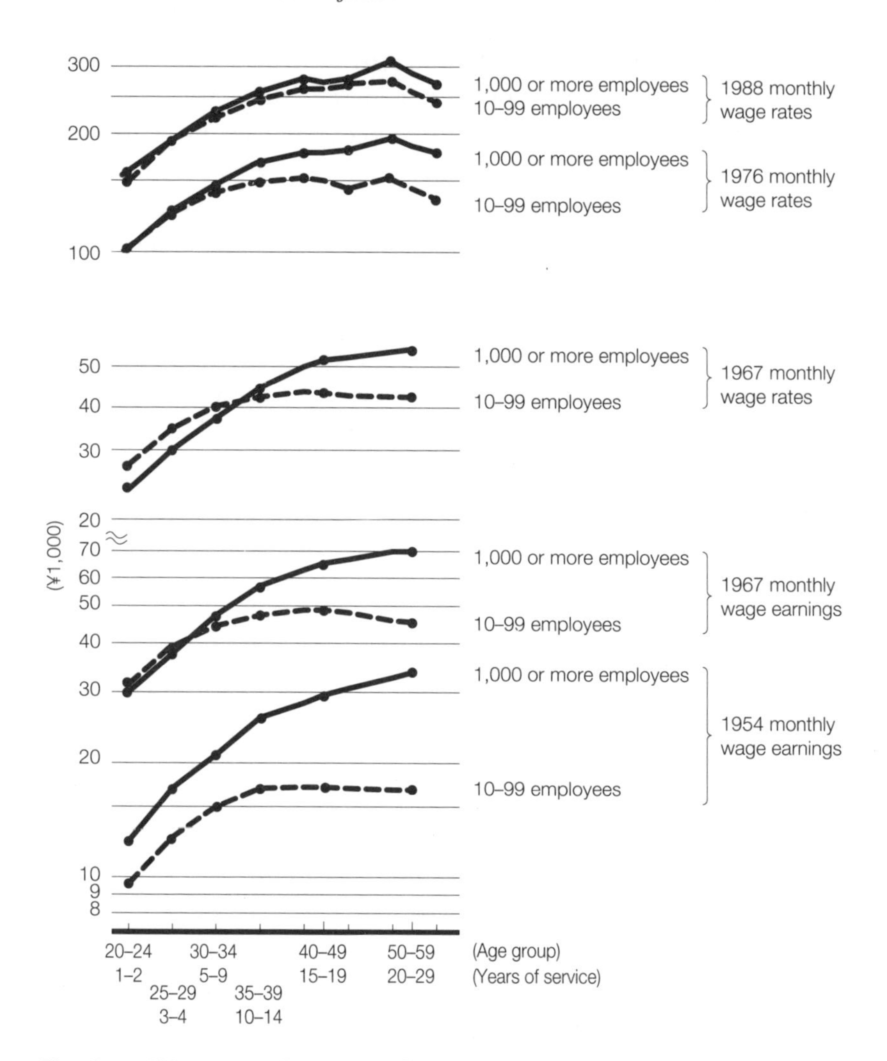

Fig. 8-1. Wages by Company Size, Age, and Length of Service for Male Blue-collar Workers of All Educational Levels in the Manufacturing Industries (1954, 1967, 1976, 1988)

Source: Ministry of Labor, *Chingin Kozo Kihon Tokei Chosa* (Statistical Survey of Wage Structure).
Note: The 1954 statistics provided figures for five classifications of company size, but no numbers for age and length of service. It is therefore difficult to recalculate figures for the three classifications for other years using the original figures. This was done, however, by using the percentage distribution of people of all ages by company size as substitute data.

in the wage curves. The gradients directly indicate the rate of increase in wages by age and length of service. Figure 8-1 tells us various things.

1. Wages rise in different ways depending on company size. In general, large companies have a seniority-based curve; at small companies wages level off for workers in their mid-30s with 10 or more years of service. These trends cause the differentials to widen.
2. Size-based differentials have clearly become smaller. In 1954, the wage gap for workers in their 40s was around 40 percent, but in 1988 it was only 5 percent. The flattening of the wage curve at small and medium-sized companies now takes place for workers in their 40s.

What has caused wage differentials to narrow? Is it because wage curves have changed? If so, has the curve become less steep for large companies or steeper for small and medium-sized companies? Alternatively, have the curves remained the same and the differentials shrunk? When did contraction take place?

The reader, moreover, should be forewarned of a small but unavoidable element in this empirical study. Wage differentials differ by company size depending on whether monthly wage rates or monthly wage earnings are used. Figure 8-1 shows that wage differentials are smaller with the former. Unfortunately it is impossible to observe size-based differentials using only one of these categories over the length of time depicted in the figure. Between 1954 and 1966, only statistics for monthly wage earnings were compiled; after 1984, only statistics for monthly wage rates were collected (collated by age and length of service). In the intervening period, statistics for both were compiled. Comparisons show a significant impact on size-related differentials depending on which statistics are used. Roughly speaking, monthly wage rates produce a smaller differential—in the 10 percent range. The way wages rise, however, is unaffected.

Rapid Narrowing and Subsequent Steadiness

Figure 8-2 shows in greater detail how size-related differentials changed over time for workers aged 20–29 (with 1–2 years of service for early 20s and 3–4 years of service for late 20s workers); aged 30–39 (with 5–9 years and 10–14 years of service, respectively); and aged 40–49 (with 15–19 years of service).

Note the two time periods, from 1954 to the late 1960s and from the 1970s thereafter. In the first, the wage gap among companies of different size narrowed rapidly. Wages for workers in their 20s at companies with 10 to 99 employees went from around 80 on the index in 1954 and exceeded wages for this age group at large companies by the mid-1960s. For workers in their 40s, the gap also narrowed, from below 60 to nearly 80.

Fig. 8-2. Trends in Wage Differentials by Company Size (wage index of male blue-collar workers of all educational levels at companies with 10–99 employees in the manufacturing industries, 1954–88, as wages at companies with 1,000 or more employees = 100)

Source: Ministry of Labor, *Chingin Kozo Kihon Tokei Chosa* (Statistical Survey of Wage Structure).

Notes: 1. Figures for workers in the "20–29" age group are the average between those aged "20–24 with 1–2 years of service" and those aged "25–29 with 3–4 years of service"; for those in the "30–39" age group, they are the average between those aged "30–34 with 5–9 years of service" and those aged "35–39 with 10–14 years of service"; and for those in the "40–49" age group they are the average for those with "15–19 years of service."

2. Until 1966, only data on "monthly wage earnings" were collected; since 1984, only data on "monthly wage rates" have been collected.

The second period saw wages remain generally steady, with slight fluctuation. Despite the acute labor shortage just before the energy crisis, the reverse differential for workers in their 20s disappeared, the size-based gap was eliminated, and thereafter wages in that age group leveled off. Even for workers in their 30s, wage differentials stabilized at less than 5 percent for wage rates and at around 10 percent to 15 percent including overtime pay. By the late 1970s, the gap for workers in their 40s was around 15 percent for monthly wage rates and probably around 25 percent with overtime pay included. Since the end of the 1970s, wage differentials for this last group have slowly narrowed to around 5 percent for wage rates.

Why did wage differentials narrow so rapidly in the first period and remain unchanged in the second? Why does a slight wage gap remain for workers in their 30s? Why have the large wage differentials for workers in their 40s continued to narrow since the end of the 1970s?

Answering these questions requires distinguishing between a narrowing of the wage gap as a whole and a narrowing caused by changes in the wage curve. An overall narrowing can be assumed from wage movements for the 30–39 age group in figure 8-2. The rapid narrowing in the first period relates to the wage gap as a whole; in the second period, the gap as a whole remains unchanged.

Figure 8-3 enables us to observe the other side of this phenomenon: changes in the wage curve. It shows the ratio of wages for workers in their 40s, with 15 to 19 years of service, to that for workers in their early 20s, with 1 to 2 years of service. In the first period, two opposite trends can be observed. The wage curve at large companies rose fairly steeply until 1961 but subsequently eased off, whereas the curve for small companies eased slightly and then stabilized. Part of the reason for the narrowing of the wage gap in the latter half of the first period can be attributed to the easing of the wage curve at large companies.

The second period can itself be divided into two time spans. During the acute labor shortage, the wage curve at large companies continued to ease. After the energy crisis, however, it more or

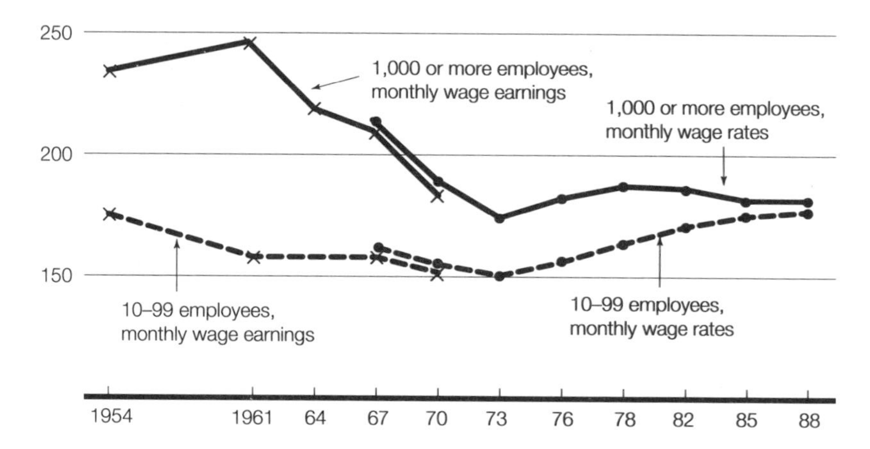

Fig. 8-3. Trends in Wage Profiles by Company Size (wage index of male blue-collar workers of all educational levels aged 40–49 with 15–19 years of service in the manufacturing industries, 1954–88, as wages for workers aged 20–24 with 1–2 years of service = 100)

Source: Ministry of Labor, *Chingin Kozo Kihon Tokei Chosa* (Statistical Survey of Wage Structure).

less stabilized. Though at times it rose slightly, in general the curve did not change. The curve for small companies, however, rose steeply, causing a narrowing of the wage gap for workers in their 40s that began at the end of the 1970s.

What caused the narrowing in wage differentials? What is the reason for the gap that remains? More specifically, What caused the rapid narrowing in the wage gap as a whole during the first period? The wage curve for large companies rose steeply until 1961 and then eased off. Why? Why did the curve for small companies remain unchanged? And why did wage differentials remain steady in the second period? In particular, why did the differentials hold steady despite the acute labor shortage in the early 1970s? Why did the reverse differential for younger workers disappear in the early 1970s? Why did the gap for workers in their 30s, though small, continue in the second period? Why did the gap for those in their 40s begin to narrow at the end of the 1970s? The chief reason is likely to be the steep rise in the wage curve at small companies, but why did it rise so steeply?

Before examining these issues, an international comparison is needed because wage differentials by company size are thought to be unusually great in Japan relative to Western Europe and North America.

International Comparison

Observations on wage differentials relative to company size have depended on figures found in the census of manufacturers in industrialized countries. This is the most important source of statistics on production, but wages are not its primary focus, and it only includes average salaries aggregated for men and women and for white-collar and blue-collar workers. The EC's 1972 survey, by contrast, provides reliable data focused on salaries. It does not cross-classify wages by age multiplied by company size, but it does collect statistics on average wages for men, women, and white-collar and blue-collar workers. Figure 8-4 is based on these data.

Wage differentials by company size exist in all countries. Claims that they are a phenomenon unique to situations without market competition and that they are thus not found in Western Europe or North America are false. Japanese wage differentials by company size for male blue-collar workers, by far the largest group, are close to the mid-range for EC countries. For male white-collar workers, Japan elicits fairly large differentials but is on the low side for female white-collar workers. Female blue-collar workers are somewhere near the middle. Wage differentials in Japan are not unusually large.

Japan's data, though, do not include term-end bonuses. Size-based differentials including bonuses are greater than monthly earnings. If bonuses are added, Japan's wage differentials would approach Italy's, then surveyed as the highest among EC countries.

There is reason to believe that the differentials are smaller than the data indicate vis-à-vis differences in the rates of internal production. The internal production rate for large Japanese companies is far lower than for Western companies because work that is done in-house in the United States, for example, is farmed out in Japan. However, suppose wage differentials for Japan and the United States were the same. In figure 8-5, the wage levels for

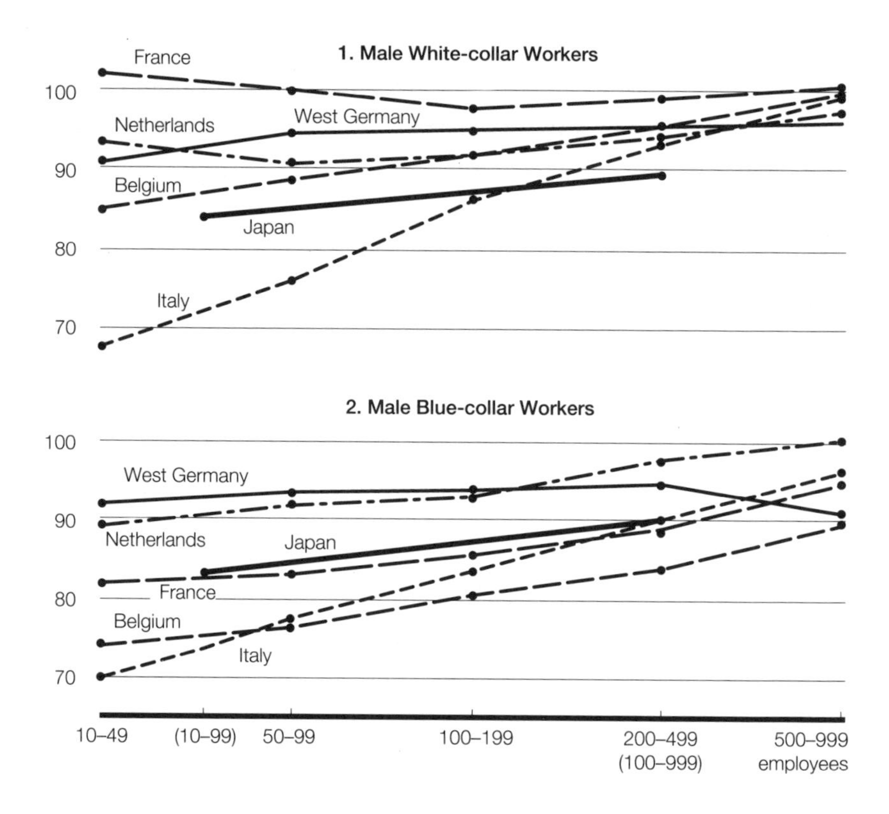

Fig. 8-4. Wage Differentials by Company Size in Japanese and EC Manufacturing Industries (1,000 or more employees = 100)

Source: Ministry of Labor, *Chingin Kozo Kihon Tokei Chosa* (Statistical Survey of Wage Structure).
Notes: 1. EC data are for establishment size; Japanese data are for company size.
2. Figures in parentheses are the size classifications for Japan.

Toyota employees and for Ford employees who do the same work as Toyota employees are 100. Likewise, the wage levels for employees at small and medium-sized related companies in Japan and for Ford employees who engage in the same type of work are 50, as are salaries at non-related companies in Japan and the United States. The real wage level at Ford thus is 75. If the level at Ford was 100, wages at small and medium-sized U.S. companies would be 67. If the level at Toyota is 100, wages at small and medium-sized companies are 50. Size-based differentials thus appear larger in Japan than in the United States. Even though

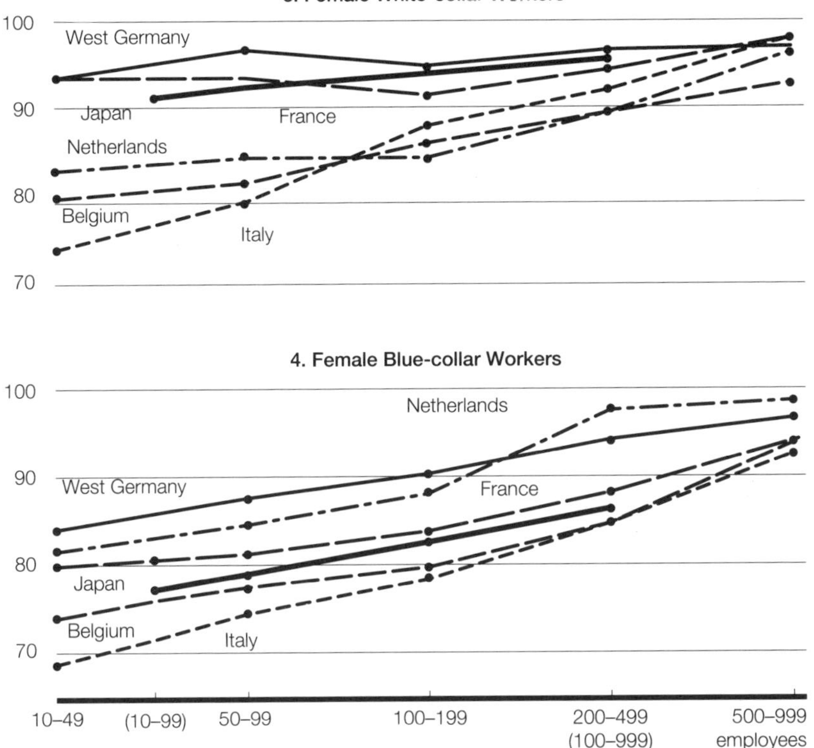

wages are the same, the difference in the rate of internal production causes wage differentials by company size that are different in the two countries.

Wage differentials by company size, moreover, have been narrowing steadily in Japan since the EC survey. It is hard, therefore, to conclude that Japan alone has unusually large size-based wage differentials. Readers are cautioned, however, that good statistical data that cross-classifies wage differentials by age and length of service or show how they change are unavailable except for Japan.

VARIOUS VIEWS

The Surplus Supply Theory

Various theories have appeared to account for wage differentials among companies of different size. Examining them will show

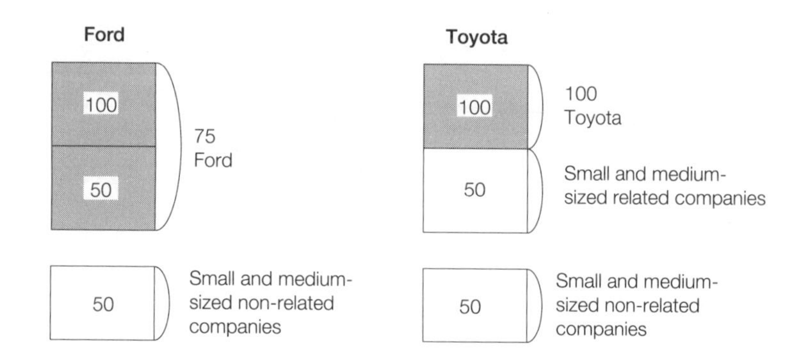

Fig. 8-5. Hypothetical Wage Differentials by Company Size and Rate of Internal Production at Toyota and Ford

how well they account for such trends as a rapid narrowing followed by a leveling off. The traditional view seeks the main cause for this phenomenon in a surplus population. Even granted that a surplus population exists, it is unclear why it should produce size-related wage differentials. This view states that a surplus population exists primarily in farming villages. After large companies select the workers they want, they close their labor markets. The pressure of the remaining surplus is then borne by small and medium-sized companies, which allows them to pay excessively low wages.

Thinking about this explanation reveals the dubiousness of its reasoning. It does not explain why large companies pay higher salaries than small and medium-sized companies. Large firms face fierce competition from companies at home and abroad. If workers at small and medium-sized firms are as efficient as their large-company counterparts, why do large companies not hire lower-paid workers? Ultimately, the reasons for this are sought through two views that focus on differences in productivity and the ability to pay.

This view's bankruptcy is obvious in its flawed logic and through a look at size-related wage differentials, which, it argues, ought to be eliminated by a labor shortage. Yet, they hardly decreased during the acute labor shortage from the late 1960s to the early 1970s. For a time, differentials among younger workers reversed themselves, but this inverse gap disappeared. In addition, this view cannot account for wage differentials for workers in their late 30s and older in the subsequent period. Nor does it explain the lack of differentials by company size before World War I, despite its stress on a labor surplus. Large differentials should have existed before World War I.

The Difference in Productivity Theory

The ability to pay theory is so widespread that no source is representative. It argues that size-based differentials arise because large companies have a greater ability to pay. This is explained by the difference in productivity theory and by the capital-concentration hypothesis advocated by Shinohara Miyohei. He argues that banks loan money to large corporations and restrict capital to small and medium-sized companies, producing a difference in the ability to pay. The difference in productivity theory is the more widespread and is discussed here, although it does not make much difference which of the two is chosen to explain the ability to pay theory.

The reasoning behind the ability to pay theory can be divided into two propositions. Differences in productivity cause differences in the ability to pay, and differences in the ability to pay cause differences in wages.

For the first proposition to work presupposes that companies of different sizes are competing fiercely and making the same products and selling them for the same prices. Minus these conditions, differences in physical productivity do not matter. If their products differ, companies of various sizes can maintain their profit rates with different prices. Only with same products and same prices does a difference in physical productivity at variously sized companies affect profit rates. This presupposition is seldom fulfilled. Even large and small and medium-sized companies that belong statistically to the same industry make different products sold at different prices.

Automakers, for example, are all big, with tens of thousands of employees. Small and medium-sized companies make parts.

There is no way a company with 200 workers could compete directly with Toyota. Likewise in the steel industry. The making of pig iron, steel, and sheet metal for automobiles is confined to the integrated steelmakers, also huge companies with tens of thousands of employees. A steelmaker with 200 employees could not compete against them directly.[2]

Men's tailoring represents the opposite side of the coin. Even a one-person operation can be competitive with a department store of over 10,000 employees in making high-quality, made-to-order suits. A tailor and big department stores, however, can coexist. In general, though, long-term competition destroys the less efficient. Why this extremely obvious point is not understood in Japan suggests, perhaps, an inferiority complex that causes people to misjudge reality.

The disparities in productivity found statistically among companies of varying sizes are a result of different products and those products' different prices. Therefore it is doubtful if differences in productivity cause differences in profits.

The second proposition also raises doubts. If there is a difference in profits, why pay it out as wages? A company that sets its wages higher than the going rate amid fierce competition is likely to go under. A small difference in salaries would be acceptable and might pay off in morale. Wage differentials by company size are thought to be abnormally large, however. If so, they could not be explained on the basis of morale. The ability to pay theory is thus not convincing.

Reder's Thesis

The most convincing hypothesis is Reder's thesis, which applies to Japan and the West.[3] In his classic, mid-1950s essay, Melvin Reder argued that various wage differentials narrow in times of prosperity and widen or remain unchanged in recessions. He explained that because information about the labor market is incomplete, some companies may pay high wages and others low wages for the same job. Moving from a low-paying to a high-paying company is difficult except when opportunities are plentiful, as in an expansionary period. Otherwise, workers might not find new jobs.

When workers move in good economic times from low-paying to high-paying companies, wage differentials shrink. In bad economic times, when movement occurs rarely, wage differentials remain unchanged. Reder's thesis does well in explaining why differentials remain unchanged during recessions, but is less satisfactory in explaining why they widen.

Reder, however, also focuses on the structure of demand. The demand for labor is not for a single job but for a ladder of closely related job clusters—a career. During expansion, when companies increase personnel, they hire workers for the easiest jobs at the bottom of the job ladder and fill the more difficult jobs internally by promoting employees one step up the job ladder. The connection with the external market is thus focused on the easiest jobs at the bottom of the job ladder. As a result, salaries for these jobs rise and wage differentials shrink. In a recession, on the other hand, workers doing higher-level jobs move down a rung on the job ladder until ultimately workers at the bottom of the job ladder are laid off; naturally salaries decrease and wage differentials increase. This explains why wage differentials widen during a recession but presupposes an internal labor market. For that reason, it is effective in explaining why wage differentials are primarily found in large companies and after World War I. But it does not explain small and medium-sized companies or why before World War I internal labor markets were not widespread.

Reder's thesis nevertheless is successful in presenting facts and is well-suited to explaining long-term differentials in North America and Western Europe, where various wage differentials shrink when business is good and widen or remain unchanged when business is bad.[4] It is also compatible with Japan's situation throughout the twentieth century judging from studies of the prewar period.[5] It applies where no internal labor market exists. But a problem remains.

Reder's thesis is quite good at explaining the postwar changes in wage differentials by company size discussed earlier. It is especially good at explaining the rapid narrowing of the wage gap in the first period. In the 1950s, the effective job vacancies to job seekers ratio was around 0.3, an extreme supply surplus. Around

1967, it approached 1.0 for the first time after the war, and the demand for labor rapidly tightened. According to Reder, wage differentials should narrow rapidly, and they did. The thesis also explains the leveling off that began in the mid-1970s, in the latter half of the second period. After the energy crisis, the labor supply suddenly slackened, falling from a high of 1.76 just before the oil crisis to around 0.6 in terms of the job vacancies-job seekers ratio, where it stayed until the end of the 1980s. That differentials flattened but did not shrink is only natural according to Reder. Reder, however, does not explain the following:

(a) At the beginning of the second period, there was an acute labor shortage from the late 1960s to the early 1970s. According to Reder, wage differentials ought to have narrowed rapidly. Instead, they flattened, and reverse differentials among young workers disappeared. Otherwise, the wage gap did not shrink.
(b) Wage differentials persisted for workers in their late 30s and older and did not narrow for workers in their 40s despite a labor shortage.
(c) Differentials for workers in their 40s began to shrink at the end of the 1970s. Labor supply and demand continued to be gloomy, with a job vacancies to job seekers ratio of 0.6. According to Reder, a narrowing of the wage gap should not have occurred.

A more effective explanation of events can be found in the nature of skills.

SKILL FORMATION AT SMALL AND MEDIUM-SIZED COMPANIES

A Mixture of Different Groups of Workers

The skills of workers at small and medium-sized companies attract little attention. The assumption seems to be that their skills are not high. It is sometimes agreed that small and medium-sized companies compete for labor with large companies, so no difference in skills is recognized based on company size. Rather than assuming that high skills are required by companies of all sizes, it is supposed that little skill is necessary at any of them. But it is inconceivable that paid labor of any kind not require some skill. Knowing that outstanding intellectual skills exist in the workshops of large companies, it becomes extremely important to discover whether they also exist in small and medium-sized companies.

Skills, however, are difficult to observe. As at large companies, the formation and nature of skills at small and medium-sized companies depend greatly on OJT in the workshop. Skill thus manifests itself in the movement of workers within a workshop or among closely related workshops. Workshop practices and, above all, intensive interviews provide the best view of skill. The observations that follow are based on nine 1978 case studies by the author of companies with about 100 workers[6] and on six 1986 studies of companies with between 100 and 300 workers.[7]

The number of case studies is small and must be supplemented with two questionnaires. Together, questionnaires, which are inevitably superficial, and in-depth case studies make up for each other's shortcomings to strengthen the observations. The questionnaires used are a 1978 survey of 429 small and medium-sized companies conducted by the Small Business Finance Corporation[8] (Chusho Kigyo Kinyu Koko) and a 1981 survey of 1,432 companies by the National Institute of Employment and Vocational Research (Koyo Shokugyo Sogo Kenkyujo).[9] Both adopted the author's hypotheses and used similar methods, but the National Institute questionnaire is the primary reference because it asked the same questions at large companies as well, enabling comparisons across companies of all sizes.

The case studies depict the skills of workers at small and medium-sized companies as follows. Noteworthy is that blue-collar workers at small and medium-sized companies can be divided into groups depending on the nature of their skills. At large companies, most blue-collar workers have the intellectual skills described in chapter 5. Not so at small and medium-sized companies. Blue-collar workers there comprise a core group with skills based on broad experience, a semiskilled group whose skills level off after around

10 years on the job, and an unskilled group whose skills do not go up.

Core Groups and Experienced Workers

Workers with skills based on broad experience, found in large companies, also exist in small and medium-sized firms. They enter companies young, gain experience of the main jobs within a workshop, then broaden their experience by moving to related workshops. Their experience seems broader than that of workers at large companies only because they generally gain experience in a greater number of workshops of smaller size than their large-company counterparts. Within 3 or 4 years, workers with potential are designated and given experience in workshops considered important. In addition, the percentage of such workers promoted to section or division chief is thought to be far greater than at large companies. This is because the corporate structure is less bureaucratized at small and medium-sized companies than at large companies, where it is exceptional for a production worker to be promoted section chief. In small and medium-sized companies, many outstanding section chiefs rise through the ranks. Their responsibilities and the number of workers under them, however, are not as great as those even of a foreman at a large company. Also, the products these workers deal with are not as diverse; the scope of their workshops is smaller.

Even so, these workers boast skills as high as those at large companies. Their income levels and the curve at which they rise thus are similar to and in some cases better than those at large companies.

The main difference is the percentage of such workers. In a large company, they constitute almost all core production workers. In small and medium-sized companies, they are a very small part of the workforce. Statistics are unavailable, but a rough estimate according to the 1978 study suggests that they account for only around 10 percent of the workers at most of the firms studied (if white-collar workers were included, this figure would rise greatly).

A far larger group comprises experienced workers. They do different jobs, mainly within one workshop, but their careers more or less stop there. Consequently, their salaries, too, level off when they reach their mid-30s, after around 10 years of experience. Until then, no significant differences exist between their salaries and those for the core group in wage levels or the way wages go up. Thereafter, the gap widens. Because of sheer number, it is their wages that are used as the averages for small and medium-sized companies.

No distinction is made between workers at hiring. Hiring and deployment during the first few years are identical. Managements seem to observe workers for several years before selecting the core group.

A third group, of unskilled workers, sees wages level off almost from the start. Initially, their salaries may be slightly higher than those of the other two groups, but when they reach their mid-20s their pay levels off and gaps widen. At a large company, unskilled workers would not be company employees. They would work for a related company or their jobs would be subcontracted. Even at small and medium-sized companies the percentage of such workers is so small that they have little impact on wage levels.

Table 8-1, compiled from a study by the National Institute of Employment and Vocational Research, facilitates a questionnaire comparison with the case studies. It uses as a loose indicator the number of those who answered "yes" to the question "Is there job rotation within the workshop?" and, as a stronger indicator, the number who gave "formation of broadly based skills" as the reason for that rotation. In both cases, the numbers decline with company size, while continuity among companies is observed. The skill-formation methods described earlier for large companies are found at small and medium-sized companies, though on a smaller scale. The same can be said for movement between workshops. The percentage of companies with long-term employees who experience most jobs within a workshop does not change, regardless of company size. Although the percentage of such workers may vary, this indicates that workers with skills based on broad experience also exist at small and medium-sized companies.

Table 8-1 Intra- and Inter-Workshop Mobility (1979)

Company size	Number of responses[a] (%) (Actual no.)	Intra-workshop mobility occurs[b]	Workers with long years of service who have experienced most of the jobs within a workshop[c]	Reason for intra-workshop mobility—broadly based skills formation	Inter-workshop mobility occurs[c]	Reason for inter-workshop mobility—broadly based skills formation
3,000 or more	100 (83)	71.1	47.0	50.1	57.8	33.7
1,000–2,999	100 (129)	66.7	44.2	41.9	63.6	39.5
300– 999	100 (259)	59.1	30.9	28.2	62.5	32.0
100– 299	100 (282)	62.4	37.9	31.9	62.0	33.7
30– 99	100 (222)	47.7	44.1	24.8	48.6	24.7

Source: National Institute of Employment and Vocational Research, *Kigyonai Rodoryoku no Yuko Katsuyo ni kansuru Jittai Chosa* (Investigation into the Effective Utilization of the Labor Force within Companies), 1982.

[a]Number of responses do not always match the original totals. Among the questions, those that received the most responses were selected. This was because there were differences in the number of responses depending on the question; in such cases, comparison between questions was not appropriate.

[b]The total of those who replied "change as circumstances warrant" and those who replied "change on a regular basis" was taken here.

[c]Those who responded "yes" to the question "Is it normal practice for male employees who have worked for 5 or 10 years to experience most of the jobs in the workshop?"

A glance at the constituent groups of workers at small and medium-sized companies helps to explain wage differentials by company size. Two problems, though, could not be accounted for by the relationship between supply and demand. First, from the late 1960s to the early 1970s, despite an acute labor shortage, wage differentials did not shrink. Why? In particular, what was the reason for the wage differentials that remained for workers in their late 30s and older? Second, despite an easing in the demand for labor in the late 1970s, why did differentials for workers in their 40s and older slowly but steadily decrease? This is thought due to the steeper wage curve at small and medium-sized companies, but why?

These questions cannot be explained in terms of supply and demand, so the nature of skills must be considered. The reason for the first problem is that small and medium-sized companies have a lower proportion of workers with skills equivalent to their large-company counterparts'. By far the largest number of workers at small and medium-sized companies are experienced workers whose skill formation is confined to one workshop, which itself is smaller than workshops at large companies. After 10 years' experience, their skills stop expanding, and, consequently, wage differentials by company size appear thereafter. Because these differentials are based on skills, they do not change, no matter how tight the demand for labor.

Although decisive evidence is lacking, the reason for the second problem is thought to be as follows. In workshops at small and medium-sized companies, the number of workers with intellectual skills equivalent to those at large companies gradually increases. No study of workers with intellectual skills was conducted in the 1970s because this concept had not yet been developed, but, according to case studies in the late 1980s, it is clear that, though small in number, workers with intellectual skills are found in the workshops of small and medium-sized companies.[10] Is it not the formation and growth of these skills that are reflected in the rise in the wage curve for small and medium-sized companies?

Chapter 9

Women and Older Workers

OLDER WORKERS

High Participation Rate in the Workforce Despite Early Mandatory Retirement Age

So far, the focus has been on workers at large and small and medium-sized companies. This chapter deals with two subgroups among them that display distinct problems and thus are deserving of special attention: women and older workers. An older worker is here defined as a male aged 55 or older and especially males in their early 60s because this is where most problems arise.

The most widespread belief about older workers in Japan is that a sharp increase in their numbers will make the seniority wage and permanent employment systems excessively costly, necessitating changes. Another belief insists that because mandatory retirement comes earlier in Japan than in Western Europe and North America and because Japan's proportion of elderly is rising rapidly, the retirement age must be extended to avoid bankrupting pension plans. The dubiousness of common perceptions of permanent employment and seniority wages has been exposed. Now onto the problem of older workers.

That the number of older workers is rising steeply is incontrovertible. According to an estimate by Japan's Ministry of Health and Welfare's Institute of Population Problems, the proportion of people aged 60 to 64 to the total population will rise from 5.4 percent in 1990 to 7.3 percent in 2010.[1] Those 65 and older will soar from 11.9 percent in 1990 to 23.6 percent in 2020. Japan's population, moreover, is aging much faster than Western Europe's.

However, rapid rises in age levels among older workers are already over. Steep rises of over 20 percent every five years took place between 1975 and 1985 for workers in their late 50s and between 1980 and 1990 for workers in their early 60s. Since then, the rate of increase has dropped sharply. It appears that a period in which counterplans can be made has been reached.

The point about mandatory retirement, too, is not straightforward. Mandatory retirement does occur earlier in Japan than in developed countries, but later than in developing countries with low life expectancy. In the United States, the 1978 Mandatory Retirement Act (originally the 1967 Age Discrimination in Employment Act) raised the age of mandatory retirement to 70. In Western Europe, the retirement age for white-collar workers at large companies is generally around 63 to 65, but usually 65. Figure 9-1 indicates that as of 1989 mandatory retirement in Japan for most workers was 60, and even earlier for the rest. And this is after a steady raising of the retirement age—in 1978, fewer than 20 percent of even large companies mandated 60 as retirement age.

Mandatory retirement implies that a worker stops working at a specified age. In Japan, the opposite is true. The rate of older workers in the same-age population—the percentage of people employed at paying jobs—is far higher than in Western Europe and North America. Figure 9-2 shows it to be higher in every age bracket. For early 60s workers, it reaches as high as 70 percent in Japan, compared with less than 30 percent in the West as a whole, and rates are declining in all countries. Japan is no exception, but its figures for every age group remain high. The percentage of older workers in the workforce, as revealed in chapter 1, varies depending on the measurement methodology—as a reflection of usual circumstances or of the actual circumstances during one particular week. But the size of the differences between Japan and the West transcend differences in methodologies.

The number of older workers despite Japan's early mandatory retirement age indicates that many work beyond official retirement.

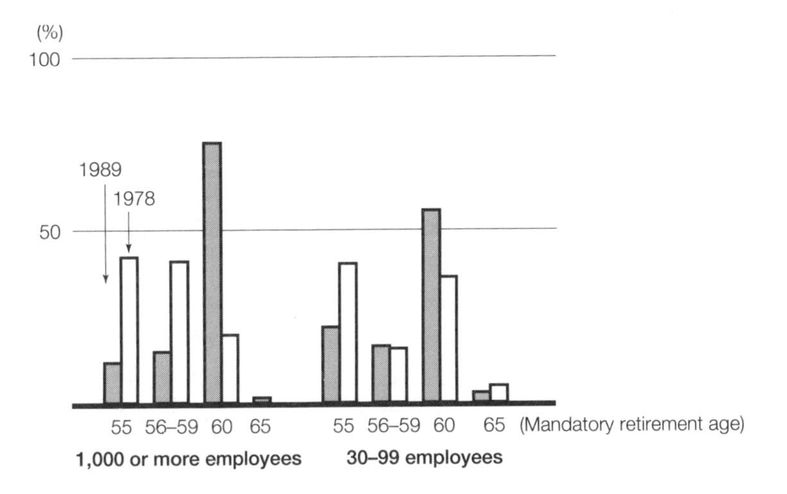

Fig. 9-1. Mandatory Retirement Age (proportion of number of companies, 1978 and 1989)

Source: Ministry of Labor, *Koyo Kanri Chosa* (Survey of Employment Systems).
Note: Proportion of the number of companies that have uniform mandatory retirement = 100.

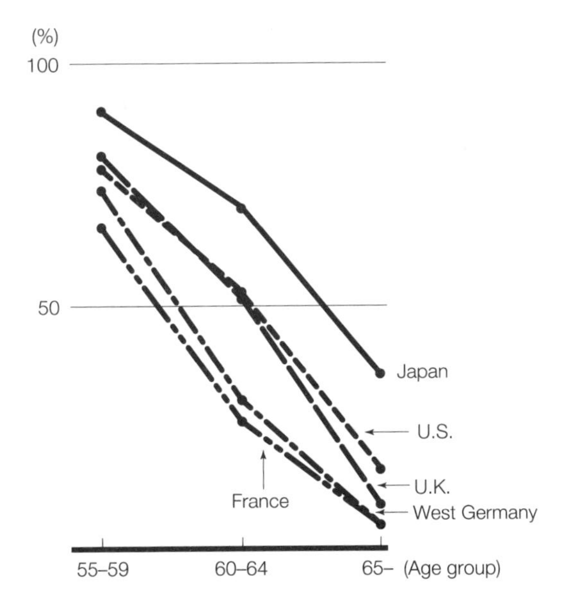

Fig. 9-2. International Comparison of the Labor Force Participation Rate for Older Male Workers (1987)

Source: OECD, *Labor Force Statistics.*

The Rehiring System

To continue working beyond mandatory retirement, a worker can be rehired by the same company, although not as a regular employee, or can find work at another company. To be rehired first involves severing the formal regular employment relationship and leaving the company. Retirement pay is issued upon formal mandatory retirement. Although deferred mandatory retirement also occurs, the primary method is to retire and then be rehired. As of 1988, around 30 to 40 percent of Japan's large companies had either a rehiring or a deferred mandatory retirement system in place, with rehiring predominant.[2] Table 9-1 shows that rehiring often entails loss of management position and lower salary, but oftentimes little change in job.

Figure 9-3 shows how much salaries decline. The data are from Japan's Statistical Survey of Wage Structure, which includes rehiring in its figures for number of years of service. The figure takes employees with 30 years or more of service and looks at how much wages declined for workers aged 60 to 64 compared with peak salaries for workers aged 50 to 54. At large companies, older workers' salaries were close to 90 percent of peak salaries in 1987. In 1974, they were at about 60 percent. Clearly, the gap has narrowed. At small companies with 10 to 99 workers, however, the rates for both years remained unchanged, at around 85 percent. The problem of a gap, as shown latter, exists only in large compa-

Table 9-1 The Rehiring System for Older Workers (1978 and 1988)

		1978	1988
Management position	Changed	62.0%	52.7%
	Unchanged	20.4	18.4
	Uncertain	17.7	26.2
Job contents	Changed	18.3	16.9
	Unchanged	61.4	60.0
	Uncertain	20.3	21.0
Salary (fixed)	Lowered	59.4	66.6
	Unchanged	24.7	15.8
	Raised	1.9	0.1
	Uncertain	13.9	15.9

Source: Ministry of Labor, *Koyo Kanri Chosa* (Survey of Employment Systems).

nies. It is important to note here that reductions in salaries are diminishing at large companies and approaching the levels found in small companies.

The reason for this is that when someone continues working for a large company, efficiency is a crucial matter. Most older, experienced workers have skills acquired through years of service. If unused, efficiency drops. Thus, in most cases job descriptions remain unchanged even in rehiring. If, however, pay is reduced for the same work and approximate level of efficiency, workers' morale and desire to work diminishes. Pay cuts of up to 40 percent were so keenly felt at one point that it seems to have led to improvement in the rehiring system. The production workers on whom the data for this survey were based, however, did not include supervisors and managers. The impact on salary of being relieved of managerial responsibilities is thus not reflected in

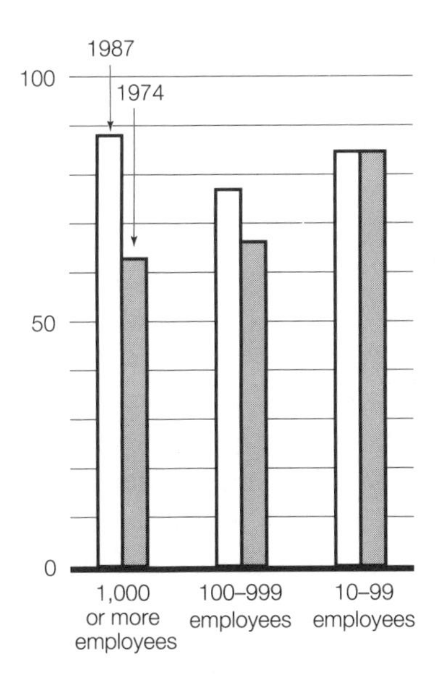

Fig. 9-3. Drop in Wages for Male Blue-collar Workers of All Educational Levels Aged 60–64 with 30 or More Years of Service in the Manufacturing Industries (1974 and 1987; peak wages for workers aged 50–54 with 30 or more years of service = 100)

Source: Ministry of Labor, *Chingin Kozo Kihon Tokei Chosa* (Statistical Survey of Wage Structure).

figure 9-3. What has been said about skills also applies to losing a management position, but an alternative policy in which older workers maintain their management positions also disadvantages middle-aged workers, who then have to wait a long time for promotion. Policy selection depends on which policy is less disadvantageous.

On the whole, rehiring accounts for a small part of the high percentage of older workers in the workforce. It was popular for only two or three years and has greatly declined at large companies. In 1973, rehiring took place at around 90 percent of companies with 5,000 or more employees; by 1989, the rate had fallen to one in three.[3] The rehiring system has been replaced by deferred retirement. In addition, many workers quit before reaching retirement age, particularly in the case of white-collar workers. Where, then, do most workers go who continue working after retirement?

Two Routes

By means of the either of two routes, most workers end up at small and medium-sized companies. Older workers either move from a large to a small or medium-sized company or continue working at the small or medium-sized firm at which they started their careers.[4]

Figure 9-4 confirms the first route. If older workers did not move from large to small or medium-sized companies, the percentage of older workers by company size would not be too different from the percentage of middle-aged workers. Look, for example, at the employment rate for middle-aged, manufacturing industry production workers by company size. Workers aged 45 to 49 in companies with 1,000 or more employees constitute 34 percent, compared with 38 percent in companies with 10 to 99 employees. Workers in their early 60s, however, drop sharply at large companies to a mere 1.6 percent and soar to nearly 80 percent at smaller firms, indicating a veritable avalanche of older workers from large to small companies. This also suggests that the age ceiling at large companies is less than 60 even for blue-collar workers.

The second route, of continuing one's employment at a small or medium-sized company, presents a problem. Figure 9-1 shows that the mandatory retirement age is earlier at small companies. A mandatory retirement age of 60 is common at 74 percent of large companies, compared with 56 percent of small companies. Conversely, a mandatory retirement age of 55 prevails at slightly more than 10 percent of large companies but at more than 20 percent of small companies. More small companies have rehiring systems, but only to compensate for earlier mandatory retirement. How is it, then, that small companies are the chief employers of workers over 60?

First, some primarily small companies do not have mandatory retirement systems. The figure was as high as 45 percent in 1973, but slowly diminished to 15 percent in 1989.[5] Although noteworthy, 15 percent is insufficient to make smaller firms the chief employers of older workers. Second, however, add to this what observation suggests are the numerous smaller companies that

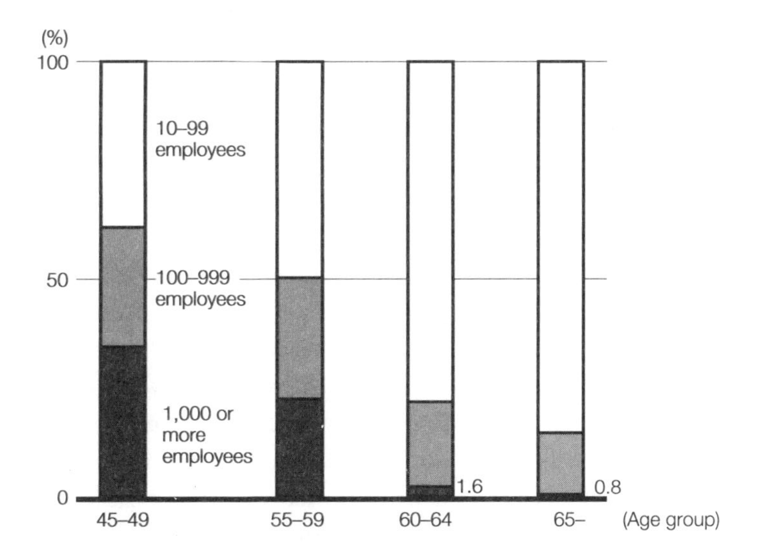

Fig. 9-4. Percentage of Older Male Blue-collar Workers of All Educational Levels in the Manufacturing Industries by Company Size (1988)

Source: Ministry of Labor, *Chingin Kozo Kihon Tokei Chosa* (Statistical Survey of Wage Structure).

have but do not enforce mandatory retirement and where workers can continue to work until nearly 70. These companies have mandatory retirement only so that workers who are ill or who wish to leave can receive lump-sum retirement pay. The number of these companies is unknown, but if it were not sizable accounting for the high proportion of smaller companies that employ older workers would be impossible.

Making Use of the Skills of Older Workers

Of the two routes described, continuing to work for the same company is better for the national economy. This route, however, is available only at small and medium-sized companies.

This is a problem because it puts into question what will happen to the high skill levels of older workers with long workshop experience at large firms who are forced to take the alternative route of moving to smaller companies. If rehired and assigned to jobs where they cannot use their skills, their loss and that of the national economy are great. Acquired skills accumulated over many years are best used in the same workshop. Continuous employment—working at the same company and doing the same job—is thus important. But it does not preclude the possibility of doing the same or similar work at a different company; even the specificity of specific skills is slight. The supply and demand of older workers worldwide, however, is such that if workers waited for suitable jobs, they might never work again. Older workers from large companies, therefore, often take jobs at small and medium-sized companies that do not utilize their skills.

Most older workers are forced to follow this route because of misapprehension about their skills. Supported by a battery of figures measuring physical strength, which diminishes with age, it is thought that ability, too, declines with age. Physical strength, however, is not of preeminent importance to today's skills. Consider intellectual skills—their deterioration is not commensurate with declines in physical strength.[6]

Japan's employment practices waste the skills of older workers and are apparent in an international comparison of wage curves of, for example, Japan and the EC in figures 2-1 and 2-2. Wages for older workers drop precipitously in Japan. Conversely, since salaries for production workers in the EC level off early it can be said that wages for older Western European workers do not go down. In Japan, the curve falls abruptly even for white-collar workers who have the same seniority wage curve, with little to no change in the EC. The common perception in Japan is that a seniority wage curve implies that wages go down for older workers. This holds true only in Japan.

Wages drop sharply for older workers in Japan because workers are forced to move from large firms to small and medium-sized companies. There, they are unable to use the skills they have acquired and must start over as unskilled labor.

Continuous Employment

Continuous employment is possible through rehiring or deferred retirement. They are similar in their use of workers' skills, but different in that rehiring entails relieving older workers of their management positions and cutting their pay. Rehiring thus threatens morale. Why should workers employing the same skills and doing the same jobs have management positions taken away and salaries cut? Ultimately, workers will feel like outcasts, and this will affect their ability to use their skills effectively. Deferred retirement, too, damages morale—of younger workers—in that it entails no change and allows older workers to continue receiving regular pay increments.

Interviews conducted at a few large companies in the United Kingdom and West Germany revealed no cases—even among white-collar, seniority wage curve workers—of retirement-age workers being relieved of management positions, taking pay cuts, or changing to jobs for older workers. It was clearly the practice to work at positions until retirement. But middle-aged and older workers who were not promoted often did stop getting regular pay increments.[7]

Large Japanese companies do not practice continuous employment because, under human capital theory, early retirement is regarded as an emergency escape route. Long-term investment in human capital presupposes that it is necessary for older workers to recoup the investment made when young in the form of salaries that exceed their skill levels. It is thus advantageous for management to let older workers go early or to lower the age of mandatory retirement. Carried out on a regular basis, however, such practices make workers aware that the long-term balance between skill and salaries has been disrupted, causing morale to drop. The emergency escape route approach is nevertheless adopted frequently in Japan.

That these practices continue possibly arises from a misunderstanding of employment practices in Japan and the West. The belief is that Western Europe and North America put ability first and have neither a seniority wage curve nor permanent employment, whereas Japan has a unique system that especially protects older workers. The real situation, therefore, goes unrecognized: Japan does not encourage the employment of older workers. Lack of awareness compounds the employment problems of older workers in Japan.

WOMEN WORKERS

An International Comparison of Women's Participation in the Workforce

Many views on women workers exist in Japan that initially appear correct. Japanese women, it is said, traditionally stayed at home, have begun working only recently, and have been slower to do so than European or North American women. The wage gap between men and women is for that reason, it is argued, much greater in Japan than in the West. In general, these views stress the late industrialization of Japan. Their corollaries are that Japan denigrates women and has achieved economic growth at their expense.

The International Labour Organization's statistical yearbook, which gives government statistics for all countries, provides data on women's participation in the workforce. The EC compiles statistics for all its member countries in Western Europe using a common method.[8] Although some discrepancies may arise depending on whether surveys ask for "usual" work status or "actual" work status "during one particular week," the differences between Japan and the West in workforce participation rates exceed differences in survey methods. Figure 9-5 reveals that findings for the mid-1980s pretty much agree with common perceptions. The rate for Sweden is clearly high; in fact, it is extremely high for all the Scandinavian countries. Western European rates fall somewhere between the United Kingdom's and West Germany's, but are above Japan's. U.S. rates, too, are higher than Japan's. More Japanese women over the age of 40, however, work than in West Germany, and their numbers are close to those in some other countries of Western Europe.

To say that Japanese women have gotten off to a late start is to misread the facts. Figure 9-6 compares trends in the postwar period in Japan and Sweden, which has the highest participation rate in Europe. Until around 1970, Japan had the higher percentage of women in the workforce. This cannot be attributed to the

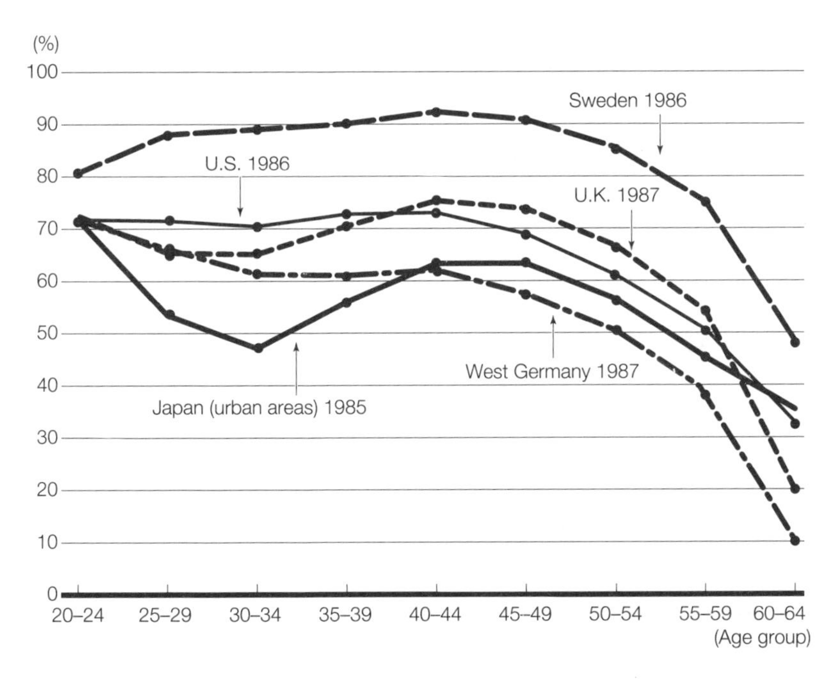

Fig. 9-5. International Comparison of the Labor Force Participation Rate for Women

Sources: United Kingdom and West Germany, EC, *Labour Force Survey*, 1987; United States and Sweden, ILO, *Yearbook of Labour Statistics*; Japan, *Kokusei Chosa* (National Census).

large number of women in agriculture because both figures 9-5 and 9-6 use data for women in urban areas only. European and North American women only began working en masse after the 1970s. This trend may well be called a phenomenon of the period of equal opportunity laws.

Figures 9-5 and 9-6 show another feature that is often said to be unique to Japan: the twin-peaked or M shape of the workforce participation rate. The line starts out high when women are young, goes down for women in their late 20s and early 30s child-bearing years, and then goes up again. The rate for Sweden differs. In 1960, the line moved down; in 1970, it flattened out; and in 1987, it continued the plateau. Japan's pattern is said to be another sign of late development, but this is not necessarily so. The graphs omit the downward slope that the participation rate took in prewar Japan. Japan's twin-peaked shape is a postwar phenomenon that is also found in Western Europe, including the United

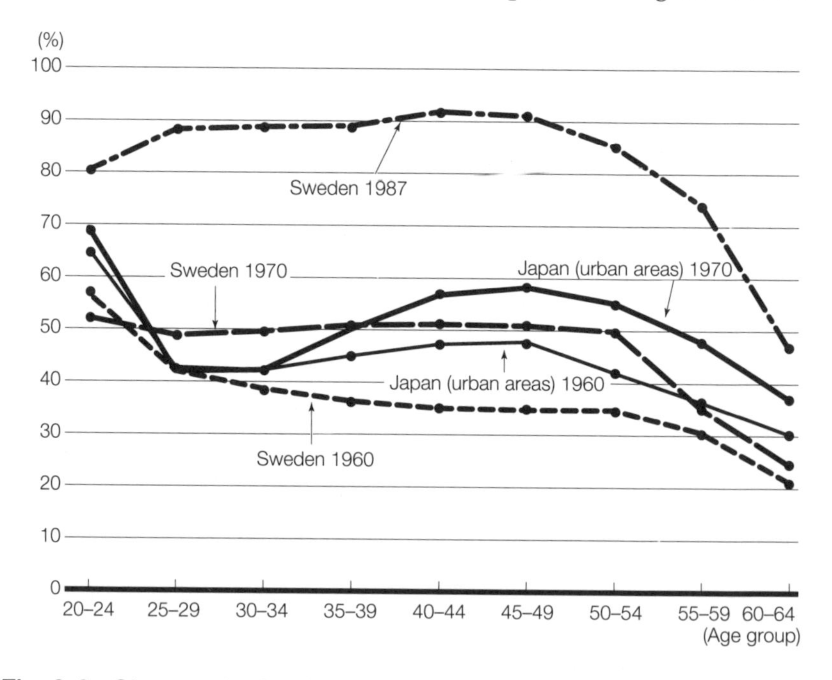

Fig. 9-6. Changes in the Labor Force Participation Rate for Women in Japan and Sweden

Sources: Sweden, ILO, *Yearbook of Labour Statistics; Japan*, *Kokusei Chosa* (National Census).

Kingdom, which has had a high percentage of women in the labor force for a longer time. A result of Japan's twin-peaked shape is that the percentage of women over 40 in the workforce is higher than in West Germany.

Both employment and its quality should be looked at. The percentages of women in managerial positions and professional occupations, as given in table 9-2, which is based on ILO statistics, serve as indicators. Note, however, that the ILO compiles government statistics from each country, so definitions of "managerial" may differ. The table cites countries that exhibit advanced industrialization. Thus, if the percentages for men and women are very different it is reasonable to conclude that definitions also differ. The percentage of those in managerial positions is so much lower in Japan and West Germany than it is in either the United States or the United Kingdom that no comparison can be made. Compared even with West Germany, whose percentages are similar, Japan has a lower percentage of women in management. Japan's figure for professional occupations, however, is not especially low.

Japan's twin-peaked workforce participation rate offers perhaps a partial explanation for differences. The percentage of women who interrupt their careers in Japan is higher than in Western Europe. Length of service is a particularly significant factor in promotion to managerial positions in Japan. Why, and what

Table 9-2 International Comparison of Women in Managerial Positions and Professional Occupations

	Japan	U.S.	U.K.	West Germany
Managerial position / Total number of employees	3.5%	10.7%	7.2%	3.4%
Professional occupation / Total number of employees	11.9	15.1	17.7	15.3
Women in managerial positions / Total managers of both sexes	11.5	38.5	19.1	20.2
Women in professional occupations / Total professionals of both sexes	43.1	50.2	41.2	43.1

Source: ILO, *Yearbook of Labour Statistics.*

Notes: 1. The dates of the surveys were 1985 for Japan, 1986 for the U.S., 1981 for the U.K., and 1984 for West Germany.

2. Survey limited to employees only.

economic significance does this have? Chapter 11 discusses these issues.

The Wage Gap between Men and Women

It has long been believed that the average wage gap between men and women is extreme in Japan. This is true if only wage averages for all age groups are looked at. The EC's 1972 survey permits for the first time observation of wage differentials by age and sex using reliable statistics. Figure 9-7 derives from these data and elucidates several points; (1) wage differentials between men and women exist in all countries; (2) the wage gap is high in Japan only for workers over 30; (3) for workers in their 20s, the gap is not much different than it is in Western Europe.

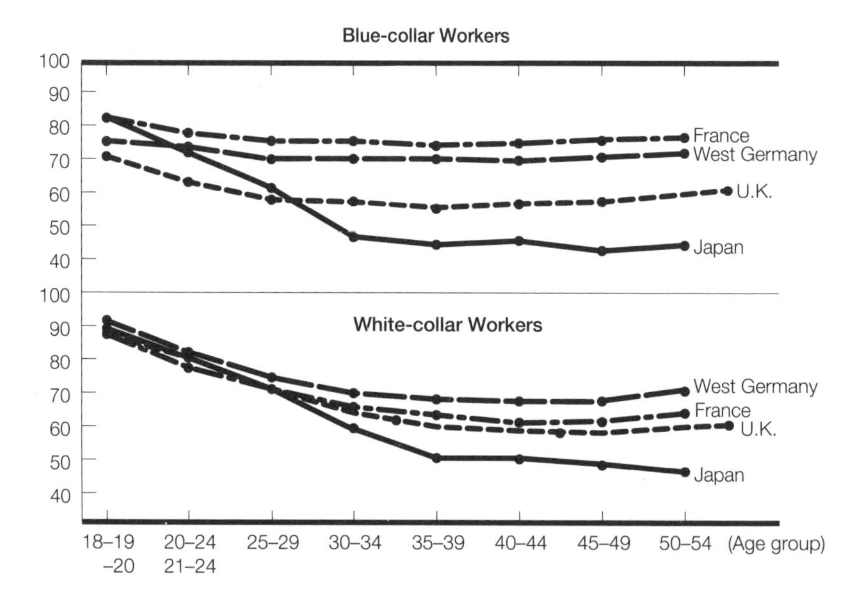

Fig. 9-7. International Comparison of Wage Differentials by Sex and Company Size in the Manufacturing Industries (1972, 1973, and 1975; wages for male workers = 100)

Sources: EC, *Structure of Earnings for 1972, 1975–1976*; Japan, *1973-nen Chingin Kozo Kihon Tokei Chosa* (Statistical Survey of Wage Structure for the Year 1973); U.K., Department of Employment, *New Earnings Survey for 1975.*

Note: Based on hourly wage earnings for blue-collar workers and monthly wage earnings for white-collar workers.

The reasons for points two and three are the same and mostly have to do with wages for men. In the discussion of the age-wage profile for male workers in chapter 2, Japan displayed a steep wage curve for blue-collar workers. In Western Europe, production workers saw their wages flatten out after reaching their mid-20s. Although not depicted, wages for most women worldwide tend to level off. The wage gap between men and women in Japan is therefore naturally greater after the age of 30 than in Western Europe. Western European white-collar workers also have a seniority wage curve; the gap in West Germany and France, for example, is slightly wider than for blue-collar workers. Because the wage curve for Japan's white-collar workers is somewhat steeper than for blue-collar workers and for European white-collar workers, the gap between men and women after 30 is far greater in Japan than in Western Europe. But what accounts for the sex-based differentials found in all countries?

The Theory of Statistical Discrimination

The theory of statistical discrimination is a brilliant theory on sex-based wage differentials. It argues that even if no bias against women's working abilities existed sexual discrimination would still occur amid companies' intensive pursuit of efficiency.[9] A far greater basis in fact for this theory exists than is commonly believed, so it deserves examination. The theory was developed in the early 1970s to account for the racial discrimination against African Americans in American society, but it is just as applicable to sexual discrimination. An understanding of this theory is a requisite to prevent discussions from degenerating into unproductive arguments dependent solely on Japan's uniqueness and late development. Plans to correct the situation can be formulated only if the remarkable rationality of discrimination is taken into account.

Applied to sexual discrimination, the theory of statistical discrimination presupposes the following. First, on average women have statistically obvious shorter working careers than men. Second, some women work for lengthy periods, but it is difficult to know in advance who they will be so the cost of finding out can be high. Third, skill requirements are high, and forming the necessary skills requires medium- to long-term OJT within the company. Some variants of the theory stress enterprise-specific skills, but the argument is fully developed on the above conditions alone.

The underlying idea of the third condition—medium- to long-term OJT—is that if a worker quits, the company incurs a loss for the OJT to that point. To avoid this, employers must choose long-term workers. According to the second condition, however, the cost of determining such individuals can be high. It is less costly to choose from groups with easily recognizable—statistically evident—characteristics: race, sex, education. The first condition, meanwhile, implies that men are more likely to work long term than women; thus they are preferentially assigned to medium- or long-term OJT. Inevitably, a skills gap opens between the sexes, followed by a wage gap. This is the price of pursuing corporate efficiency.

The applicability of these three conditions is widespread. The first applies wherever women bear and raise children and particularly in advanced countries, where women cannot get help with housework without paying high salaries because wage differentials by educational level are low. The second condition, too, is commonly applicable, as is the third condition, which applies equally to developing and advanced countries.

That these three conditions are so universally applicable makes achieving sexual equality in employment extremely difficult. The first condition is surmountable only by middle- or upper-class women in developing countries who can afford household help. Companies that ignore the third condition do so at their peril. The key to solving sexual discrimination probably rests with overcoming the difficulty inherent in the second condition. How is Japan attempting to do so?

The Promotion Test Method

Laws mandating sexual equality in employment originated in the United States with the Civil Rights Act of 1964. The original objective had been to prohibit racial discrimination, but after achieving results in that area the objective was expanded to include sexual discrimination. Many American companies were sued and forced to change their employment practices.[10] Then, in the 1970s, the women's rights movement swept across Western Europe, prompting nation after nation to enact sexual equality laws.

Japan finally enacted a similar equality law in 1986. What distinguishes it is that of its provisions many involve merely an obligation to make an effort toward equality and few of these are subject to enforcement. Companies must comply only with provisions for hiring, severance, and formal off-JT. Promotions, transfers, and OJT fall in the obligation to make an effort category. Nevertheless, the response of even large Japanese companies was rapid.

The preferred method among large businesses is to distinguish between ordinary career track (*ippanshoku*) and comprehensive career track (*sogoshoku*). Upon entering a company, women and men choose between a comprehensive career track toward management or an ordinary career track offering limited prospects but involving no cross-area transfers. Companies then train and promote employees based on their choice. Another method, the promotion test method, used in businesses such as supermarkets and department stores, has, meanwhile, demonstrated a quiet effectiveness. Men and women take formal tests at stages of their careers and are promoted if they pass. Examining these two methods throws light especially on the second condition of the theory of statistical discrimination [illegible]

The promoti[illegible] extremely effec-[illegible] second condition. The [illegible] understanding of promotion tests. In [illegible] study, tests were administered three times. To assume a supervisory position, a graduate of a four-year college could apply to take the first test two years after entering the company. Passing the second test was a condition for promotion to chief clerk. And passing the third test was a condition for promotion to section chief. Decisions about an employee's future were never made immediately upon entry to the company; they came after each promotion test.[11]

The promotion test method greatly reduces the cost of determining whether employees will continue working for the following reasons:

1. It is an appropriate way of confirming workers' intentions. Childbirth and child rearing are a part of most women's lives, and a woman is probably not sure how long she will work until she has a child. But she and the company must at least have the opportunity to confirm that she will not quit for several years. A test at stages of a worker's career provides that opportunity in an appropriate fashion because taking it is solely the employee's decision.
2. It is open, transparent, and public. It is open because the opportunity to confirm an intention to stay with the company for a certain period is available to all employees. It is transparent and public because the worker's commitment and its timing are made known throughout the company. The company thus cannot ignore the results. If the worker passes the test, the company must promote her.
3. The commitment is made based on full disclosure. The opportunity to commit comes only after the worker has been informed of all that a supervisory position entails. Similarly, the worker can commit after she has a child.

These points are clarified when the test method is contrasted with the customary [illegible] by a superior. A performance appraisal lacks openne[illegible] scrutiny. If a woman's good merit rating is no[illegible] employer is under no pressure to respond publicly, so her p[illegible]tion is not guaranteed. Conversely, an assessment by a superior includes valuable information about work performance that is unavailable through a test, since the superior works with her in the workshop. The more objective the test, the greater its transparency, but this gain comes at the expense of measuring real job ability. If, moreover, the worker concentrates her energy on passing a test that has little to do with her job, her efficiency will suffer. Promotion tests should be implemented in conjunction with performance appraisals.

The comprehensive track, ordinary track method fulfills the conditions of transparency, public scrutiny, and comfirming workers' intentions. But the third point—full disclosure—is a problem. Typically, this method forces a woman to make a decision upon entering a company, when it is difficult to have a good understanding of the job. Likewise, when most women enter a company they have not yet had or raised children, so their decision is not a true commitment. To avoid this problem, workers should periodically be offered the opportunity to switch from ordinary track to comprehensive track by means, perhaps, of, if not a promotion test, a test close to it. Despite its failure to measure job ability, the promotion test method is effective in raising sexual equality.[12]

Part-time Workers

This discussion has so far dealt only with regular, full-time workers. Part-time workers, however, have risen dramatically in number to account for a significant portion of Japan's workforce. They constitute more than one-fourth of female employees. According to the Basic Survey of Employment Structure, part-timers—those who work less than 35 hours a week and those who work less than 200 days a year, excluding seasonal workers—composed 27.5 percent of all employees in 1987. The figure for 1971 was 11.9 percent, so this is an astonishing growth rate. Increases in part-time workers are common to all countries. In the United States, so-called contingent workers, including part-time and temporary workers, exhibit the greatest growth.[13] A possible reason is that for white-collar jobs, unlike in blue-collar workshops, layoffs by reverse order of seniority are breaking down, making it harder to eliminate personnel.

In Japan, however, there are indications that the aggregate percentage of those who want home work and of those who want part-time jobs remain unchanged.[14] It can thus be said that a consistent percentage of women want to work, but not as regular, long-term employees. Companies, naturally, are looking for workers whose positions can easily be eliminated depending on the business cycle. In the past, temporary workers fit the bill.

Table 9-3 Differential in Hourly Wage Earnings between Part-time and Full-time Female Blue-collar Workers of All Educational Levels in the Manufacturing Industries (1988)

Age group	Wage for part-time worker/Wage for full-time employee	
	1,000 or more employees	10–90 employees
20–24	84	93
25–29	70	91
30–34	65	94
35–39	63	94
40–44	67	92
45–49	69	92
50–54	74	90

Source: Ministry of Labor, *Chingin Kozo Kihon Tokei Chosa* (Statistical Survey of Wage Structure).

The number of de facto regular workers even among part-timers, however, has, in fact, increased greatly. Statistics show that the number of long-service part-timers has risen at an astonishing rate. Observations of workshops reveal that the jobs they do are indistinguishable from those done by full-time employees. In some cases, part-timers even have managerial positions. Part-timers with 5 or 10 years of experience handle more important jobs than relatively inexperienced full-time workers. They are necessary and, indeed, strategically important to companies, which diligently cultivate them. Companies provide them with regular pay increments, bonuses, and other benefits on a par with full-time employees.

How, then, do part-time wages compare with full-time wages? Because the statistics lump together two groups of part-time workers, only the average wages are known. As shown in table 9-3, this average results in rates as low as around 70 percent of the hourly income for full-time workers at companies with 1,000 or more employees for most age groups, whereas at companies with 10 to 99 employees rates are between 90 and 94 percent. Some studies show that wages for part-time workers in the United States are around 80 percent of those for full-time employees.[15] So, it cannot be said that part-time wages in Japan are especially low.

Soon, and maybe it has already happened in places, shorter working hours only will distinguish part-timers from full-timers;

the job and the ability to do it will be the same. The trend toward similar hourly wages, too, will steadily continue to grow. This sort of part-time worker is often found in Sweden, where the percentage of women in the workforce is extremely high.

Chapter 10

The Transferability Overseas of the Japanese Way of Working

THE ISSUE

Needs

This chapter explores the extent to which the Japanese way of working can be transferred abroad. The high-minded reason for doing so is the belief that the Japanese way of working can help to raise the standard of living in other countries. National economic development is largely dependent on skill formation. Production and economic well-being ultimately depend on international competitiveness. Poor competitiveness reduces a country's ability to import goods and raw materials, causing economic contraction. Many elements integral to competitiveness—money, machinery, and raw materials—can be borrowed or bought. A supply of trained workers, however, must be localized; they cannot, for the most part, be imported.

Economic efficiency is affected by workers' skill levels. Are Japanese skills and the methods of forming them effective outside Japan? If so, how can they be transferred? Generally speaking, can Japan contribute to the economic development of other countries?

These are important considerations for international economic development and for Japan's further economic expansion. Japan's overseas trade and direct investment is so comprehensive that economic success or failure abroad affects life in Japan. Direct investment especially involves setting up factories abroad, hiring local workers, and producing goods overseas. Success hinges on local workers' skill levels. The effectiveness of applying Japanese methods to form overseas workers' skills has thus become a pressing issue.

The biggest trade problem facing Japan is the enormous trade deficits that other countries have with it because of insufficient purchasing power to buy Japanese goods. It is not only the United States that has a trade deficit with Japan. Among the members of the Association of Southeast Asian Nations (ASEAN), for example, most of Thailand's trade deficit is with Japan, and its ratio to GNP is far higher than that of the United States.[1] Note, however, that the popular belief in Japan's dependence on exports is mistaken; exports account for only 10 percent of GNP in Japan, compared with between 20 and 30 percent in the countries of Western Europe and ASEAN.

The elimination of trade deficits calls for basic improvement in a country's economy. Japan's chief contribution in this respect is direct investment. But when direct investment is too successful, it results in over presence, causing tension and other problems stemming from a perceived threat to sovereignty. This makes economic cooperation, which classifies skill formation as technical cooperation, significant.

Conventional Wisdom

According to conventional wisdom, Japan's technical cooperation entails so many problems that only significant modification of Japanese methods will facilitate transfer abroad. The same problems apply to industrialized Western countries and to developing countries:

1. Other countries are qualifications oriented. Workers acquire high, formal qualifications in training courses outside companies that are the basis for assignment to high-level positions in companies. In Japan, skill formation centers on OJT.
2. Workers elsewhere do only what they are told. In Japan, they are characterized by the diligent attention they pay to their

workshop tasks. This stresses cultural differences—in thought and behaviour.

3. The order and means by which a job is done and the authorized limits of workers' duties are standardized and precisely documented in other countries. In Japanese workshops, nothing is written down, and the limits of authority are vague.

Do these perceptions correspond with fact? Skill formation in U.S. workshops also centers on OJT. And as for non-Japanese workers doing only what they are told, this corresponds to an earlier discussion of workshop practices where some blue-collar workers are unable to do unusual operations. To argue otherwise is tantamount to asking whether intellectual skills found predominantly in large Japanese companies can be formed in other countries. Standardization and documentation, too, refer to an earlier discussion of dealing with workshop problems. These perceptions require study.

A few excellent studies of these perceptions as they relate to the developing and Western countries are available from among the abundant papers that are mostly confined to observations on Japanese firms.[2] Studying the transferability of Japanese work methods demands more than observations on Japanese companies abroad. The workshop practices of locally owned and operated companies must also be studied to avoid speculative conclusions. Direct comparisons must be made between Japanese companies in foreign countries, indigenous firms, and Japanese companies in Japan. Few studies have attempted this. The pertinent findings of these few follow.

JAPANESE CORPORATIONS IN THE UNITED STATES AND THE UNITED KINGDOM

Takamiya's Research

The studies done on the United Kingdom by Takamiya Makoto and Malcolm Trevor are foremost. Their research overlaps and forms two groups. The first is Takamiya's project in the late 1970s, in which Trevor participated. The other is the research primarily done by Trevor in the early 1980s, after Takamiya's untimely death.

Takamiya's pioneering work commands attention for its methodology. He studied four U.K.-based television assembly plants: two Japanese, one American, and one British.[3] To shed light on national differences, he made the conditions as similar as possible. The study involved, first, a questionnaire of 1,000 employees at the four plants, for which he achieved the impressive response rate of 70 percent; second, interviews with around 200 employees, from managers to machine operators; and third, observations of workshop practices and the gathering of documents. His findings were as follows:

1. The Japanese companies were clearly more efficient than the U.K. or U.S. firms, demonstrated by the number of TV sets assembled daily and by the defect rate. Japanese companies are often said to be more efficient, but little proof has been offered to support this assertion. Takamiya's figures are valuable for confirming this in one industry.
2. This efficiency was the result of neither generous compensation and welfare benefits nor of greater job security. The mobility rates at the Japanese companies differed little from those at the British or American firms, and Japanese employees had no special sense of job security. In short, it was difficult to account for higher efficiency in terms of permanent employment, generous company benefits, or a seniority wage curve. In fact, sick leave was unavailable at the Japanese plants, making benefits there inferior to those elsewhere.
3. Production; the ability to make adjustments between divisions; and the one-factory, one-union system, but most of all, production, and primarily product quality, were, for Takamiya, the keys to higher efficiency. For example, if three people worked together as a team, one of them was always assigned to check product quality. If defects persisted, it was this worker's responsibility to report them to a supervisor so that the cause could be found. It was not that worker's job to find the cause, nor was there emphasis on the skills to do so. Takamiya

makes almost no observations on skills except to indicate that machine operators would help maintenance personnel or technicians with their jobs.

Takamiya's other observations were conventional wisdom later refuted by Trevor. Takamiya sought to account for the smooth adjustments between divisions on the basis of employees moving between divisions at the Japanese plants. Trevor showed that this was not unique to Japan.[4] He also showed that there was nothing particularly Japanese about a one-factory, one-union system; it was common at new factories, even of U.K. and U.S. firms.[5]

Trevor's Work

Trevor took Takamiya's original study, in which he had participated, a step further after Takamiya's death. Together with Michael White, he expanded the scope to three U.K.-based Japanese manufacturing companies and one U.K.-based German company.[6] Although this later study observed white-collar workers in the nonmanufacturing sector, it did not draw direct comparisons with British companies. This discussion is thus confined to the manufacturing sector. The primary data for the study derived from a comprehensive, take-home questionnaire that asked the same questions of employees at the Japanese, U.K., U.S., and German firms.

The study's findings for the most part supported Takamiya's. British blue-collar workers at Japanese companies gave their companies higher ratings than their counterparts at British, American, or German firms. Like Takamiya's, Trevor's study made it clear, through workers' perceptions, that the reason was not particularly good wages or benefits; in fact, rules and discipline at the Japanese companies were more severe than elsewhere. Instead, employees' high assessment stemmed from reasons related to production, corresponding with Takamiya's findings. British workers were impressed by the emphasis on product quality and appreciated that Japanese engineers responded to their questions by teaching them carefully, even explaining why operations were done in specific ways.

The observation that Japanese corporate efficiency relates to production hits the mark. But Trevor's study did not ask how production boosts efficiency; it, too, overlooked workers' skills. This is perhaps because the companies surveyed had not been in operation long enough for the formation of intellectual skills. The authors, however, did not even explore the requirements for the formation of intellectual skills: compensation and merit rating systems that provide the incentives to acquire such skills. Lacking appropriate compensation, neither workers' interest in production nor high efficiency can be maintained. Since there was no interest in such arrangements, the authors felt no need to make in-depth observations of production or workshop practices.

Nevertheless, this study is significant in that it demonstrates, statistically, that British blue-collar workers rated parts of the Japanese system highly. British white-collar workers, however, gave low ratings to Japanese firms, an issue dealt with in the next chapter.

A Japanese Automobile Company in the United States

No study appears to exist that makes a direct comparison between American and Japanese automobile companies in the United States. However, Shimada Haruo's research on New United Motor Manufacturing Incorporated (NUMMI), the joint venture between Toyota and General Motors, comes close.[7] Unlike Takamiya and Trevor, Shimada does not directly compare Japanese and American plants. NUMMI's antecedent, though, was GM's Fremont plant, whose employees were retained and whose machinery differed only slightly. The contrast with the GM period probably provides a more rigorous basis for comparison. And instead of questionnaires, the method used was to enter the workshops and interview American workers.

Shimada's study showed that efficiency at NUMMI increased 50 percent over that at the GM plant, differences in products and partial changes in machinery considered. The improvement related to the way employees worked on the production line, which can be attributed to the following. First, production workers were empowered; the initiative that they showed in doing their jobs led them to constantly improve standard procedures. Second, workers found solutions when problems occurred. Third, workers partly repaired and maintained the machinery, previously the exclusive domain of maintenance personnel.

All three points relate to dealing with problems—the second and third, directly, and the first, indirectly. Because problems occur unexpectedly and responses to them cannot be standardized, empowering workshop workers underlies dealing with problems.

Unfortunately, this study has two problems. It did not explore workers' skills as techniques for dealing with problems, as it did not seem to regard problem solving as a skill. And it did not recognize the importance of compensation in stimulating the formation of the intellectual skills needed to deal with problems. These skills are not likely to develop unless encouraged. Incentives are essential. They should include merit ratings and regular pay increments; in short, paying blue-collar workers the same as white-collar workers. Because Shimada did not understand this, he made no observations on skills.

Ishida Mitsuo, on the other hand, drew attention to these factors in his study of Japanese automobile factories in the United States.[8] Although he offered no comparison with local U.S. plants, he provided a detailed look at the overseas workshops of Japanese companies, the skills involved and their formation, deployment and rotation, compensation, and other personnel practices. Ishida makes it clear that these companies had no personnel policies of promotions or merit ratings to stimulate the formation of skills for dealing with problems.

Ishida's study was an interim report and draws no conclusions. But its implications are clear. The U.S. social system, especially its labor-management relations, impedes the transfer of Japanese methods. Unlike in countries such as those in Southeast Asia with a short history of industrialization, in countries where industrial relations and workshop practices are firmly entrenched it is difficult to get blue-collar workers to accept the incentive programs needed for intellectual skill formation—merit ratings and yearly pay increments. Intellectual skill formation thus is also difficult.

Indeed, the United States, the countries of Western Europe, and other areas that have lengthy histories of labor-management relations may have difficulty adopting regular pay increments, performance appraisal, and other incentive programs to promote skill formation. It would be a mistake, though, to conclude that this is a manifestation of cultural differences. In white-collar workplaces in Western Europe, as mentioned earlier, regular pay increments and merit ratings are common, and the percentage of white-collar workers is steadily rising. It will take time for these methods to spread to blue-collar workers in the West. But if local workers approve, and the Japanese company pushes, implementation is not impossible. There are reports that merit ratings have already been accepted by British blue-collar workers. In 1977, a mere 2 percent of the U.K.-based companies surveyed appraised performance; by 1986, 24 percent did so.[9]

There are, in fact, many examples of efficiency being raised by changing production methods and adopting some Japanese workshop practices. To maintain and raise levels of efficiency, however, workers require the skills to deal with problems and change. Implementing compensation for the formation of these skills will take a long time.

SKILL FORMATION IN SOUTHEAST ASIA

The Groundwork Has Been Laid

A careful study of Southeast Asia was made using the framework outlined in chapter 5.[10] It compares Japanese companies in Japan with indigenous Thai and Malaysian firms and with Japanese companies in those countries and is thus a rarity.[11] Its strength is that it compares the workshop practices of non-Japanese companies not influenced by Japanese methods with workshop practices in Japan.

To make the conditions of the comparison as similar as possible, industries were selected from the main technological categories and observations were made of two workshops from companies manufacturing similar products in the same industry. Companies that manufactured car batteries provided examples of mass-production assembly lines, especially their pasting machine shops and assembly shops. Conventional machine tool workshops provided examples of non-mass-production machine processing; food processing and cement production, of the process industry; and bank lending offices, of the service sector. Partially structured interviews were the method.

It is worth noting that the people interviewed about their jobs and careers were those most familiar with the workshop: mainly foremen, sometimes workers. Workshops were visited several times on different days. The number of places visited, however, did not amount to the number that guarantees statistical significance. But in total, 20 companies were visited and more than 100 interviews were conducted. Chapter 5 is based on the findings of this study.

The workshop of an indigenous Thai battery maker is the basis for a discussion of the study's research findings. Trends revealed there were mostly shared with the other case studies. It was assumed that long-term job attachment was needed for intellectual skill formation. Workers' responses to questions about length of service revealed astonishingly stable tenure. A Malaysian case study suggested at first glance that Malaysian workers were more mobile, but this proved true only during the first two years of employment; thereafter, Malaysian workers, too, showed considerable stability.

Few entered the Thai company with skills acquired elsewhere. Workers acquired their skills through OJT after entering the company. As for breadth of experience, nobody did only one job. The pasting workshop involved regular rotation among three to five jobs, and around half of the nearly 20 workers in the assembly workshop moved daily between their own and the shop's three other lines. They did so on their own initiative, knowing from daily production schedules what lines were likely to have bottlenecks. Awareness of problems, they said, stemmed from having worked there a long time and from knowing that the foreman was observing, grading, and submitting appraisals of their performances, on the basis of which they were promoted to higher positions.

Promotions were as high as foreman. In Thailand, almost all foremen surveyed had risen through the workshop ranks. In Malaysia, the percentage dropped to nearly half. In general, medium-sized or larger companies in developing countries often promote an elite with higher education or other qualifications to foreman over blue-collar workshop workers. This is the case in local companies in India and Singapore.[12] Japanese and their joint companies, however, promote foremen from the rank and file. This practice not only says much about the level of workshop production workers, it is also worth noting for its incentive value. Malaysia and especially Thailand are among its biggest practitioners.

In that most important area—dealing with change and with problems—perhaps only 1 or 2 out of 10 of the Thai workshops' blue-collar workers could handle unusual operations. A separated system existed, but so did a recognizable trend toward an integrated system. Both blue-collar workers and quality control specialists, for example, conducted tests and dealt with defects. Moreover, workers in Thai workshops pass their expertise on to other workers in their groups. Their solutions were self-taught, not something learned in a training course. Indeed, what they knew cannot be learned in courses, especially courses run outside the company.

Companies had compensation schemes to promote skill formation and to encourage broader experience. These took the form of a pay raise system based on merit ratings. Workers capable of dealing with problems were promoted, ultimately to foreman.

Similarities and Differences

This comparative study of Japanese and indigenous companies in Thailand and Malaysia exposed similarities and differences. General trends related to skills and the methods of forming them were identical. A dependence on OJT made the companies studied alike in providing workers with experience over the long term. Similarities were also discernible in the early development of an integrated system. But major gaps exist between countries. Breadth of experience was narrower in Thailand and Malaysia than in Japan, and depth of experience shallower—only a few Thai and Malaysian blue-collar workers can deal with problems or change.

Differences arise naturally from the dissimilar histories of industrialization in Japan and in Thailand and Malaysia. The formation of intellectual skills especially demands a firm history of industrialized society. Intellectual skills require basic scholastic ability: the ability in particular to learn by oneself as a prerequisite for self-teaching in the workshop. Japan's period of high growth suggests a minimum of nine years of schooling. Young people in and around Bangkok are close to this level, and young people in Malaysia have just about surpassed it. Corporate history, too, is necessary. Skills are formed through customary practices, such as rotation within workshops. These practices, however, must first be established, over as long a period as 10 to 15 years. Provided companies have taken the time to cultivate these practices, the necessary conditions for skill formation will fall into place. Beyond that, these practices need only be promoted.

The problem is that such practices are not always recognized as integral to skill formation. Few academics, government officials, or industrialists are aware of them. Worse is the possibility that policies may be adopted that will stymie the establishment of these practices. These practices must be supported as the true methods of skill formation that they are.

DOCUMENTATION

Written in the Manual

Attention has to this point focused on skills. Documentation, too, must be considered. Japanese assert that in the West and elsewhere job methods are standardized and documented to the last detail. And that, as a result, no matter the country or the nationality of the workers the work requires merely following an operating plan. By contrast, jobs at Japanese companies are neither standardized nor, for that reason, documented—Japanese can understand Japanese without documenting or saying anything. Overseas, this does not work. Another argument suggests that work methods are group oriented in Japan, with each member's job limits undefined. This, too, is unlikely to work abroad. The transferability abroad of Japanese methods makes documentation unavoidable.

The presupposition is that efficiency rises when the way a job is done is standardized and recorded. Taking into account what chapter 5 shows actually happens in a workshop, this assumes that an unexpected occurrence can be foreseen and a response to it standardized. As shown, these assumptions are questionable. Unexpected events are just that. They cannot be fully predicted. And they occur two to three times more frequently in workshops than predictable events. Moreover, they today require so complex a response that any standardization would be so gross an over-simplification as to have an adverse effect on efficiency.

The usual measures adopted are to standardize and document most usual operations, but not to do so for unusual operations. Standardization and documentation may be possible for unusual operations that occur frequently and for which solutions have been found. But it is not possible to standardize all responses to the unexpected. Even if it were, efficiency would be retarded. In general, when Japanese companies do business overseas most of their local workers are ordinary people with the minimum required education. Japanese managers thus must use the local language. To avoid misunderstandings that result from attempting to communicate orally in a foreign language, they must convey their intentions in writing far more often than they would in Japan. Documentation thus is essential. It is a mistake, however, to say that efficiency will decline if everything is not written down.

It is commonly thought that documentation is rare in Japanese workshops. Observation reveals, however, that considerable documentation exists.[13] Even such usual operations as the installation of a new machine are recorded in detail. Blue-collar workers also write reports on dealing with problems that are discussed and studied in the workshop. Yet, because all operators acquire the ability to do usual operations there is no need for documentation. Operators, moreover, make such frequent improvements to operating procedures that manuals quickly become obsolete. And there is no need to document unusual operations that everyone in the workshop understands; reports are needed only for complex or severe problems.

Summary

In general, permanent employment, seniority wages, and other textbook practices cannot be transferred abroad because they do not exist in Japan. No Japanese company hires only recent graduates and employs them until retirement. And it is unlikely that any Japanese company implements the strange practices of salary increases and promotions determined solely by workers' years of service.

By contrast, long-term employment, experience gained by doing several jobs in a workshop, constantly rising skill levels, and regular pay increments based on merit ratings exist not only in Japan but also fairly extensively elsewhere. They are found among white-collar and blue-collar workers at medium-sized and large companies in Southeast Asia and among white-collar and some blue-collar workers in the West. In short, the best features of Japanese workshops today—a skill formation system that enables workers to accumulate experience in a company over time and to develop a style of working based on it—are thought to be fairly universal.

These features, however, cannot be easily transplanted. A system is necessary to promote them—to make it advantageous for workers to raise their skill levels by acquiring experience in a company over the long term. The system entails a fair evaluation of upgraded skills and compensation based on the assessment; in other words, an arrangement for promoting workers and for pay increments based on increases in skills. Transferring and implementing such a system especially among Western blue-collar workers will take time.

This discussion has focused primarily on blue-collar workers and on pay increments and promotions based on merit ratings. Since this system exists everywhere for white-collar workers, few problems would appear to be involved in transferring Japanese practices abroad. Studies of Japanese companies, however, indicate that it is white-collar workers who have the biggest problems with

Japanese methods. This issue is explored in the next chapter. First, another aspect of technical cooperation needs to be investigated.

TECHNICAL COOPERATION

Defining Technical Cooperation

Technical cooperation is part of the economic cooperation provided by advanced countries to developing countries. Economic cooperation varies with the nature of the money that is used: When only government funds are loaned under far better than market conditions and the pure grant rate is high, the aid is called official development assistance (ODA). In essence, economic cooperation is aid given to a country to support its efforts at economic development without any thought of making a profit, and it is technical cooperation that is high in grant elements in economic cooperation.

A country's contribution is expressed in terms of the percentage of its ODA to GNP. In 1988, Japanese aid was 0.32 percent of GNP, slightly less than the 0.35 percent average for the members of the OECD's Development Assistance Committee (DAC), but nothing to be ashamed of. France had the highest contribution rate, at 0.72 percent of GNP, but this includes funding for French language teachers that should probably be subtracted. If comparisons were made in all the DAC categories, the definitions would have to be reconsidered, but the present ones must suffice for now. Elsewhere, the U.K.'s contribution rate was 0.32 percent, the same as Japan's; Germany's was slightly higher, at 0.39 percent; and the rate for the United States was only 0.20 percent. Countries with high contribution rates, such as Belgium, included many former colonial powers, indicating a fairly high connection between aid givers and former colonies.[14]

ODA can be divided into either financial assistance or technical assistance depending on the nature of the aid. Note that when aid is money to buy machinery and other kinds of technology, it is categorized as financial assistance; technical assistance means the transfer of skills and techniques needed to operate equipment.

Technology in this sense is embodied in people. Technical assistance thus can only occur through the transfer of people who have or who hope to have skills and techniques and consists of sending and receiving—the dispatching of experts and peace corps volunteers, on the one hand, and the hosting of primarily industry trainees and foreign university students, on the other. Grants of materials and mechanical equipment are also included, but the percentage is small; the emphasis is primarily on skill formation. Technical cooperation accounts, on average, for only one-fifth of the DAC's ODA, but the grant rate is so high that technical cooperation constitutes an important part of economic cooperation.

It is essential for Japan to promote technical cooperation because its chief element is skill formation, whose importance is emphasized by the saying that the essence of nation building is human development. On visits to developing countries, Japanese prime ministers promise Japanese technical cooperation and, in fact, are asked by those countries for technical cooperation in the belief that it underlies Japan's growth in the absence of natural resources. Indeed, careful observation of Thai and Malaysian workshops reveal that hourly productivity in Japanese workshops is several times higher despite those countries' use of the same and sometimes even newer equipment than Japan.[15] The role of skills is enormous.

International Comparisons

DAC statistics compiled since 1966 facilitate a comparison of technical cooperation in Japan and the West. Figures 10-1 through 10-4 compare the number of foreign students and trainees received and experts sent by the major industrial countries. In 1979, DAC stopped compiling separate sets of statistics on trainees and foreign students; more recent figures show a combined total for these two categories.

The figures distinguish between a French and U.K. and a Japanese and West German pattern of aid. France and the United Kingdom, both former colonial powers, focus on foreign students, as did the United States in the 1960s, but their numbers there subsequently dropped dramatically. By contrast, the number of foreign students hosted by the United Kingdom and France increased despite those nations' economic problems.

Japan and West Germany, meanwhile, emphasize training. They host more trainees than foreign students and in increasing number. West Germany ranked first in 1979, far outstripping other countries, and the rate at which trainees' numbers were growing was also high. But since the early 1980s, the combined totals for foreign students and trainees suggest that Japan ranks first as the host of trainees.

Technical cooperation in the United States is in a state of change and even decline. In the 1960s, U.S. technical cooperation was outstanding. That country ranked first as a host of foreign students and second as a host of trainees and in dispatching experts. It dropped in all three areas in the 1970s, and despite a slight recovery in the 1980s it is today a second-class contributor of technical cooperation.

Why do Japan and West Germany, with their high economic achievements and few former colonies, emphasize trainees over foreign students? Foremost is the language barrier—a foreign university student would require a good working knowledge of either country's language. French and English, in contrast, are international languages. English, in particular, has been the undisputed international language since the British Empire spanned the globe and, subsequently, as a result of the economic and military strength of the United States. The United Kingdom and France thus can make proficiency in their respective languages a prerequisite for government scholarships. Language proficiency undoubtedly contributes greatly to the success of foreign study, but neither Japan nor West Germany can impose such a prerequisite.

A more positive reason for Japan's and West Germany's emphasis on training is the belief that university study is merely a foundation for skill formation in the workshop. Overmuch emphasis on a university degree mistakenly implies that it is the aim of skill formation, when the real focus is extensive OJT in the workshop. Training programs in West Germany and Japan, moreover, include not only engineers but also foremen and workshop leaders because efficient production starts in the workshop. The technical cooperation programs of these two countries are therefore right on track.

The two countries, however, differ in their training methods. Although research is insufficient, West Germany seems to emphasize off-JT and Japan OJT, for which it has been unjustly criticized.

Training Programs Centered on OJT

The Association for Overseas Technical Scholarship (AOTS) is the largest of the organizations managing Japan's ODA training programs. The Japan International Cooperation Agency (JICA) hosts more trainees, mainly through public-sector arrangements, but AOTS, a private organization, leads all organizations in arranging workshop-level technical transfers with private Japanese companies. During the first five weeks of their stay in Japan, trainees stay in an AOTS dormitory and take an intensive course in the Japanese language. The next four months involve OJT at the host company.[16] The length of the training period differs little from ODA training periods in other countries. AOTS staff members periodically visit the trainees to ensure that training methods and living conditions meet the standards for government funding (about 75 percent of the direct expenses are government subsidized). They also ask the trainees for their opinions.

Trainees' main complaint is about OJT. It is work, they say, not training. College graduates complain about being assigned to a production line or about the lack of full-time instructors. Their view of skill formation and of training is based on textbooks. They think that off-JT is the true method of skill formation, that skills are best learned from a teacher in a classroom. Unfortunately, many intellectuals in Japan share this belief, fueling the discontent with OJT programs.

These complaints arise from ignorance of the facts. An emphasis on OJT in skill formation is not unique to Japan; it occurs in the United States as well. Workshops in Southeast Asia also rely heavily on OJT; indeed, off-JT plays a smaller role there than in Japan. It would be more productive to promote the distinctive qualities of OJT than to foment discontent with it.

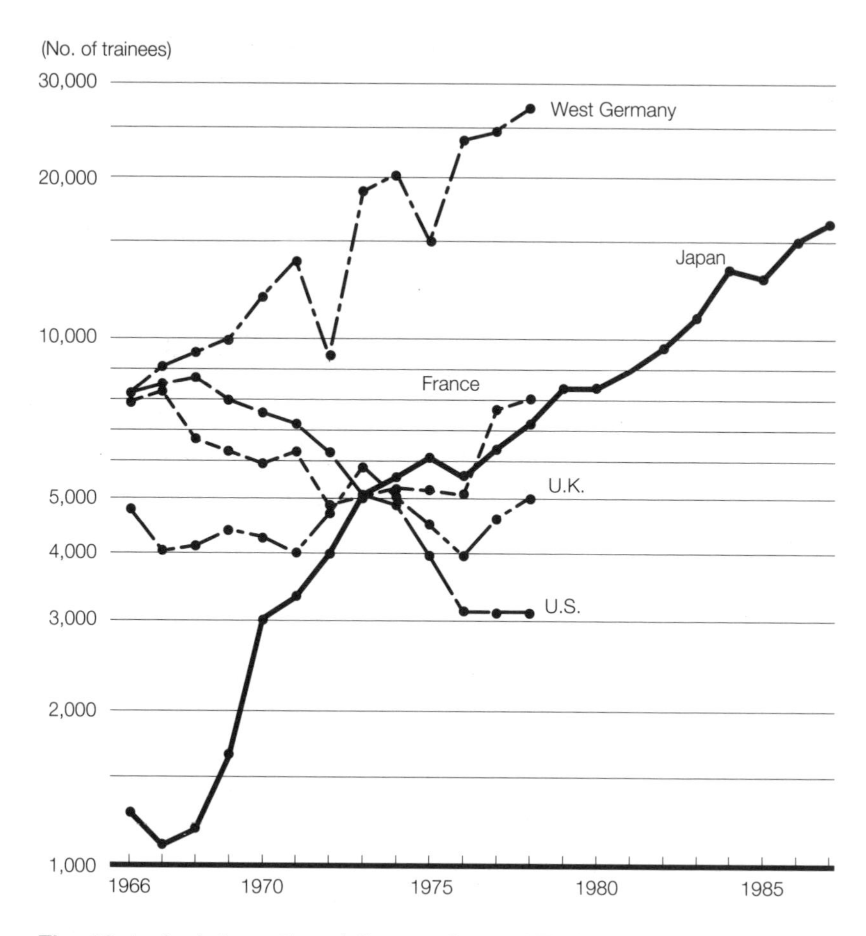

Fig. 10-1. An International Comparison of Trainees (1966–78)

Sources: OECD, Development Assistance Committee (DAC), *Economic Cooperation* (yearly). Recent statistics for Japan are from Ministry of International Trade and Industry, *Keizai Kyoryoku no Genjo to Mondaiten* (Present State of Economic Cooperation and Problem Areas) (yearly).

Two problems, however, remain:

1. It is too easy for OJT programs in Japan to be confined to Japanese companies and their business associates. Because the system involves admitting foreign trainees into workshops, implementation depends on corporate relationships. How Japan can conduct independent technical transfers with, for example, employees of a local Southeast Asian firm remains an

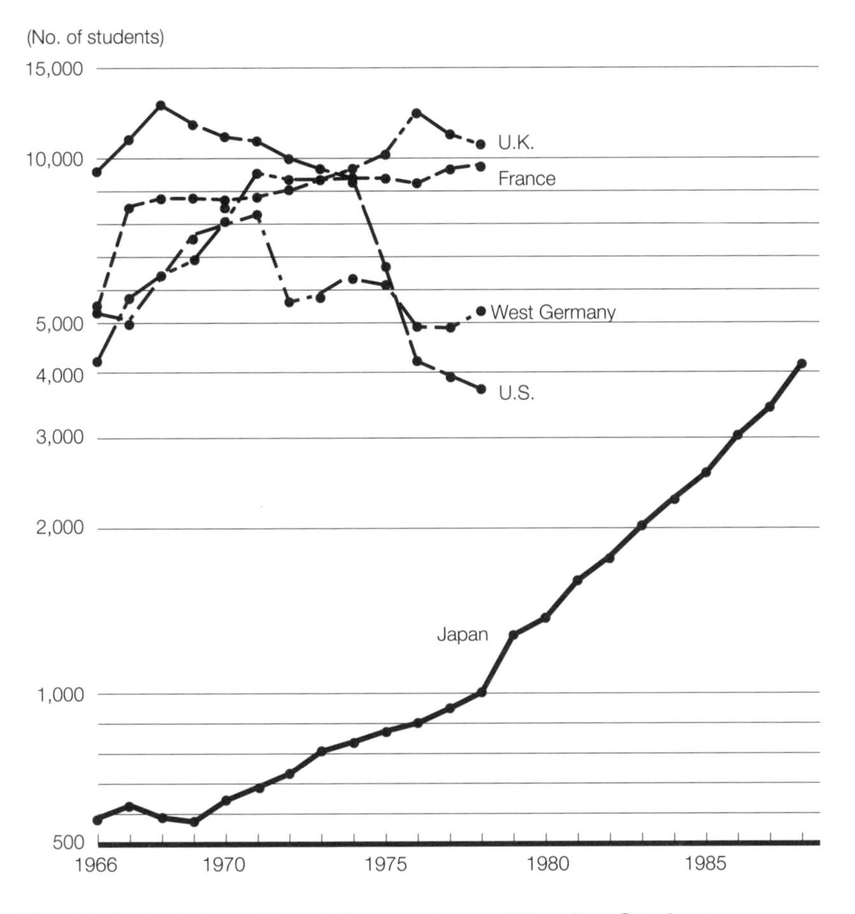

Fig. 10-2. An International Comparison of Foreign Students (1966–78)

Sources: OECD, Development Assistance Committee (DAC), *Economic Cooperation* (yearly). Recent statistics for Japan are from Ministry of International Trade and Industry, *Keizai Kyoryoku no Genjo to Mondaiten* (Present State of Economic Cooperation and Problem Areas) (yearly).
Note: Limited to foreign students studying at the expense of the host government.

issue. Dispatching experts to the country in question is one method. But how best to do that is the largest stumbling block faced in technical cooperation.

2. It is difficult to incorporate OJT into government policies on technical cooperation involving the dispatch of experts. Sending experts instead has usually included building vocational training centers in developing countries; equipping them

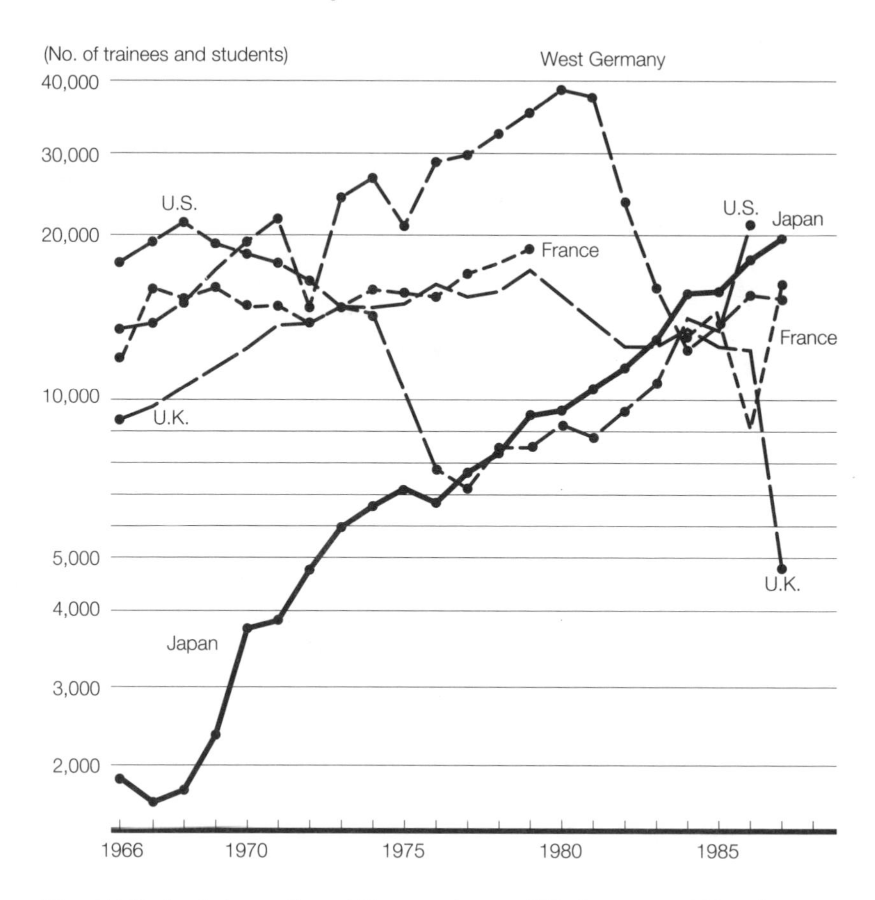

Fig. 10-3. An International Comparison of Trainees and Foreign Students (1966–87)

Sources: OECD, Development Assistance Committee (DAC), *Economic Cooperation* (yearly). Recent statistics for Japan are from Ministry of International Trade and Industry, *Keizai Kyoryoku no Genjo to Mondaiten* (Present State of Economic Cooperation and Problem Areas) (yearly).

with machinery and textbooks; stationing people to train instructors; and offering a one- or two-year preemployment, off-JT course. This approach is common among all countries. For Japan, however, it deviates from the usual skill formation methods in Japanese workshops and makes no use of the most effective skill formation method: OJT. Off-JT courses are not useless—they are very important especially in developing countries where secondary education is not yet widespread—

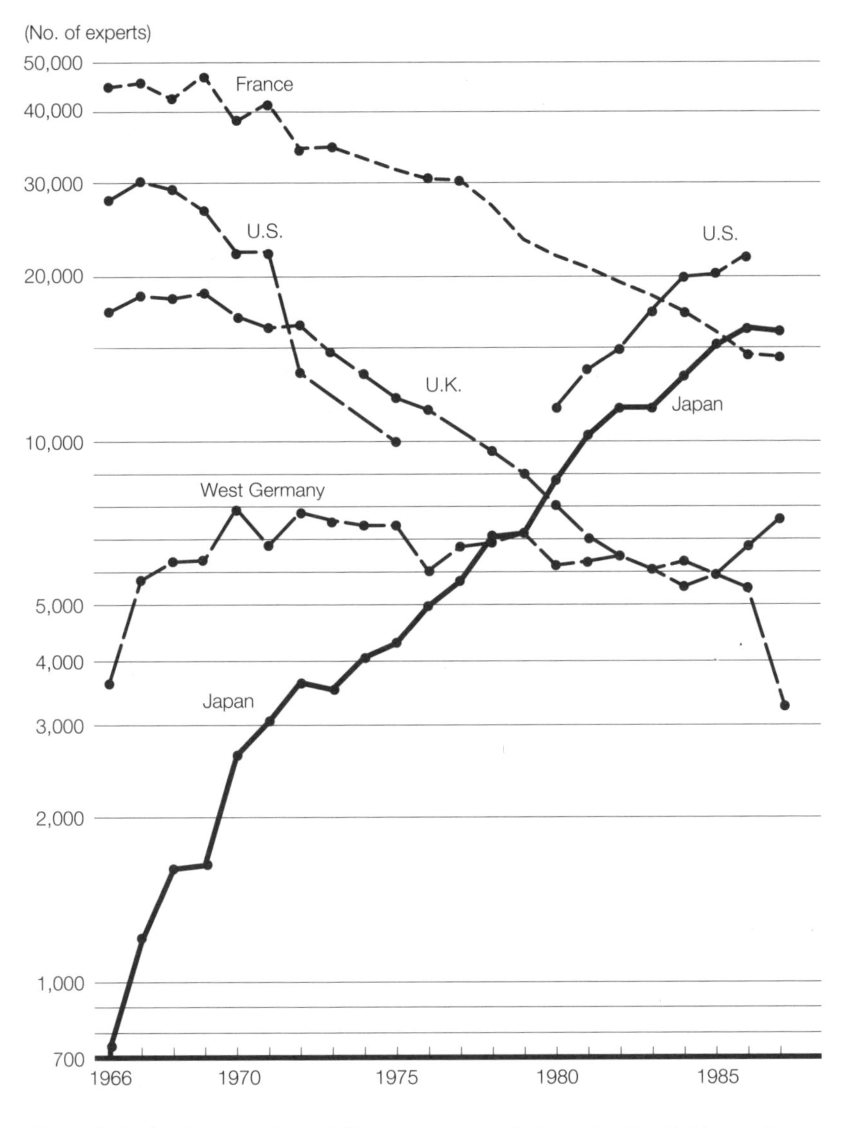

Fig. 10-4. An International Comparison of Experts Sent Abroad (1966–87)

Sources: OECD, Development Assistance Committee (DAC), *Economic Cooperation* (yearly). Recent statistics for Japan are from Ministry of International Trade and Industry, *Keizai Kyoryoku no Genjo to Mondaiten* (Present State of Economic Cooperation and Problem Areas) (yearly).

> but overmuch emphasis on off-JT leads to the mistaken belief that it can alone form skills and develop full-fledged craftsmen when, in fact, it is merely the foundation for skill development through OJT.

OJT, however, is difficult to incorporate in technical cooperation programs chiefly because distinguishing it as training and not work is impossible. On-the-job training is just that; it cannot be separated from work either by time or place. OJT instructors, moreover, are not professional teachers. They are senior shop workers usually engaged in their own jobs who instruct whenever trainees do not understand something about their assigned jobs. In addition, OJT involves experiencing different jobs in the workshop. Since job rotation is a normal workshop practice, it is hard to formalize as training.

Despite the difficulty, including OJT in technical cooperation programs is vital. The following serve as guidelines for how to do so:

- Convey a constant supply of positive information about OJT to developing countries. Since OJT forms careers, include case studies from Japanese workshops in the major industries of careers based on OJT. Careers each have unique features, but a general pattern needs to be communicated. Case studies should outline career details and show how a career can change and be encouraged. Encouraging careers entails, at the very least, the following:

  1. A job matrix. Chapter 5 reveals that this involves charts showing workers' progress in upgrading their skills.
  2. Remuneration linked to the acquisition of higher skills. This means a pay-for-job-grade system with range rates, a yearly pay increment system, and merit ratings.

- Assign consultants to overseas training centers who can give advice on career formation. Career case studies offer only typical examples. Individual firms should take environmental conditions, stage of development, and other factors into consideration and make adjustments accordingly. A consultant can advise on these matters.

- Incorporate short, off-JT courses at training centers or elsewhere into OJT. OJT is essential for the formation of high-level skills but is insufficient by itself. To form intellectual skills, workers must understand machinery and the production process. The best way to consolidate their workshop experience and to teach them theoretical concepts is through short, off-JT courses.

These proposals could well be the substance of technical cooperation programs carried out with government funds. If OJT is the basis of skill formation, direct investment involving people working together is the ideal form of technological transfer. Policies of developing countries that restrict the admission of Japanese engineers and technicians hinder technological transfer by limiting the opportunities for OJT.

Chapter 11

College Graduates in Industry

TRANSFERABILITY ABROAD

The Frontline of Business

This chapter considers the careers of white-collar college graduates, now an important element of Japanese companies. It also examines the many problems related to white-collar workers, especially in the overseas activities of Japanese firms.

In 1973, college graduates (including graduates of the prewar higher school system[1]) accounted for 20 percent of the employees at companies with 1,000 or more workers. By 1986, they had risen to 30 percent. This, however, is merely the average for all age groups; truly spectacular growth is found among young people in their late 20s: exceeding 50 percent.[2] Their growth has been especially high in the service sector: 80 percent in banking, 72 percent in wholesaling and retailing, and 60 percent in service. In fact, city banks stopped hiring male high school graduates some time ago.

The number of young people attending universities is increasing rapidly worldwide, especially in Japan and the United States. No other industrial societies have so many college graduates working in businesses. Japan's situation provides a glimpse of global trends. Unlike U.S. businesses, which hire many MBA graduates, Japanese companies hire few holders of advanced degrees beyond engineers. Large Japanese firms instead appear to be establishing a corporate culture based on uniformity of educational background.

Little research has been done on white-collar college graduates, for whom career studies are rare. Conventional wisdom, though, is firmly entrenched. The myth of Japanese uniqueness in this area is based on an implicit contrast with the problems faced by Japanese methods abroad when applied to foreign white-collar workers. The preceding chapter showed that Japanese methods, rated highly by blue-collar workers at home and abroad, are dissatisfactory and problematic for non-Japanese white-collar workers.[3] Japanese managers, in turn, have many complaints about these workers. Tomita Teruhiko's painstaking questionnaire survey refutes the contention that foreign white-collar workers are dissatisfied.[4] First, however, the conventional wisdom on this topic must be examined:

1. Promotion in Japan is based on seniority, whereas in the West it is based on ability. Promotion is important for white-collar workers in all countries. The claim that in Japan it is based on seniority implies an absence of competition, with workers promoted solely because of length of service and regardless of ability. If they lack competition, how is it that Japanese firms are more efficient than Western firms, where ability determines promotion? This claim emphasizes Japanese uniqueness and exposes the problem of the vertical aspect of a career.
2. Japan prefers generalists, whereas the West prefers specialists. This is an oft-heard claim of Japanese businessmen with much overseas experience. Japanese white-collar workers experience many aspects of their companies, it is argued, while Western workers are confined to specialized areas of expertise. Japanese white-collar workers do their own jobs and raise efficiency by helping one another. Do Japanese white-collar workers, in fact, acquire the skills to master diverse jobs? Is the scope of their jobs so undefined? The problem here relates to the breadth of a career.
3. The workforce in Japan is stable, whereas in the West it is mobile. This claim stresses a fundamental difference depending on whether or not a career is formed within a single company. Seasoned overseas Japanese businessmen complain that Western workers are too mobile and have no long-term perspective. The problem here relates to where a career develops.

I-House Press

Recent Works and Perennial Favorites

Unmasking Japan

I-House Press is the commercial imprint of
the International House of Japan,
a leading publisher of English-language translations
of Japanese nonfiction.

財団法人 国際文化会館
International House of Japan

I House Press

New!

The New Paradox for Japanese Women

Greater Choice, Greater Inequality

Tachibanaki Toshiaki*
Translated by Mary Foster

2010. 316 pages, hardcover. ¥3,000 (¥2,858 + tax).
ISBN 978-4-903452-17-3
Originally published in Japanese in 2008 by Toyo Keizai, Inc., as *Jojo Kakusa*

*Here and elsewhere, the names of Japanese individuals active in Japan appear in the traditional Japanese sequence of surname followed by given name.

"Economic recession since the 1990s, together with neoliberalist political reform, has brought about not only increasing gender inequality but also disparities among women. Women have been polarized into elite and non-elite in the name of diversity and freedom of choice. Tachibanaki Toshiaki, a leading economist, vividly describes multiple realities of women based on statistical evidence. His analysis proves that the Japanese family myth of a workaholic businessman husband and a full-time housewife is now no longer the case."

Ueno Chizuko, University of Tokyo

Demystifying Pearl Harbor

A New Perspective from Japan

Iguchi Takeo
Translated by David Noble

2010, revised and expanded edition. 366 pages, hardcover. ¥3,000 (¥2,858 + tax).
ISBN 978-4-903452-19-7
Originally published in Japanese in 2008 by Chuokoron Shinsha as *Kaisen Shinwa*

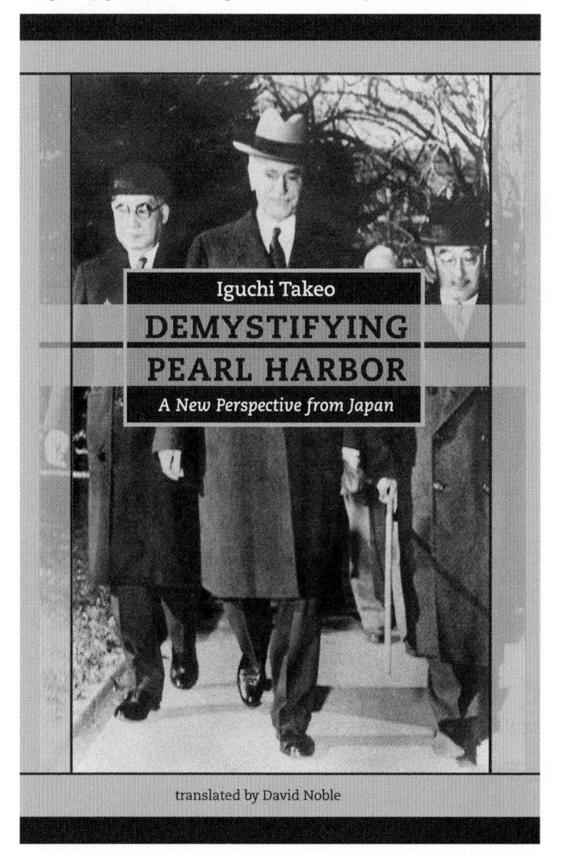

"This is a valuable addition to the literature on Japan's Pearl Harbor attack. The author has three qualities in unique combination. First, on 7 December 1941, he was in Washington, DC, where his father worked for the Japanese embassy. . . . Second, he himself later became a diplomat and is intimately familiar with the bureaucratic workings of the Foreign Ministry and of overseas embassies. Third, he also is a specialist in international law, having written and taught on the subject for many years after retiring from the foreign service."

Akira Iriye, Harvard University

The Edo Inheritance

Tokugawa Tsunenari

Translated by Tokugawa Iehiro

2009. 212 pages, hardcover. ¥2,500 (¥2,381 + tax).
ISBN 978-4-903452-14-2
Originally published in Japanese in 2007 by PHP Kenkyujo as *Edo no Idenshi*

The 18th head of the house of Tokugawa demonstrates how Japan was in many ways ahead of the West during the extended peace and prosperity of the Edo period.

Japan in Trade Isolation

1926-37 and 1948-85

Ikeda Michiko

2008. 378 pages, hardcover. ¥3,000 (¥2,858 + tax).
ISBN 978-4-903452-07-4

This groundbreaking work examines the harsh environment that enveloped Japan in the years from 1926 to 1937 and again from 1948 to 1985.

A Nagging Sense of Job Insecurity

The New Reality Facing Japanese Youth

Genda Yuji

Translated by Jean Connell Hoff

2006. 218 pages, paperback. ¥1,400 (¥1,334 + tax).
ISBN 4-903452-00-X
Winner of the Suntory Prize; originally published in Japanese by Chuo-koron-Shinsha in 2001 as *Shigoto no Naka no Aimai na Fuan*

The author critiques Japan's youth-unfriendly job market.

Kabuki

Baroque Fusion of the Arts

Kawatake Toshio

Translated by Frank and Jean Connell Hoff

2006, revised and expanded edition. 388 pages, paperback, color photos. ¥2,000 (¥1,905 + tax).
ISBN 4-903452-01-8
Originally published in Japanese in 2001 by the University of Tokyo Press as *Kabuki*

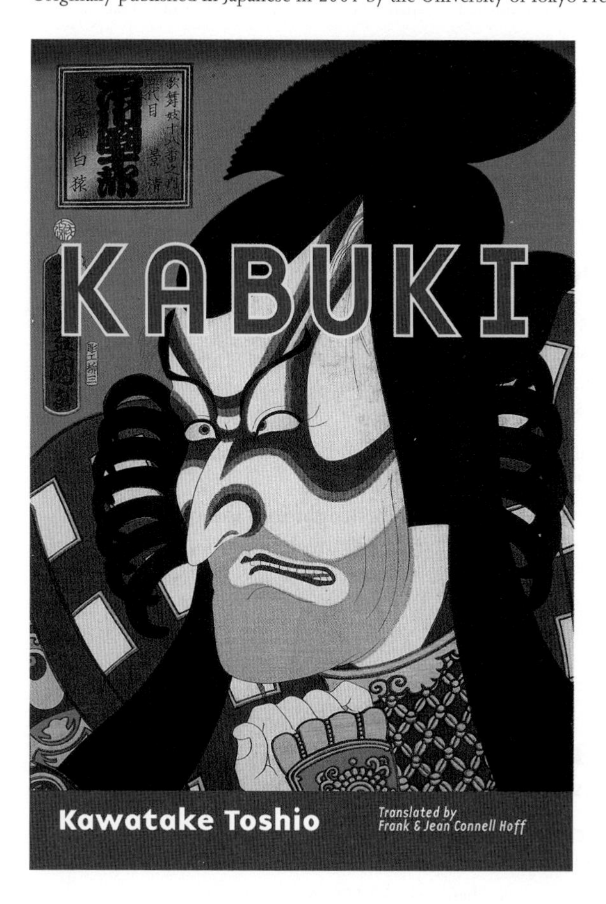

"As kabuki, grounded in tradition, proceeds boldly forward into the new century . . . its distinctly Japanese beauty will be disseminated to the rest of the world, and kabuki will continue to move and entertain audiences in Japan and worldwide."

From the afterword

Escape from Impasse
The Decision to Open Japan

Mitani Hiroshi
Translated by David Noble

2008, revised and expanded edition. 388 pages, hardcover. ¥3,000 (¥2,858 + tax).
ISBN 978-4-903452-06-7
Originally published in Japanese in 2003 by Yoshikawa Kobunkan as *Peri Raiko*

Here is the drama that followed Perry's arrival in Japan.

Japan's Lost Decade

Yoshikawa Hiroshi
Translated by Charles H. Stewart

2008, revised and expanded edition. 267 pages, hardcover. ¥3,000 (¥2,858 + tax).
ISBN 978-4-903452-12-8
Originally published in Japanese in 1999 by Iwanami Shoten as *Tenkanki no Nihon Keizai*

The reader will gain new insight into the policy failures that caused Japan's decade-long economic malaise.

Maruyama Masao
and the Fate of Liberalism in Twentieth-Century Japan

Karube Tadashi
Translated by David Noble

2008. 222 pages, hardcover. ¥2,500 (¥2,381 + tax).
ISBN 978-4-903452-10-4
Originally published in Japanese in 2006 by Iwanami Shoten as *Maruyama Masao: Riberaristo no Shozo*

The subject emerges as a champion of Japanese democracy.

Doing It Our Way

A Sony Memoir

Ohga Norio

Translated by Brian Miller

2008. 144 pages, hardcover. ¥2,000 (¥1,905 + tax).
ISBN 978-4-903452-11-1
Originally published in Japanese in 2003 in a somewhat different form by the Nihon Keizai Shimbun as *Sony no Senritsu*

Especially interesting is Ohga's account of brand building.

Shrinking-Population Economics

Lessons from Japan

Matsutani Akihiko

Translated by Brian Miller

2006. 214 pages, paperback. ¥1,500 (¥1,429 + tax).
ISBN 4-903452-03-4
Originally published in Japanese in 2004 by the Nihon Keizai Shimbun as *Jinko Gensho Keizai no Atarashii Koshiki*

The author tells how to cope with demographic change.

The Meiji Constitution

The Japanese Experience of the West and the Shaping of the Modern Japanese State

Takii Kazuhiro

Translated by David Noble

2007. 216 pages, paperback. ¥2,000 (¥1,905 + tax).
ISBN 978-4-903452-04-3
Originally published in Japanese in 2003 by Kodansha as *Bummeishi no Naka no Meiji Kempo*

A cross-cultural approach informs this important study.

Competing to Be Really, Really Good

The Behind-the-Scenes Drama of Capability-Building Competition in the Automobile Industry

Fujimoto Takahiro

Translated by Brian Miller

2007. 167 pages, paperback. ¥2,000 (¥1,905 + tax).
ISBN 978-4-903452-05-0
Originally published in Japanese in 2003 by Chuokoron-Shinsha as
Noryoku Kochiku Kyoso: Nihon no Jidosha Sangyo wa Naze Tsuyoi no ka

An expert in the field probes the roots of competitiveness.

Learning for Life

The Kumon Way

Kinoshita Reiko

2008. 250 pages, hardcover. ¥3,000 (¥2,858 + tax).
ISBN 978-4-903452-13-5
Originally published in Japanese in 2006 by Iwanami Shoten as
Terakoya Gurobarizeshon

A journalist surveys the phenomenal, global permeation of the Kumon method of learning.

Japan and Its Worlds

Marius B. Jansen and the Internationalization of Japanese Studies

Martin Collcutt, Kato Mikio, and Ronald P. Toby, editors

2007. 312 pages, hardcover. ¥3,000 (¥2,858 + tax).
ISBN 978-4-903452-08-1

Friends and former students laud the great Japanologist.

The Japanese House

In Space, Memory, and Language

Nakagawa Takeshi

Translated by Geraldine Harcourt

2006, revised and expanded edition. 282 pages, paperback, color photos. ¥2,000 (¥1,905 + tax).
ISBN 4-903452-02-6
Originally published in Japanese in 2002 by TOTO Shuppan as *Nihon no Ie: Kukan, Kioku, Kotoba*

THE JAPANESE HOUSE
In Space, Memory, and Language
Nakagawa Takeshi
Professor, Department of Architecture, Waseda University
Translated by Geraldine Harcourt

A renowned architectural historian revisits the Japanese house in 25 essays illustrated with color photos. He shows how the quality of life has suffered in Japan's transition to modern architecture and offers proposals for restoring some of the lost amenity.

Contradictions of Globalization

Democracy, Culture, and Public Sphere

Tessa Morris-Suzuki, editor

2008. 176 pages, paperback. ¥1,500 (¥1,429 + tax).
ISBN 978-4-903452-09-8

Insights from prominent figures in academia, media, and NPOs in the Asia-Pacific region present fresh perspectives on globalization and on related issues.

Ridashippu to Kokusaisei

(Leadership and Internationalism)

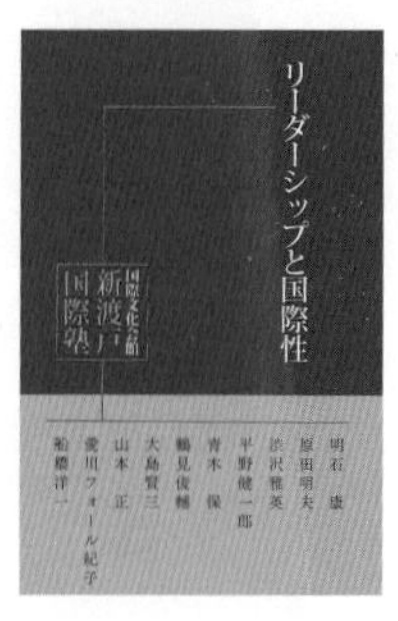

Nitobe Kokusai Juku, International House of Japan, editor

2009. In Japanese, with some English. 304 pages, paperback.
¥1,600 (¥1,524 + tax).
ISBN 978-4-903452-15-9

Ten leaders prescribe positive ways for Japan to assert a higher profile in the international arena.

International House of Japan

Cultural Bridge Between East and West

International House of Japan, editor

2009. 112 pages, paperback. ¥1,000 (¥952 + tax).
ISBN 978-4-903452-17-3

More than 300 photographs detail the history of the International House of Japan. An essay describes a friendship that spawned the organization.

I House Press

How to Order I-House Press Books

Online

Access the I-House Press Order Form by clicking on one of the "Click to order" buttons at **www.i-house.or.jp/en/publications/ihousepress**.

By fax

Fax the following information to...
+81-3-3470-3170

- The I-House Press title(s) that you want
- The number of each title that you want
- Your name
- Your address
- Your phone and fax numbers
- Your e-mail address (optional)

Inquiries

I-House Press
c/o Program Department, International House of Japan
5-11-16, Roppongi, Minato-ku, Tokyo 106-0032, Japan
Phone: +81-3-3470-3211 or -9059
Fax: +81-3-3470-3170
E-mail: press@i-house.or.jp
Url: **www.i-house.or.jp/en/publications/ihousepress**

Noh mask photo courtesty of Iba Teiichi

May 2010

None of these claims is supported by reliable data. The remainder of this chapter is devoted to examining what is known of white-collar college graduates based on the research done so far. Comparisons with other countries focus on graduates who are managers or professionals and not on college graduates because the diffusion rate of a college education differs from place to place.

Stability versus Mobility

The issue of a stable versus a mobile workforce was examined by Trevor.[5] Trevor studied the job histories of 31 British and 22 Japanese managers at three Japanese companies in the United Kingdom: a manufacturing, a retail, and a trading company. All but 1 of the British managers had changed companies four times on average, whereas none of the Japanese managers had ever changed employers. This agrees with the conventional wisdom about Japanese job attachment versus Western mobility. Trevor points out that managers at large British companies did not move as often as is claimed, but he offers no evidence for this assertion. The complaints of Japanese businessmen abroad thus appear to be substantiated.

How then to reconcile these findings with the EC data on job attachment in Western Europe in chapter 2? That data, for companies of all sizes, shows that though many Western European workers have short terms of service, Western Europe actually has more long-term workers than Japan. Two reasons for this are conceivable. First, the difference is based on company size. The EC data does not specify company size, but Trevor's study involved only small companies. The three Japanese companies' U.K. offices or factories are small. British managers had no place to move within those facilities, let alone up to the head office. They consequently saw their companies as small. And their rate of mobility was commensurate with that of small firms.

Unfortunately, the EC study does not cross-classify statistics on length of service by company size. A comparison by company size thus must use data for Japan alone. Table 11-1 takes college graduates in their late 40s and early 50s—the age group most indicative of managers and of job attachment—and compares

Table 11-1 Length of Service for Male White-collar College Graduates Aged 45–49 and 50–54 in the Manufacturing Industries by Company Size (1987)

	10–99 employees		1,000 or more employees	
	45–49	50–54	45–49	50–54
Aggregate	100	100	100	100
–4 years	19.5	20.9	1.2	2.4
5–9	15.2	13.3	1.6	1.3
10–14	13.9	12.1	2.1	2.1
15–19	14.1	12.2	6.8	4.8
20–24	27.3	12.6	88.4	7.8
25–		28.8		82.1

Source: Ministry of Labor, *1987-nen Chingin Kozo Kihon Tokei Chosa* (Statistical Survey of Wage Structure, 1987).

their length of service with the sizes of their companies. Whereas the companies in Trevor's study were all old, famous large corporations, table 11-1 uses data from ordinary large companies. Nearly 80 percent of the college graduates at companies of 1,000 or more employees had worked for the same company since graduation. Those few who had worked elsewhere did so when quite young and only for a short time. Fewer than 30 percent of those surveyed at small companies were long-term employees; 20 percent had worked at their present place of employment for fewer than five years. Company size thus can account for significant differences in the careers of Japanese college graduates.

The second reason for the difference is mobility while young. In general, many managers, even at large companies in the West, changed jobs while young. The number of changes increases in line with the time young workers spend searching for jobs. At large Western companies, managers' careers evolve through internal promotion; thus, even after changing jobs while young they build up considerable job attachment within the firms they settle on. Japanese companies must expect some mobility until their overseas operations are of a suitable size, and their policies should reflect this.

Generalists versus Specialists

Trevor's study examines the issue of generalists versus specialists. He makes it clear that the careers of the Japanese managers studied, including their job experiences in Japan, were specialized and little different from those of the British managers studied. Of the 22 Japanese managers, only 2 had experience of two areas—gained in Japan. One had worked in financial affairs and personnel; the other in design engineering and sales engineering. The rest remained within machine processing, quality control, accounting, and marketing. Even in the nonmanufacturing trading company managers were confined to a single product group in the United Kingdom and Japan. Of the 31 British managers, only 3 had changed functions before entering their Japanese companies. By percentage, no difference existed between the British and Japanese managers.

This, however, may only be a trend in small companies in the United Kingdom. Closer examination of British white-collar workers' careers and, indeed, of white-collar workers elsewhere and more widespread testing of the findings are needed.

EARLY SCREENING SYSTEM

Career Research in the United States

Careers are not easy to study. They are the result of largely unwritten practices within a company. What is documented is unreliable, and observing company practices is difficult. Nonetheless, many career studies exist, most done in the United States, and more often in sociology than in economics. The finest will be used to explore corporate practices to compare them with Japan's. The emphasis is chiefly on managers instead of white-collar workers to better target personnel who correspond to college graduates in Japan.

Research on the intraorganizational careers of American managers began in the 1960s. Initially, researchers advanced the concepts of contest and sponsored mobility, using mobility because promotion connotes movement within an organization. Contest mobility suggests that since many people are candidates for promotion they are in contest with one another, the winner being promoted. Sponsored mobility maintains that promotional eligibility is more or less predetermined by such factors as the employee's alma mater, degrees earned, and family background. Both of these concepts are oversimplifications, and since the late 1970s a more effective model has garnered support because it reflects prevailing practices in U.S. companies. Its premise is that an employee's performance right after entering a company determines later promotional opportunities.

James Rosenbaum is responsible for this model, known as tournament mobility.[6] He analyzed the careers of 671 people who had entered a large company of more than 10,000 workers in the early 1960s and were still employed there in 1975. His study followed their careers over a long period of time and is a superb example of the analysis of panel data. What Rosenbaum discovered was that performance at the beginning of a career is decisive; those who fall behind then do not contest for later promotion. Once defeated in battle, they can never reenter the lists—thus, tournament mobility.

Rosenbaum's findings correspond to practices frequently seen in large U.S. companies and have subsequently become established theory. There is an arrangement at large U.S. companies that is usually referred to as the fast track. Employees recognized by superiors within three or four years after entering a company are rapidly promoted, while most others are promoted at a more leisurely pace. Rosenbaum's model accurately reflects this.

Superb data such as Rosenbaum's were hard to come by until 1987 and J. Benjamin Forbes's study.[7] Forbes analyzed the careers of 180 white-collar workers who were hired between 1968 and 1970 at a large company of 22,000 employees and were still employed there in 1981. Forbes concluded that tournament mobility did not apply as firmly as claimed. The impact of performance at the start of an employee's career was strong, but not decisive.

Widespread

The tournament model is not unique to the United States. The gist of interviews conducted with many personnel directors at large companies in Western Europe and Southeast Asia about their selection procedures—which have not been written up because one-time interviews provide insufficient evidence—is that a U.S.-style early screening system is almost universal.[8] An obvious example is France, where major banks and other large firms rapidly promote some graduates of the *grande e'coles* to important divisions and cultivate them as generalists. The *grande e'coles* in this case are not the famous Paris Ecole Normale Supérieure or the Ecole Polytechnique. Since few graduates of these schools enter corporations, those who do are treated more as decoration than employees. The number of graduates of the ordinary *grande e'coles* who enter large companies is roughly equivalent to the number of graduates of Japan's old university system who went into business prewar. As a result of their preparation for entering the *grande e'coles,* they are one or two years older than graduates, say, of the University of Paris when they graduate and enter companies.[9]

In Southeast Asia, a typical large Thai company exhibits early screening by promoting a few college graduates shortly after they are hired. Their standing at graduation—among, for example, Chulalongkorn University's top engineering graduates—is crucial.

In addition to being common worldwide, it is thought that the early screening system also is quite old, although research lags. Even Japan's large prewar companies employed this system, with graduates of the old imperial universities being promoted early.

In all of the studies cited, no mention is made of whether companies have internal promotion. This is because internal promotion is thought so natural that no effort has been made to confirm its existence. If internal promotion was not natural, the focus on managers within a company would make no sense. That does not mean that internal promotion systems abroad are like Japan's. A difference is that intercompany mobility seems to occur more frequently among young workers overseas than in Japan. Unfortunately, U.S. statistics to confirm this are unavailable.[10]

Internal Promotion in Large British Companies

Fortunately, the EC's *Structure of Earnings in Industry* classifies different management-level positions by age and by length of service, as does Japan's Statistical Survey of Wage Structure. A comparison of the statistics should make it possible to corroborate the use of a screening system. West German statistics typify the EC and are compared with Japan's in figure 11-1. Management positions are difficult to compare, so only general observations are possible. Upper management in Japan appears to consist of older employees, while younger employees make up middle management, suggesting a late screening process. West German upper- and mid-level managers, however, show a consistent age distribution, suggesting early screening.

A study of management positions in British companies is also available.[11] It shows that presumably large British companies have an internal promotion system based on merit ratings and regular pay increments for 5 to 7 years at the same job. Another study based on interviews with 80 managers at two large British companies offers a look at mid-career managers with an average of 15 years experience and a profound understanding of their jobs and their companies and is valuable because nothing like it exists.[12] It focuses on the problems managers face in dealing with career-related matters. The interviews reveal internal promotion to section chief and department chief.

Managers were asked what factors were important for internal promotion. Of the 11 items cited, the top 3 were "improve one's qualifications," "choose jobs that are stepping-stones," and "improve interpersonal relations." Contrary to conventional thinking, as in Japan the reference to "qualifications" is to "experience and technical knowledge...relevant to the...organization." When managers were asked what determined advancement, "several emphasized the importance of gaining experience and training in management." "Jobs that are stepping-stones," they said, implies assignment to a valued post with future prospects. "Improve interpersonal relations" is explained as "good relations with one's immediate superior and drawing one's capacities to his attention in a tactful way" and also involves "getting better

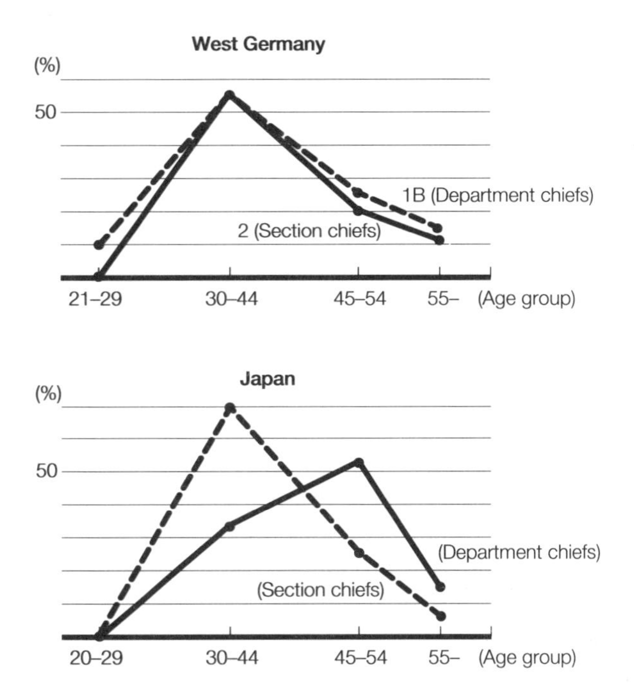

Fig. 11-1. Age Distribution of Managers in Japan and West Germany

Sources: EC, *Structure of Earnings in Industry*, 1972; Japan, Ministry of Labor, *1976-nen Chingin Kozo Kihon Tokei Chosa* (Statistical Survey of Wage Structure, 1976).

Notes: 1. Job rank 1B in the EC statistics seems to be equivalent to upper-level department chiefs; job rank 2 seems to correspond with the remaining department chiefs and with section chiefs. This can be surmised from the percentage of white-collar workers.

2. The statistics for Japan are the averages for manufacturing companies with 100 or more employees; for West Germany, they are for manufacturing companies with 10 or more employees.

known to people, especially...seniors, as an intelligent and cooperative person."[13] This study illuminates more similarities than differences with Japanese companies.

None of the cited studies, however, refers to career breadth—the generalist versus specialist argument—because skill formation was not their aim. Conjectures, though, are possible. Generalists are promoted rapidly and specialists slowly. It is wrong to conclude that Western European managers are specialists. And it should be remembered that general managers experienced in many divisions are promoted early.

This foregoing is a general overview of chiefly U.S. and U.K. managers' careers made possible by the still early research in this area. What follows is a look at the special features of college graduates in industry in Japan.

PROMOTION WITHIN A JAPANESE CORPORATION

Two Stages

Career studies of white-collar college graduates in Japanese businesses have just begun. Only a present-day description thus is possible, using case studies of personnel officers and managers in accounting, marketing, planning, and other departments from fewer than 60 mostly large companies, but including medium-sized firms of several hundred employees. Interviews were conducted in 1987 and 1988 based on guidelines furnished by a sampling of the career records of employees with 10 and 20 years of service at some dozen typical large Japanese firms. The study was then gradually expanded to include companies where such records could not be obtained.[14]

Most of the firms studied used the late screening system: The screening that determines assignment to management positions occurs late, around 15 years after a worker enters the company. Careers thus have two stages. The first covers the years before screening, during which most white-collar college graduates are promoted. A few drop out, and distinctions are evident among the many who remain, but, superficially, these are minor—a 2- or 3-year delay in promotion to upper job grades after 3 or 4 years of experience. Everyone is aware of this. The assertion that promotion in Japanese companies is based on seniority or length of service corresponds fairly closely to the situation during this first stage.

Among the companies surveyed were two notable exceptions to the late screening system. The first occurred in large companies in the extremely traditional spinning and electric power industries. They continue to cultivate college graduates as executive material while employing fewer college graduates than other industries. The second occurred frequently in medium-sized companies, where managers typically started out in different careers. At a car dealership, for example, key managers generally started out elsewhere or were supplied from a large automaker. Apart from these exceptions, late screening is widespread.

In the second stage of a career, the pace of selection speeds up, and a gap grows even among employees with the same length of service. The assumption that Japanese companies do not differentiate between workers on the basis of ability is only true if this second stage is ignored. By this stage, employees are divided into three distinct career tracks: central management, departmental management, and nonmanagerial. The important few chosen for central management are groomed to run the company, but departmental managers predominate. If a company grows and if few of its white-collar workers are college graduates, many of the latter will become departmental managers. If these two conditions break down, however, the nonmanagerial group will steadily increase.

Career breadth differs for each group. Central managers must acquire wide-ranging experience, but employees in the other two groups will probably forge more specialized careers. They may branch out slightly, but their main area will be clear.

Broad Specialization

Broad specialization is a distinctive feature of careers during these two stages.[15] Employees change jobs every few years within a single specialized area, gaining considerable experience in doing so. A specialized area for a building engineer, for instance, could be any of site operations, planning and design, structural engineering, or interior work. Once the area is chosen, the engineer would remain there. Broad specialization in, for example, the case of site operations would entail supervising the construction of a variety of structures. A site engineer would experience building condominiums, factories, stores, schools, hospitals, etc., or, in civil engineering, such public works facilities as roads, harbors, housing sites, and railroads; everything except dams and tunnels, whose construction requires so much specialized technology that they must be built by specialists.

At large trading houses, each product group—steel or chemicals, textiles or energy—is an area of specialization. Employees are assigned to an area, and that is where they remain unless something extraordinary happens. They broaden their experience by handling two or more of their group's products; through different postings; and by mastering two transaction types from among exports, imports, or domestic or overseas trade. Someone in the steel department, for example, might switch from importing scrap iron to overseas trade.

In a department store, product groups such as menswear, women's wear, and furniture are each specialized areas. Increasing breadth of experience in menswear, for example, would involve handling formal wear, shirts, and neckties and other accessories.

In the food wholesale business, domestic sales would be a specialization, and employees would broaden their experience by changing sales districts every three to five years. Such a change involves new retail customers with different clients and product lines. Indeed, the type of facility and transaction may vary greatly from district to district, from supermarkets to hotels or both, so that employees experience diverse clients, products, and transactions.

General areas of specialization in the manufacturing industries include general affairs, personnel, accounting and finance, domestic sales, overseas sales, information systems, buying, advertising, international operations, legal affairs, public relations, distribution, services, product development, research, design, production technology, and production control. Some companies might either combine or, for very specialized career formation, further subdivide some areas. A company that exports heavily might designate export regions as specialized areas, and employees would gain experience with each region. Accounting might encompass general accounts, cost control, budgetary control, and financing, several of which employees would experience. Employees in personnel would acquire experience of education and training, union negotiations, welfare, salaries, recruitment, etc.

In smaller companies, the breadth of specialization is the same as or narrower than in large firms. The area of specialization of a site engineer at a small firm, for example, changes in scope only. An engineer at a large company deals with a greater variety of projects because large firms get commissions for bigger and more complex structures. The assertion that smaller firms provide a more varied range of work experience is not always correct.

Dealing with Diversity

The specialization discussed above contrasts sharply with the common perception of the Japanese white-collar worker as a generalist. Studies confirm, however, that specialization exists and that white-collar workers have a main area of specialization even when they have experience of several different areas.

Knowing why specialization exists would facilitate predictions of trends. If a college graduate is active on the leading edge of business, reasons for specialization are easy to guess. A college graduate in industry must acquire specialized skills. Constant job changes prevent their development. This suggests, however, that a narrower area of specialization is better.

Why, then, broaden experience? Three reasons are conceivable: dealing with diversity, dealing with change, and the multiplier effect. Important career assignments often require diverse skills. Overseas postings on behalf of a trading house are an example. Overseas staffs are, of course, smaller than home office staffs, so each person must deal with many products. The main product groups do not change, but the diversity of products each employee is responsible for increases. Alternatively, if a company that a manufacturer does business with moves overseas, the manufacturer's domestic sales staff must learn to handle foreign sales if the business relationship is valued. This aspect of diversity is obvious.

Many aspects of diversity, however, are not so obvious. Take, for example, the wholesale business, where the most important skill is that of consulting retailers. Wholesalers take into consideration the trade areas of retail stores and suggest effective product displays. Since trade areas are unique to each retailer, only through experience of many different retail outlets, say veteran salespeople, can consultants develop the know-how to deal with retailers' individual needs. Site engineers provide a further example. Although they may deal with a single building type, soil characteristics and building conditions differ at each site. The skill to handle this diversity, say experienced architects, comes only with diverse experience.

Dealing with Change

The most obvious type of change is change in demand, either cyclical or ongoing. The latter—long-term change—is more difficult to deal with. Public works projects, for example, used to be chiefly railroads and harbors, but have shifted to housing site development and highways. A company that specialized in each of these categories would thus have too many employees in some and too few in others. Layoffs would result in excessively high costs for employees and firms, and breadth of experience is in this case problematic because the costs of training for such broad experience are prohibitive. Broad specialization is much more important.

Other changes occur in technology and in products. Despite technological changes, many of the same principles and theories apply, as, consequently, do many specialized skills. And new skills can be developed from existing knowledge; the ability to deal with diversity is a good foundation for handling changes.

The Multiplier Effect

The multiplier effect refers to the interplay between closely related activities. After 10 years in over-the-counter sales, an employee in the menswear department of a department store, for instance, might move to buying, which encompasses purchasing and product development. Buyers envision products with sales potential and commission designers and manufacturers. Initially, buyers specialize in one product, such as shirts, for which they do the buying nationwide. Every few years, they move to another, related item. Their increasing experience broadens their familiarity with makers, designers, and wholesalers and improves their ability to negotiate.

It is not uncommon for buyers to return to sales; the areas are closely related. This is where the multiplier effect comes in. Successful buyers are aware of consumer demands, and over-the-counter sales offer direct contact with consumers. Salespeople, likewise, are aware of buyers' importance in increasing sales.

Salespeople experienced in buying know manufacturers and wholesalers and can refer orders to them. For the multiplier effect to work, the training costs of moving from field to field must be reasonable. Thus the importance of limiting movement to closely related areas.

In general, a long-term career is meaningless unless it involves the multiplier effect. Companies that opt for internal career development must encourage this effect. Those that do not encourage it ought instead to rely on outside specialists or temporary help, but must not expect the multiplier effect to occur.

Careers among white-collar college graduates result from the way the skills described previously are formed. Skill formation depends not only on OJT but also on off-JT courses at each stage of workers' careers. As a rule, white-collar skill formation is similar to that seen earlier for blue-collar workers. The difference is in degree. The experience of change and diversity is similar, but occurs more frequently for white-collar workers and requires more skill. This is probably the reason compensation systems for white-collar workers and blue-collar workers at modern Japanese companies differ very little in wage structure and yearly pay increments. The differences are that white-collar workers have more demanding careers and a slightly steeper wage curve than blue-collar workers.

Problems Overseas

If Japanese companies employ the late screening system overseas, it will be difficult for them to attract young local talent because in the West and in the developing countries they interpret late screening badly. Since corporate success overseas depends on attracting and cultivating local talent, this is a problem.

To replace late screening with early screening, however, would be enormously costly because late screening offers extraordinary benefits. Above all, it intensifies long-term competition and raises skill levels in individual employees.

The late screening system reduces bias and promotes competition. For competition to be effective, the criteria for measuring job performance must be fair. If promotion is determined without regard for worker diligence, workers won't make the effort. Devising fair and objective criteria to measure white-collar job performance in a large corporation, however, is difficult because of the complexity of the work. Ultimately, companies worldwide depend on assessments by workers' immediate superiors. No amount of pretension can disguise that this is a subjective, biased opinion and that bias makes merit ratings a doubtful incentive. However, if the period involved is extended using the late screening system, and if the assessors and the assessed move within an organization assessment data mount up. The number of assessors increases, and merit ratings accumulate in the personnel department, making it possible to eliminate unduly biased assessments. Assessors are themselves assessed, creating a kind of assessment market amid a system that stimulates competition.

Late screening also promotes the upgrading of skills. During the lengthy period before decisive screening, workers are compelled to constantly upgrade their skills. They do so knowing that it influences screening. Moreover, the incentive to upgrade skills is widespread, involving many workers, not just a few elite. Early screening robs the majority left behind of incentive for skill improvement.

The late screening system, however, does have shortcomings. It does not help to form an elite. Early screening allows those selected to be assigned early in their careers to important posts where their leadership potential can be developed. This is advantageous in dealing with abrupt changes in the business climate.

Trends, however, favor the late screening system. Advances in computerization are freeing workers from repetitive work to deal more with change and diversity. Since workshop efficiency depends on workers' handling of change and diversity, increasing importance will be given to honing skills among the majority rather than an elite few. To replace the late screening system, which stimulates skill advancement in the majority, would thus be a mistake.

In addition, as the number of universities increases worldwide college graduates are becoming less of an elite. They will constitute the core and even the majority of the business workforce.

Corporate survival will depend on cultivating this large group, something for which the late screening system is well suited.

Late screening is neither a Japanese tradition nor an expression of Japanese culture. Prewar Japanese companies used early screening, and Japan's ministries and government offices still use it today. Detached as it is from Japanese culture, nothing prevents use of late screening abroad. Yet, problems remain with how best to attract young non-Japanese employees. Following are some suggestions:

1. Start out at a level that will advance the local situation and do not try to reach Japan's level all at once. Pay serious attention to the local situation.
2. Explain carefully and repeatedly to local management candidates how the late screening system works in Japan. Stress its merits, general applicability, and costs.
3. If local management candidates have the ability, give them the same opportunities for promotion—either in the head office or elsewhere—as Japanese candidates. This will eliminate impressions of exclusivity toward Japanese and allow local candidates to experience Japanese methods firsthand. It would also be effective in curtailing mobility among foreign employees, who quit when they see no prospects for promotion even in the small overseas branches of Japanese companies. Broadening their careers to include the Japanese head office would increase their prospects dramatically. Giving capable employees, Japanese or foreign, equal opportunities should be the keynote of personnel policies in the globalization of Japanese corporations.

Chapter 12 Labor Unions in the Workplace

LABOR DISPUTES: AN INTERNATIONAL COMPARISON

The Enterprise Union Theory

Some point to a trend away from labor unions, but unions' important role continues. Working people invest time and energy in their workplaces; the importance they place on their jobs is immense. Having a say in how their jobs are done, in day-to-day operations, or in company policy is a key issue, just as is the impact of workers' input on economic efficiency and on industrial society. Workers voice their say through their labor unions.

Because of the importance of labor unions, criticism of Japanese industrial society focuses on what is known as the enterprise union theory. Japanese labor unions are company unions, the argument goes, and therefore not true mouthpieces of workers—Japan's economic growth has been achieved at workers' expense.

This criticism originated in Japan based on the assertion that enterprise unions are organizationally flawed. It holds that labor unions transcend companies, are industrywide or trade related, control the labor market, and confront management. Company unions, it says, cannot control the labor market outside the company and are unable to resist management. Enterprise unions thus have little say in management and at best can only collaborate in production.

This theory is based on several assumptions: first, Japanese labor unions only exist at the company level; second, unions in the West are either industrywide or trade related, not corporate; and third, Japanese unions are less independent than European or

North American unions. Obviously, an examination of Japanese labor unions involves a study of Western labor unions. Here, the study will be confined to labor unions in the United States and West Germany.

Workplace labor unions follow three patterns:

1. Formal labor unions and, above them, industrywide unions. Formal implies that they have legal standing and can collect union dues and employ full-time union officials. Unions in the United States and Japan are good examples.
2. Worker organizations at the establishment level. Found in West Germany and France, these are not legally labor unions; they are vehicles for employee participation in management. Functionally, however, they are labor unions. French establishments may also have a branch of a formal labor union, so the two may coexist. Historically and developmentally, worker organizations are older.
3. Informal unions at the establishment level. Informal implies that they cannot collect dues; the United Kingdom provides examples.[1]

The discussion that follows looks at the United States as an example of the first pattern and West Germany as an example of the second. The preceding by itself refutes the conventional wisdom on labor unions, but it is based on observations from a few case studies. A comparison requires statistical evidence. The statistics available concern labor disputes and participation rates in trade unions. To test whether Japan's labor unions are particularly weak, statistics on strikes are required.[2]

Japan's Strike Rate is about Average

Figure 12-1 shows the number of workdays per 1,000 employees lost as a result of industrial disputes. It is based on International Labour Organization (ILO) statistics. The ILO compiles government statistics on strikes in each country under the categories number of strikes, number of workers involved, and number of workdays lost. Data for the first two categories may vary by coun-

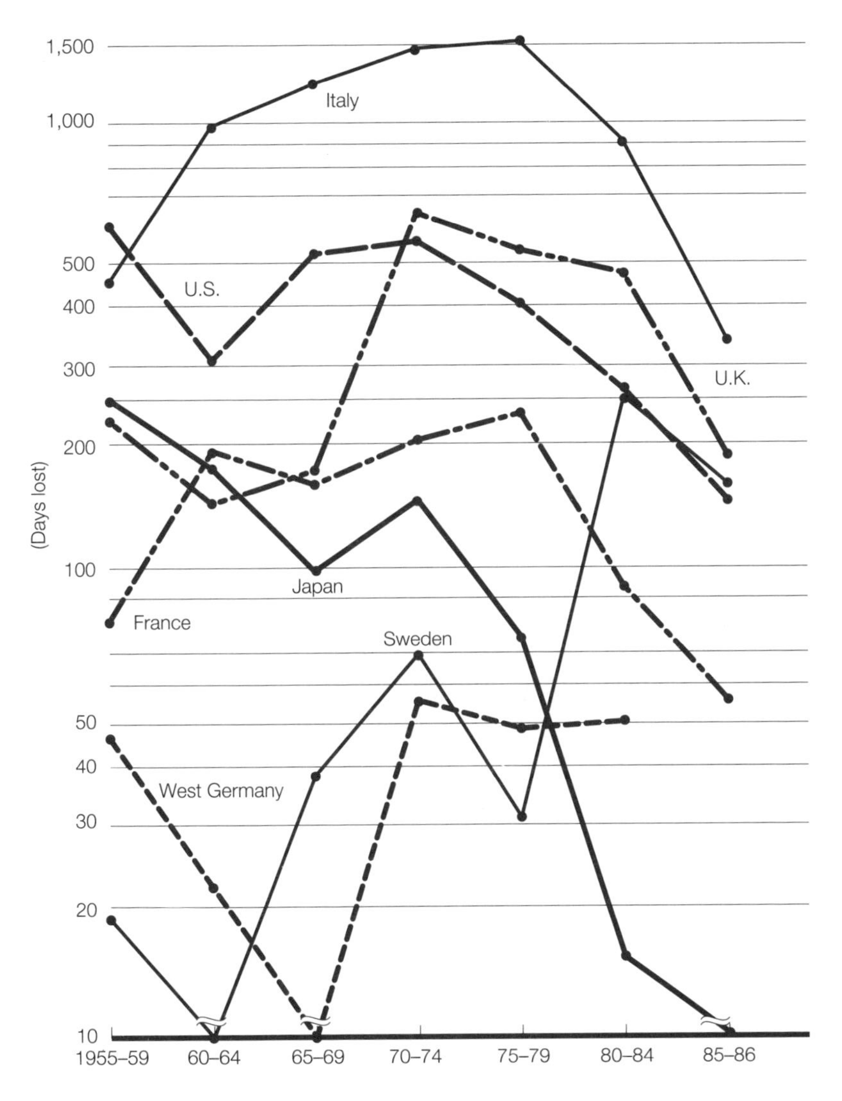

Fig. 12-1. An International Comparison of Strikes: Number of Workdays Lost per 1,000 Employees (five-year averages)

Source: ILO, *Yearbook of Labour Statistics.*

try depending on how a strike is defined. And countries differ in their handling of short, small-scale strikes. These differences, however, are negligible in calculating the number of days lost. By averaging large annual fluctuations and instead using five-year averages, the figure has been made easier to read.

The figure reveals that Japan's strike rate is not especially low. In the 1980s, Japan did have the fewest strikes of any country. But in the 1950s and 1960s, its rate compared with the United Kingdom's and France's; in fact, Japan's surpassed the United Kingdom's in the late 1950s. That Japan has fewer strikes than the United States is true, but then the United States and Italy have the most strikes. West Germany and Sweden, by contrast, had fewer strikes than Japan until the mid-1970s. If industrial relations are harmonious in Japan, they are ultraharmonious in these countries. Japan's decline in strikes after the energy crisis is shared by many countries; only the rate of the decline has been greater in Japan.

Statistics are also available for the union participation ratio (the percentage of employed workers who are union members). As of 1989, Japan's ratio was a low 25.9 percent. Since peaking in 1970 at 35 percent, the ratio has gradually declined. Cross-culturally, the old unionization rate of one in three is not low; it is normal for independent labor unions. Running unions solely off membership dues is difficult for all but larger companies; otherwise, it is impossible to support full-time officials who advise and file grievances for members.

The U.S. unionization rate began to drop even earlier than in Japan, from one in three to 17 percent. Statistics are unavailable for France, but the ratio is said to be around 20 percent. The United Kingdom and West Germany have declined recently from a peak of between 40 and 50 percent. Northern Europe features an extraordinarily high rate of between 80 and 90 percent, the result, it is thought, of the difficulty nonunion members have collecting unemployment benefits.

The overall decline in union participation rates is said to result from the rise in service industries and a trend away from unions.[3] Service industry establishments are too small to support full-time union officials. In addition, new labor laws and standardized personnel practices have eliminated the differences between unionized and nonunionized workplaces, reducing the need to belong to and heightening the trend away from labor unions.

The percentage of employed is nonetheless increasing, and the importance of a voice in operations—and thus of labor unions—has not diminished. This is corroborated by Richard Freeman and James Medoff.[4] Economics has hitherto regarded labor unions as a monopoly that obstructed the optimal distribution of resources in disregard of the national welfare. Freeman and Medoff argue against this view with a theory that proved labor unions contribute to economic efficiency. Their work is based on Albert Hirschman's exit-voice model.[5] Exit refers to workers who quit when dissatisfied, and voice refers to those who vocalize the reasons for their dissatisfaction instead of quitting. Voice is assumed to be more conducive to raising efficiency since management knows of problems through workers' input and can rectify them. Freeman and Medoff substantiated this using data from the United States.

Labor unions affect not only economic efficiency but also social structure. Work underpins industrial society, whose structure is influenced by input from workers. Seizing on this vital point, foreign observers have severely criticized Japanese industrial society. This criticism is unwarranted in terms of strikes. But strikes are only a fraction of the union activities that must be examined but for which no statistics exist.

LOCAL UNIONS IN THE UNITED STATES

A Single Organization for Each Establishment

Most Americans believe that U.S. labor unions are industrywide or trade related. Observation, however, reveals a multilayered structure, with a basic organization at the plant or company level overseen by an industry union. Apart from such as the building trade and its tradition of craft unions, this structure prevails in U.S. manufacturing and service industries.

The basic blue-collar organization in each U.S. business establishment is the local union. For most Americans, this is a labor union. Local does not connote the establishment, it is traditional labor union terminology from the nineteenth century, when most unions were craft unions whose regional branches were called local unions. Today's building and other craft unions retain regional local unions, and the longshoremen's union has regional chapters. Other industries, however, do not have regional basic units.

For each U.S. establishment, regardless of industry, to have a single organization contrasts sharply with Japanese assumptions. But this is so obvious to specialists on American industrial relations that they never explain it.[6] For that reason, the explanation that follows relies on case studies gleaned from interviews.[7]

Each U.S. company often appears to have dozens of unions. The local union at each plant of a large, nationwide firm may be affiliated with a variety of industry unions; U.S. industry unions' jurisdictions are not confined to single industries. In addition, the maintenance departments of individual establishments may have workers who, being the inheritors of traditional crafts, belong to the remnants of different craft unions. Despite appearances, most of these unions are incorporated into a single local union.

Although local unions cut across occupational categories, not everyone joins. Compared with Japanese labor organizations, membership among higher-ranking U.S. personnel is low. In Japan, white-collar workers up to around chief clerk become union members. U.S. union members are primarily blue collar; the few white-collar workers who join unions usually form their own.

On the other hand, U.S. membership limits are wider than in Japan, where union membership is limited to regular core employees, whose numbers are smaller than in the United States. In Japan, regular core employees work alongside workers from related companies. In the United States, most employees on company premises are company employees who can become union members after a three-month probation.

Full-time Union Officials and Their Salaries

Labor union activities are affected by the presence of full-time officials and by the costs of their services. Workers join a labor union and pay union dues to ensure that there is someone to turn to when problems arise. A full-time union official should always be available for consultation in an establishment. To listen effectively to workers and negotiate with management on their behalf, the official must know the work and the workplace well and possess many years of negotiating experience. Documentation on whether local unions have full-time officials and the means to pay their salaries is scarce in the United States, so a small sampling of interviews must suffice.

A local union at an establishment with roughly 1,000 or more employees has full-time union officials. Their numbers are smaller than for a comparable union in Japan, but, as in Japan, are mostly drawn from the employees of the establishment. Unlike Japan, in most cases the top official at a U.S. local union is released from employee status. Top officials thus were once employees and know the work and the workplace well. The major difference between the two countries is the source of union officials' wages. In Japan, union officials are paid from union dues; dues pay only a portion of U.S. union officials' salaries. If a 3,000-member U.S. local has five full-time officials, one would be paid entirely by the union, and the rest would receive half their salaries from dues, half from the company. In this respect, Japanese unions are more independent of management than their U.S. counterparts.

As formal unions, U.S. locals collect dues, which they pay to industrywide unions that, in turn, refund enough money to cover locals' operating expenses. In Japan, company organizations control dues and pay industrywide organizations from them. This is the difference between industrywide unions and federations.

Industrywide organizations are not neatly divided along industry lines. Jurisdictions cross, and unions compete for members. Territorial disputes among industry unions are a serious problem. Which industrywide union a local union joins often depends on which organizer contacts it first.

Important Problems Handled at the Establishment Level

Local and industry unions have separate functions. The distinction is clear, and industry unions do not get involved in local matters. Most problems, in fact, are the concern of local unions.

Promotion, entailing a raise in pay, is an important concern for workers and is entirely a matter for local unions, which negotiate and conclude plant-level agreements covering progression lines, promotion procedures, and order of promotion. Transfers and layoffs are also local matters. Since plant-level negotiation determines which jobs are assigned what job grades, locals set wages for jobs. How high to set pay rates for each job grade, however, is decided through negotiations between companies and industry unions. This, though, is not an industrywide negotiation. An industry union may be party to the negotiations, but the outcome applies separately and may differ from company to company.

Industrywide unions negotiate general changes in wage levels. Contrary to the common misperception in Japan, industrywide unions do not negotiate salaries for all of their members, including those at small and medium-sized companies. In the steel industry, for example, negotiations involve only the largest companies. This corresponds to the collective bargaining of Japan's private railroad companies. These practices date only to the late 1970s, when the U.S. steel industry was being overtaken by Japan's. In other industries, enterprise-level negotiations are normal. Negotiations even at big companies in the automobile industry, for example, are at the company level. The results, however, especially in wage levels, are identical for all big companies. It is thus fair to call these de facto industrial negotiations. The situation is virtually the same in Japan.

The difference between the United States and Japan is the strength of workers' say in corporate affairs. This has two sides. U.S. labor unions have a strong say in working conditions. They allow little scope for managerial discretion in decisions on promotions, transfers, layoffs, or salaries. Workers' job performances are irrelevant in determining the order of promotions or layoffs, and there is no merit pay for blue-collar workers. U.S. unions, however, have little say in management policy. In fact, it has been union policy not to get involved in management policy. But threats to employment appear to be compelling unions to seek a say in this area.[8]

U.S. unions seemingly have been changing since the beginning of the 1980s. As the U.S. economy endured painful, employment-threatening adjustment, labor unions conceded heavily to management. The leading U.S. steel and automobile unions stopped asking for raises and even accepted pay cuts. This is not a change in U.S. labor union policy, only a response to dramatic downsizing that has threatened the jobs of even longtime workers. Employment reduction in the United States is carried out in reverse order of length of service—workers with the least seniority bear the brunt of layoffs, while longtime workers enjoy job security. The unions' moves resulted from a threat to this system. If longtime workers are laid off and forced to seek new employment, the loss would be immense. Unions merely made inevitable concessions to prevent this loss.[9]

WORKS COUNCILS IN WEST GERMANY

Worker Participation in Management

Labor-management relations at companies in West Germany consist of worker participation in management. The laws that prescribe this and, more importantly, the gap between them and practice must be looked at. Worker participation in management involves participation in either corporate boards of directors or in an association of employees at each establishment. An explanation of employee associations suffices for a study of workplace labor unions, but an examination of worker participation in boards of directors is important in viewing future trends in industrial relations.[10]

The 1951 Co-determination Act, the 1952 Law on the Constitution of Business Undertakings, and the 1976 New Co-determination Act contain legislation on worker participation in boards of directors. The 1951 Co-determination Act (*Mitbestimmungsgesetz* or *Montangesetz*) targeted large companies of 1,000 or more employees in the then key coal and steel industries and sanctioned high worker participation.

Under the Law on Stock Companies, workers' representatives make up half of companies' supervisory boards (*Aufsichtsrat*). Of the 11 board members, 5 are from labor and 5 from management; the board chairman is approved by both sides. The labor representatives include 2 union and 2 employee representatives and a neutral person recommended by labor. This is the law. It works because the number of large companies is limited. The distinction between union and employee representatives is easier to understood if it is known that in West Germany labor unions have officers only at the industry and regional level. Workplaces instead have a works council that functions as a management participation organization, not as a labor union. Its leaders are the board's employee representatives. The board's labor union representatives are thus not company employees.

Supervisory boards, unlike auditors in Japan, have the legal right to choose company presidents and boards of directors and to determine corporate policies. They are, however, part-time organizations that meet only four or five times yearly. Opposition from labor can pose serious problems, but studies thus far show that board decisions are deferred until unanimity is achieved. The worker director (*Arbeitsdirektor),* moreover—the top human resource management officer—is chosen on recommendations from labor.

Only West Germany accepts this much participation by labor.[11] Its system therefore attracts attention. Far from being an obstacle to corporate activities, the system appears to have reduced problems by winning workers' cooperation. In restructuring and downsizing the coal industry, for example, circulating information among workers is said to have helped defuse a difficult situation.

Non-coal and non-steel industry companies of 500 or more workers are governed by the 1952 Law on the Constitution of Business Undertakings (*Betriebsverfassungsgesetz*). It states that 1 out of 3 members of a firm's supervisory board must be a labor representative, but does not stipulate how to determine that member. Consequently, almost all labor representatives were employee representatives. How to strengthen employees' roles later became an issue. Labor unions demanded that the scope of the Co-determination Act be widened, but management was opposed. The New Co-determination Act enacted in 1976 provided that 1 out of 2 members of supervisory boards be from labor, but it classed middle management (*leitende Angestellte*) as labor. Middle-management representatives thus give management a majority.

Worker participation in management has long been an issue. Jobs are enormously significant, and since workplace conditions affect workers' lives a say in running workplaces is important. Workers must be encouraged to express their views and guaranteed a hearing. The West German system of worker participation in corporate management is therefore worth studying.

De Facto Unions: Works Councils

The employee organizations at each company, stipulated in the 1952 Law on the Constitution of Business Undertakings, are another aspect of West German worker participation in management. Under this law, every establishment of more than 5 employees must have a works council (*Betriebsrat*) whose members are employee elected. In practice, works councils exist in establishments of 100 or more employees. They are misinterpreted in Japanese as meetings at which labor and management discuss management problems. However, they are clearly only for employees or, rather, for employees' elected representatives.

Employees are divided into blue-collar and white-collar workers, who elect their own representatives. Some representatives are freed from their jobs to serve as full-time officials. Their salaries are company paid, allowing them to devote themselves to works council activities. The number of full-time officials is legally stipulated according to company size, but the actual number seems slightly higher than that prescribed. Companies bear the full cost of works councils, including salaries for full-time officials and secretarial staff and office and operating expenses.

Works councils function just like labor unions in the eyes of the law. The Law on the Constitution of Business Undertakings stipulates three functions:

1. The right of codetermination on welfare matters. Management cannot implement programs with which the works council disagrees.

2. The right to consultation on personnel matters, including dismissals, transfers, salary, and other working conditions. With dismissals, for example, this ensures that the company must first negotiate with the works council. Unlike under codetermination, however, management can enforce its will without works council consent. The works council, though, can appeal to a labor court.
3. The right to an explanation of economic matters. The works council can ask for an explanation of corporate business conditions.

Several studies have examined these functions in practice. They show that works councils have roughly as much say in company affairs as prescribed by law and even somewhat more. In many instances, management obtains the works council's agreement before implementing policies not only on welfare matters but also on personnel matters, where the law requires only consultation. Management also holds joint discussions on economic matters.

Works councils thus resemble Japanese unions. West Germany and Japan are also similar in the strength of workers' say. Measuring this is difficult, but, in general, two indicators are available. The first is whether workers' say limits the scope of management discretion. West Germany and Japan differ from the United States in allowing considerable scope to management. Because seniority is not a factor in determining who will be let go in West Germany and Japan, managements there can exercise discretion in dismissals and transfers. The second indicator is how many matters workers have a say in. Workers in West Germany and Japan have a say in many issues.

West Germany differs from Japan in not using merit ratings to determine blue-collar wages; on that point, management there has less discretion. Whether this means that workers have less say in company affairs is uncertain—Japanese blue-collar workers are paid what are white-collar wages in West Germany, and West German white-collar workers do have merit ratings.

In function and organization, the works councils are de facto company-level labor unions. They differ from unions in Japan chiefly by being company funded, as under the law they are not labor unions. This legal standing prohibits works councils from striking, but this should not be taken at face value; works councils can strike. In West Germany, however, even legally recognized labor unions strike infrequently, making the right to strike unimportant. The law also prevents works councils membership in umbrella organizations. This appears to cut works councils off from industrywide labor unions, but a subtle relationship exists. Almost all the blue-collar members of a works council are union shop stewards (*Vertrauensmann*), a common denominator in labor unions everywhere. Chosen in each workshop, they form the grass roots of labor unions. They are workers' representatives in management participation organizations. Other than this, no strong tie with industry unions exists. Works councils have even resisted industry unions.

ENTERPRISE UNIONS IN JAPAN

Multilayered Organizations

As of 1989, Japanese unions had 12.23 million members, for a unionization rate of 25.9 percent, a decline from 35 percent in 1970.[12] The reasons for the steady decline are not unique to Japan. The unionization rate increases with company size: 62.0 percent in companies of 1,000 or more employees, 25.7 percent in companies of between 100 and 999 employees, and 2.1 percent in companies of 99 or fewer employees. It is often said that because Japanese unions are enterprise unions, they are concentrated in large companies, but union concentration in large companies seems to occur everywhere.[13] Statistical evidence to support this is unavailable, but serving union members requires a full-time official in the workplace; unions that can do this are most likely to be found at larger companies.

Unions of more than 12 million members are divided among several levels by industry, company, and establishment in Japan and elsewhere. To say that Japan has only enterprise unions and no other labor organization is untrue. Japan has grassroots organizations at the company level. In general, Japanese establishments of 1,000 or more employees have one or more full-time union officials who are elected by union members and whose salaries are paid from union dues. Unlike West German works councils or American locals, Japanese unions are entirely self-funded. Japanese grassroots organizations thus are financially more independent of management than organizations elsewhere. And they are not confined to the company level. Japan also has regional or trade organizations, such as the National Federation of Construction Workers' Unions (Zenkensoren), a true craft union for workers in the building trades—primarily carpenters—because it is an association chiefly of craftsmen rather than salaried company employees.

Above the workplace unions are industrywide unions. Their numbers depend on the method used to count them, but slightly fewer than 80 is the usual count. Most have less than 50,000 members, but there are larger unions. Topping the list is the All Japan Municipal Workers' Union (Jichiro), with 1.25 million members, followed by the Federation of Japan Automobile Workers' Unions (Jidosharoren), with 0.72 million; the Japanese Federation of Electric Machine Workers' Unions (Denkiroren), with 0.69 million; the Japan Teachers' Union (Nikkyoso), with 0.64 million; and the Japan Federation of Textile Workers' Unions (Zensendomei), with 0.52 million members, ranging from textile workers to supermarket employees. Unions of more than 100,000 members account for around 60 percent of Japan's union membership. Compared with the United States, this distribution by size is not particularly distinctive.

As in all countries, operating expenses and staff costs for industrywide unions in Japan are paid from union dues. What is distinctive about these organizations in Japan is that they are called federations. This difference manifests itself in their funding. Union dues are collected and administered by grassroots unions, which pay a portion to industrywide unions. Only because of this distinct funding mechanism is it appropriate to call Japanese unions enterprise unions. Independent examination is needed to determine if being an enterprise union interferes with union functions.

Separation of Functions

Most of what is important to union members is negotiated at the workplace. In this respect, Japan does not differ from the United States or West Germany. Dismissals, transfers, wages—all are negotiated within the company. The success of negotiations, however, varies with the union. Japanese unions are thought to be weaker than U.S. unions and similar to West German unions.

Important matters are negotiated at the workplace for obvious reasons. Skills are the most important issue. They develop through experience in the company and lead to promotions through which further experience is acquired. Transfers and dismissals that impede skill formation occur in every company. These are internal matters, so they differ from company to company and must be negotiated at the workplace. This holds true in Japan, West Germany, and the United States—wherever an internal promotion system exists.

What, then, do industry unions do? In Japan, industry unions negotiate general changes in wage levels, as do their U.S. counterparts. These negotiations take two forms. The first is a group bargaining system among the big companies similar to that used by U.S. steelmakers since the 1970s. Labor and management in the private railroad and textile industries, for example, bargain by group. The second sees both sides bargain at the company level, as did U.S. steelmakers before the 1970s. Actual negotiations, though, occur at the industry level. Most industries in the United States and Japan employ the second form.[14] As a result, pay increases differ little, if at all, from company to company in percentage or amount. To say that Japan's enterprise unions cause wage levels to vary significantly from company to company is untrue in two regards:

1. In Japan, pay increases are surprisingly similar among competing companies.

2. In West Germany and the United States, fluctuations in wage levels are not uniform across companies. Unfortunately, a lack of published data on wage fluctuations by company and of reliable figures on wage levels at companies in the United States and Japan makes it impossible to corroborate this observation.

Industrywide Wage Determination

Japan's Ministry of Labor publishes a survey of pay raises at some 300 major companies, all of which have labor unions and a tradition of industrial relations. The survey makes it possible for persons outside the companies to understand their wage increase practices.

The Japanese Federation of Iron & Steel Workers' Unions (Tekkororen) has long been the leader in wage negotiations in Japan. Table 12-1 shows the results of the agreement it reached in 1983 with Japan's big five steelmakers. Although negotiations were conducted company by company, the wage increase was identical at all five companies, as it always is. The increase was ¥6,800 for a standard worker—the index used by steel companies

Table 12-1 Wage Increase Agreements at Japan's Big Five Steelmakers (1983)

1. Basic pay increase	¥6,800		
Increase in rates	¥3,200	(Standard worker aged 35 with 15 years of service)	
Yearly increment	¥3,600	(per person average)	
apportionment of basic wage rate[a]	Basic pay	¥1,600	
	Job pay	¥1,600	
2. Retirement pay	¥400,000 increase for a blue-collar worker aged 57 with 32 years of service (an increase from ¥11.4 million to ¥11.8 million)		
3. Workers' compensation contributions (additional payment at the company level)	Accidental death or disability categories 1–3	¥1 million increase	¥19 million
	category 4	¥700,000 increase	¥3.5 million
	category 5	¥600,000 increase	¥2.9 million
	⋮		
	category 14	¥100,000 increase	¥2.5 million

Source: Ministry of Labor, *1983-nen Shiryo Rodo Undo-shi* (Documentary History of the Labor Movement, 1983).

[a]Only Sumitomo Metal Mining Co., Ltd., showed slight differences: The apportionment to basic pay was ¥1,613 and to job pay, ¥1,587.

is a hypothetical worker aged 35 with 15 years of service and average performance.

The increase was even apportioned the same. Of the ¥6,800, ¥3,200 represented a raise in the basic wage rate and the remaining ¥3,600 was the periodical increment. The distinction is not meaningful unless there are annual pay raises. In general, a periodical increment includes merit ratings and an increase in the basic wage rate does not. If no pay raise occurs in a year, a gap arises: only the periodical increment is paid; there is no increase in the basic wage rate. Of the ¥3,200 increase for 1983, all five companies added ¥1,600 to the base rate and another ¥1,600 to the job rate. Increases in retirement pay and in the additional payment of workers' compensation insurance to social security also were the same at all five companies. Wages for job grade, length of service, and managerial positions differed slightly among the companies, but this was also true for U.S. steelmakers. In addition to dealing with Japan's big five integrated steelmakers, the Japanese Federation of Iron & Steel Workers' Unions also concludes slightly lower agreements with open hearth makers, rolling mills, specialty steelmakers, and other groups in the iron and steel industry.

Japan's electrical machinery and automobile industries have the largest industrywide labor unions in the private sector. The electrical machinery industry can be divided into an all-round group, where such firms as Hitachi, Toshiba, and Mitsubishi produce from home appliances to heavy industrial machinery; a heavy industrial machinery group; a home appliance group, including such makers as Matsushita; a computer and information-related group; and a communications equipment group. Despite company by company negotiations and differences in products, the rate of increase for all but one of the companies in the five groups was 4.9 percent in 1983. The exception was a company whose business was very bad. Although negotiations are company by company, in essence they occur at the industry level for electrical machinery.

In the automobile industry, pay increases vary, slightly, among companies. In the early 1950s, auto industry union leaders were strongly communist. Long and bitter strikes were the union's downfall, and today it lags all other Japanese industry unions. Table 12-2 reveals different wage amount and percentage increases for Japan's nine automakers. For ordinary passenger car makers, the pay raise is ¥9,900 for Toyota and Toyo Kogyo, ¥200 less for Nissan, and ¥300 less for Honda. The differences are nominal, but do exist. The other automakers produce light cars, trucks, or buses and do not compete with the makers of ordinary passenger cars.

Workers' Voice in Management

Although Japan's situation thus far differs little from that in the United States, differences exist. The largest is workers' say in management and production. Japanese industrial relations are characterized by the diffusion of a joint labor-management consultation system at companies and plants. Table 12-3 shows that this system exists in almost all large companies and in small companies and even in some establishments without labor unions, which suggests very small firms. Indeed, slightly more than 40 percent of companies with 100 employees that did not have labor unions did have a labor-management consultation system.

The system has two functions. First, as indicated in table 12-4, consultation plays a preliminary role in collective bargaining. Labor and management negotiate labor conditions and other mat-

Table 12-2 Wage Increase Agreements in the Automobile Industry (1983)

Company	Agreement date	Amount of increase	Percentage of increase
Toyota	April 12	9,900	5.0
Nissan	April 12	9,700	4.96
Honda	April 12	9,600	5.39
Toyo Kogyo Co., Ltd	April 12	9,900	4.80
Isuzu	April 13	8,000	4.46
Fuji Heavy Industries, Ltd.	April 12	9,450	4.96
Daihatsu	April 19	9,450	4.96
Suzuki	April 13	8,000	4.53
Hino	April 12	9,000	4.83

Source: Ministry of Labor, *1983-nen Shiryo Rodo Undo-shi* (Documentary History of the Labor Movement, 1983).

Table 12-3 Percentage of Establishments with a Labor-Management Consultation System (1984)

Company size (number of employees)	
All sizes	72.0%
5,000–	94.2
1,000–4,999	83.6
300–999	74.4
100–299	57.6
With labor union	87.9
Without labor union	40.7

Source: Ministry of Labor, *1984-nen Roshi Komyunikeshon Chosa* (Labor-Management Communications Survey, 1984).

Table 12-4 Items Discussed under the Labor-Management Consultation System (1984; percentage of establishments)

	With labor-management consultation system	Items for consultation	Items agreed upon
Basic business policies	100%	63.1%	8.7%
Basic plans for production and sales	100	65.7	12.6
Reorganization of company	100	62.5	15.1
Introduction of new technological applications, rationalization of production, office work, etc.	100	61.6	20.8
Transfers, intercompany loans	100	66.6	33.4
Temporary layoffs, personnel reductions, dismissals	100	65.0	57.5
Workshop safety	100	86.3	60.7
Wages, bonuses	100	72.8	62.8
Education and training	100	61.0	23.1

Source: Ministry of Labor, *1984-nen Roshi Komyunikeshon Chosa* (Labor-Management Communications Survey, 1984).

ters. Unresolved issues are handled in collective bargaining. That no topic has a 100 percent consultation rate, despite its importance, is not the fault of the unions; the important issues are left to collective bargaining. Most labor unions negotiate issues such as dismissals and personnel reductions. A two-thirds discussion rate means that an issue is designated for collective bargaining from the outset. The higher a topic's level of discussion, the greater the percentage of consultation and agreement.

The system's second function deserves the most attention: workers say in business conditions and management policies, including basic policy, production, and sales plans. As many as two-thirds of workplaces discuss these matters, but discussions are low level and confined to receiving explanations and voicing workers' views. This is perhaps inevitable given the nature of the issues.

Unlike in West Germany, a say in management and production has no legal standing in Japan. No laws prescribe the labor-management consultation system; it is a spontaneous development whose support derives from employees' and union members' strong interest in management. Almost every five years since 1972, the Ministry of Labor has conducted a Labor-Management Communications Survey that asks workers about their interest in management. Figure 12-2 has been compiled from these surveys. Workers who answered "yes" to the question "Would you like to know about management policy and business conditions in your

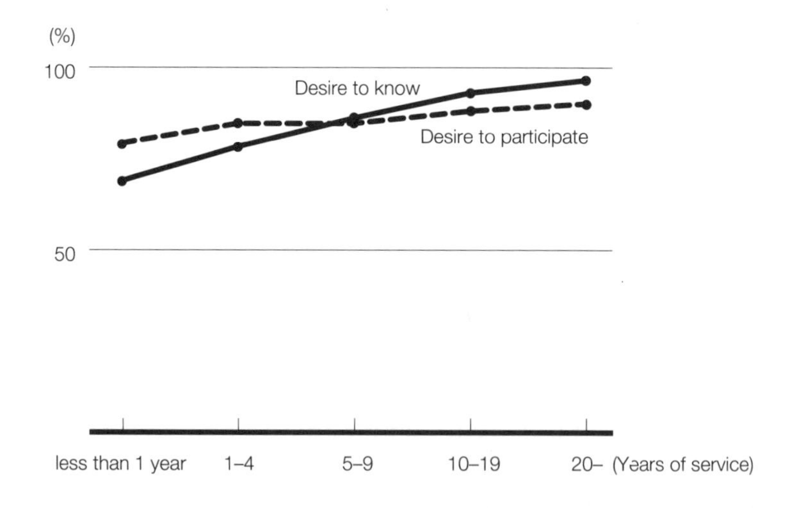

Fig. 12-2. Workers' "Desire to Participate" Rates (1984; percentage of workers)

Source: Ministry of Labor, *1984-nen Roshi Komyunikeshon Chosa* (Labor-Management Communications Survey, 1984).

company?" are the "desire to know" category. Those who answered "yes" to the question "Should the views of ordinary workers be reflected in management policy at your company?" indicate "desire to participate." The longer a worker works for a company, the higher the positive response. Workers with 10 or more years of service exceed a 90 percent positive response rate. The desire to participate underpins the labor-management consultation system, and labor union functions in Japan directly reflect members' desires. Comparisons with other countries are impossible, but the high degree of interest for Japan is undeniable.

Risk-Sharing Model

A risk-sharing model for labor-management relations is needed.[15] Understanding such a model requires an explanation of the classic model of industrial relations. It was long believed that a labor union's function was to strike to raise the market wage rate, no further interest in company business was needed. Union members at companies not paying the going rates could move to others that did. For workers, this entailed no loss because they possessed general skills common to all companies and occupations. Companies, however, lost their investment if they dismissed workers, whereas workers who were dismissed incurred no loss. Bankruptcy, too, was a loss for management, but success brought it rewards. Risks and rewards were thus managements'. Workers, it was thought, faced no risk from dismissal or a move to another company.

It is unrealistic, however, to downplay especially dismissal losses. The loss, particularly when enterprise-specific skills are involved, is so great that workers make every effort to avoid dismissal or quitting the company. Skill formation is of importance not only to workers, it is also integral to corporate success. Fast-growing companies promote workers rapidly, and workers rapidly expand their skills. At slow-growth firms, promotion is delayed, skills do not develop, and the risk of dismissal rises. Even workers with no company loyalty must thus have some interest in their employers' fortunes. Japan is often contrasted with the classic model, with critics proposing a community model instead. But the community model implies no dismissals. Given Japan's fierce market competition, it is impossible for companies to survive like communities without letting some workers go.

Companies that avoid dismissing workers must invest to increase productivity. Investment involves risk, especially in a competitive society. If companies invest badly, they will be forced to dismiss workers. Because employees share in the risk, they should have an interest and a say in management decisions and in selecting those who decide management policy. This applies anywhere that workers have any degree of enterprise-specific skills acquired through experience and promotion within a single company. In Japan, these workers are the core workforce in large companies. Consequently, worker interest in management policies now characterizes Japanese industrial relations. But this is by no means a Japanese phenomenon. It is merely more widely diffused and highly developed in Japan than elsewhere.

Chapter 13

Changes in Wage Levels and Unemployment

WAGE LEVELS

The Phillips Curve

In addition to grouping and observing workers according to attribute, workers must be examined collectively. To start, consider how wage levels are determined and how they change.

A discussion of this sort must begin with the Phillips curve, the first theory of wage determination developed based on statistical evidence. Previous theories on wages were guesswork based on observation. Adam Smith noted that wages were lower in Scotland than in England despite Scotland's more severe winters and higher cost of living. He therefore assumed that wages in England were barely beyond subsistence. In 1958, however, A. W. Phillips, of the University of London, proposed a model for determining wages based on their annual rate of change over the nearly 100 years between 1861 and 1957.

Like all good models, the Phillips curve (fig. 13-1) is clear and concise. The vertical axis is the manufacturing sector's rate of change in money wages from the preceding year. The horizontal axis is the unemployment rate. Data for each year of a nearly 100-year period form a neat curve. Phillips's theory was obvious—when unemployment rises, wages increase little and occasionally decline; but when unemployment declines, wages rise greatly—but he was the first to provide statistical proof.[1]

The theory was refined several years later in an article by Richard Lipsey.[2] Lipsey restated it in this form:

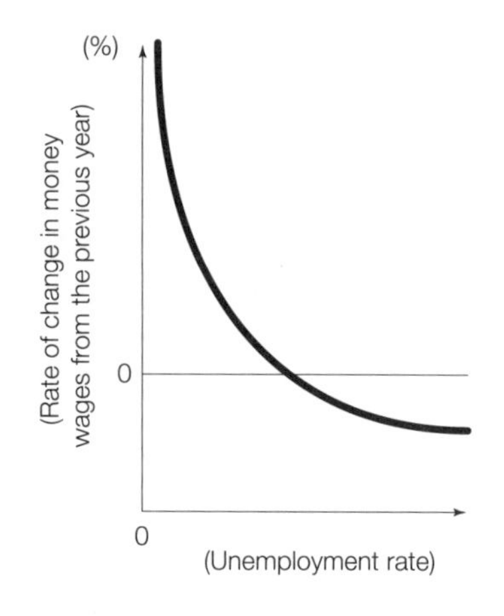

Fig. 13-1. Phillips Curve

$$\dot{W} = f(U, \dot{P}, \dot{U}),$$

where W is the rate of the change in money wages from the previous year, U the rate of unemployment, $\dot{P}$ the rate of price increases, and $\dot{U}$ the rate of change in unemployment.

This formula considers the cost of living and the rate of change in the unemployment rate and shows slight improvement beyond the trend line when business conditions improve and slight decline when conditions deteriorate. Since this formula makes it possible to predict the rate at which wages will rise—or, conversely, the rate of price increases from the rate of wage increases—Phillips curves have been estimated for many countries.

As a feature of many econometric studies, the Phillips curve has expanded in two respects. First is the addition of the profit element. Nicholas Kaldor argued that since wage determination is the result of negotiations with labor unions, the statistical significance of profit can be confirmed as a proxy indicator for collective bargaining. Second is the thinking that observing the impact of wage spillover approaches actual practices. In Japan, in the United States, and in some views in the United Kingdom, too, there are certain industries or industrial sectors that are pattern setters for pay raises—changes in wages there affect wages elsewhere. It is thus possible to estimate wage changes by distinguishing between pattern setters and followers. Otto Eckstein and Thomas Wilson best illuminate this thinking.[3]

Estimates for Japan

Of the many econometric studies of Japan, that of Sano Yoko, who has compiled estimates of unemployment, prices, and profit each year since the mid-1960s, will be referred to.[4] Noteworthy is that Sano's estimates of profits for industry as a whole are more significant than those for a particular industry in explaining wage determination in an industry. The significance of profit suggests ability to pay, but this theory does not apply. It appears instead that business conditions and other aspects of the overall economic climate have an effect on wage spillover and that spillover is effective in explaining wage determination.

After the energy crisis, Koshiro Kazuyoshi showed that the Phillips curve still applied in Japan.[5] In the West, neat Phillips curves no longer exist. According to Phillips, when business is bad unemployment increases and wages—an important part of costs—decrease, such that prices ought not to rise greatly. After the energy crisis, however, price increases continued despite bad business conditions and an unemployment rate two to even four or five times higher than before the oil crisis. Attempts to explain what was called stagflation have failed.

Stagflation becomes a bit clearer when global competitiveness is looked at over the long term. Explaining stagflation in terms of a closed economy and over the short term is difficult. It is more telling to consider what happens when many countries compete globally long term. If a country's labor unions are strong and raise salaries substantially in the short term despite high unemployment, prices rise, and the country's international competitiveness declines. As trade deficits mount, the country becomes unable to import materials for economic growth, and its economy contracts. Long term, unemployment rises, and the unions, no matter how strong, can no longer raise wages substantially. In a country with continuing stagflation, the growth rate decreases. But in an internationally competitive country, growth is maintained even when wages rise. Ultimately, real wages increase. Long term, real wage increases and economic growth roughly correlate. Figure 13-2 plots data before and after the oil crisis. Countries where the growth rate is generally or periodically high experience large increases in real wages.

This partially explains why the Phillips curve still applies in Japan. A country that implements wage increases in line with short-term economic conditions, such as those that shape the Phillips curve, maintains its economic competitiveness and can achieve long-term economic growth. The study of global economics seems only now aware of international competitiveness.[6]

Long-Term Trends

Yearly wage increases yield astonishing wage levels after several decades. Figure 13-3 shows that real wages in Japan in the mid-1960s were roughly four times higher than around 1900. Differences in wage increases between countries are thus likely to be enormous over the long term. Even if a country's wage levels were low at the beginning of its industrialization, subsequent increases might enable it to outstrip levels in other countries.

Wage levels, however, are not easily compared. If wages are a part of costs, it suffices to convert them from yen into dollars or

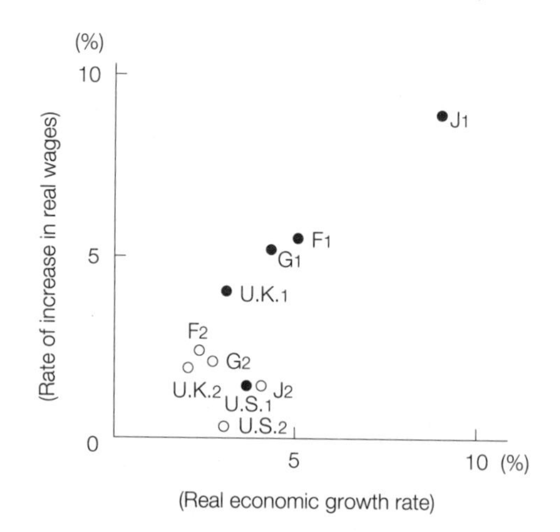

Fig. 13-2. Rate of Wage Increases and Economic Growth

Source: ILO, *Bulletin of Labour Statistics.*
Note: Figures for period 1 are the averages for 1965–1973; those for period 2 are the averages for 1974–1989.

pounds using current exchange rates. But if wages reflect standards of living, comparisons are difficult because lifestyles vary by country. Real wages are calculated by dividing money wages by the consumer price index. The way the latter is compiled is a problem. What items it includes and how much weight each gets are crucial. When the consumer price index is compiled for a country, the importance of each item can be estimated from household surveys indicating what items are consumed in what quantities by workers and their families. But when comparisons are between countries with different lifestyles, the choice of items differs, and even if they were the same their importance would differ. Beef, for example, is important in the United States, whereas fish is less so. As an expedient, figures for U.S. lifestyles are often averaged with figures for Japanese lifestyles. This may work for food, but it is hopeless for housing. Comparisons of size will not do; consideration must be given to the various conveniences of location. Price comparisons between a big, rural house and a small, city house, however, are difficult even in Japan. The convenience of life in a

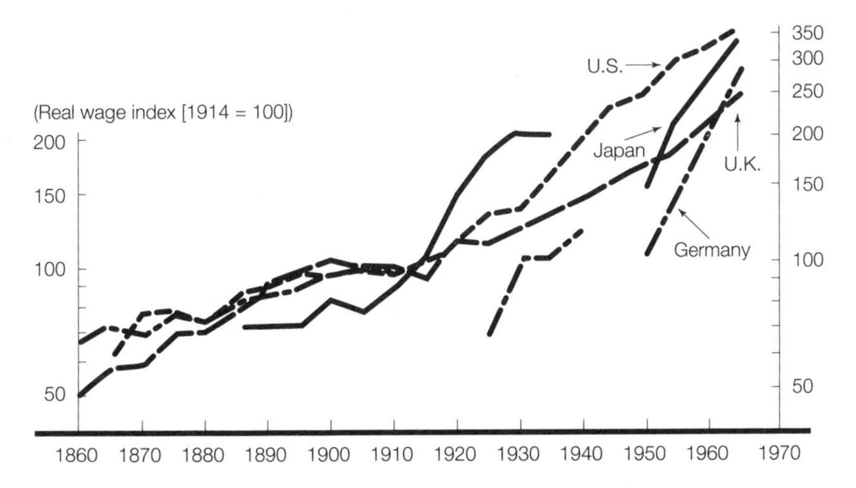

Fig. 13-3. Long-Term Trends in Real Wages for Japan, the U.S., the U.K., and Germany (five-year averages)

Sources: Japan, prewar: Umemura Mataji (1961), *Chigin, Koyo, Nogyo* (Wages, Employment, Agriculture), p. 65., and postwar: government statistics; U.S., Bureau of the Census, *Historical Statistics of the United States, Colonial Times to 1957* (Washington: 1960); Germany, Gerhard Bry, *Wages in Germany, 1871–1945* (Princeton: Princeton University Press, 1960); U.K., B. R. Mitchell and P. Deane, *Abstract of British Statistics*, 1962. Recent figures for the U.S., U.K., and West Germany are based on ILO statistics.

large Japanese city is generally high, so calculations are not easy and will not be dealt with here.[7]

At best, trends in wage increases can be observed. Data for Germany during World War I and for Germany and Japan during World War II are fragmentary, but the rapid development of historical statistics after World War II makes possible highly reliable data. That for Japan in figure 13-3 is based on the work of Umemura Mataji.[8] Before the time span depicted in the figure, real wages in the early industrializing countries appear, at about mid-nineteenth century, to have begun their upward trend after stagnating for several decades following the industrial revolution. In Japan, late industrialization meant that stagnation and a rise in real wages would be retarded. Stagnation in Japan seems only to have occurred at the end of the nineteenth century.

Japan's period of stagnation, however, proved shorter than elsewhere, and real wages in Japan began to rise as early as the beginning of the twentieth century. An increase around World War I exceeded a later 4 percent rise amid high economic growth after World War II. There is thought to have been a sizable labor shortage before the war, but popular arguments stressing low-level wages overlook the prewar increase in wages. During World War II, wages dropped to starvation levels. After the war, increases were steep as wages recovered. Even if this recovery is ignored, the 4 percent increase beginning in the mid-1950s, when wages returned to prewar levels, was higher than in the West. This is Japan's period of so-called high-level growth. Afterward, labor demand tightened, and, as shown in figure 13-2, there was a striking 9 percent rise in wages before the first oil crisis.

Errors in historical statistics encourage broad observations only. But it is clear that since the beginning of the twentieth century Japan has, almost without interruption, seen the highest real wage increases of any industrialized country. And this is by no means a postwar phenomenon alone.

This is only an introduction to Umemura's findings, begun as early as 1953 and redone in 1961. Their significance is obvious amid the then prevailing view among Marxist and neoclassical economists that prewar wages had been stagnant. The assumption was that industrialization had occurred rapidly in Japan; a large surplus population existed in farm households; and, unlike in the West, wages in Japan were barely at subsistence levels. This made it unlikely that wages could rise as depicted by Umemura. This deeply entrenched belief caused economists to overlook the significance of Umemura's work.

In the absence of other works worthy of attention, Umemura's clear and simple model helps explain Japan's long-term wage trends. The discussion of the Phillips curve drew attention to unemployment. Because wages are prices that are determined by the labor market, they are affected by market supply and demand, of which unemployment is an indicator. This logic is unchanging, so the long-term supply and demand of labor should play a leading role in determining wage increases. Umemura's model is as follows:

$$\dot{W} = f(\dot{L}d / \dot{L}s).$$

$\dot{W}$ is the rate of increase in real wages, $\dot{L}d$ the rate of growth in labor demand, and $\dot{L}s$ the rate of growth in labor supply. Using data for each period, Umemura explained why the rate of increase in real wages is higher in Japan than in the United States, the United Kingdom, and West Germany.[9] Nothing subsequent challenges Umemura's model.

UNEMPLOYMENT

Measuring Unemployment

Given that changes in wage levels are affected by supply and demand in the labor market, unemployment must be studied. Questions, though, are often raised about Japan's unemployment rate. It is too narrow, it is claimed, not to consider unemployed anyone who works for a single hour during the week of the survey—unemployment in Japan is probably much higher.

Two ways exist to measure unemployment in industrialized countries: the labor force survey method of the United States and Japan and the public employment agency registry method of

Western Europe. The former's superiority is such that Western European countries are adopting it. The latter classes as unemployed only persons looking for jobs at public employment agencies who meet such conditions as having no job or of working a minimal amount. Those who do not register at public employment agencies are thus not counted as unemployed. The labor force survey method is a random statistical sampling of households nationwide and is thus broader in scope.[10]

Disputes have arisen over differences in the labor force survey method in the United States and Japan.[11] It is said that Japan does not consider unemployed a person who works for a single hour during the survey week, providing too narrow a definition. But this is irrelevant to U.S.-Japanese comparisons. The surveys in the two countries are identical. The method used in Japan originated during the U.S. occupation, and the definitions in both countries are alike. People are unemployed if, despite the desire and ability to work, they claim not to have worked during the survey week, a definition that is more circumscribed than the one hour usually referred to in Japan's case. And both countries regard graduates of their compulsory education systems as having the ability to work; desire is confirmed by answering "yes" to the question "Are you looking for work?"

Subtle differences as a result of variations in employment practices have led to the contention that Japan's unemployment figures would be higher if redone following American practices.[12] However, such differences ultimately make no major difference.

Japan counts fewer unemployed than the United States not because of differences in definition, but because of a difference in the way its questionnaire is laid out. At the beginning of the Japanese questionnaire, respondents to the question of whether they attended school or did housework during the survey week are instructed by an arrow to skip to a later question and omit the question about looking for work during the week. Instructions that anyone who did look for work should not skip this question even if they did housework or attended school are easily overlooked. As a result, many who looked for jobs while doing housework or attending school are not counted. In the U.S. questionnaire, the questions are ordered so that people who answer that they did housework or attended school must also respond to whether they looked for work. If this formatting problem was rectified, Japanese unemployment figures might rise slightly, but the discrepancy in unemployment between the two countries is greater than can be accounted for by this minor problem. It is logical to conclude that unemployment is lower in Japan than in the United States because of differences in the countries' economic growth.

The Structure of Unemployment

The quality of unemployment also requires attention: Is it serious, or does it merely indicate that people are looking for better jobs? If the former, government policies are needed immediately. The latter, however, suggests a high degree of freedom in the labor market, giving workers the latitude to look for better jobs. The percentage of either type of unemployment changes depending on people's attitudes toward unemployment and on the government's unemployment-benefits system.

UV analysis is a method to distinguish between serious and not-so-serious unemployment. Developed in the United Kingdom, UV analysis utilizes British unemployment statistics.[13] Such statistics for Western Europe rely on the public employment agency registry method. Companies with job openings and workers looking for work are registered at public employment agencies. UV is thus an abbreviation of unemployment, represented by job seekers, and vacancies, represented by job openings. Plotting unemployment monthly or yearly results in a trend like the UV1 curve in figure 13-4. In a buoyant economy, unemployment

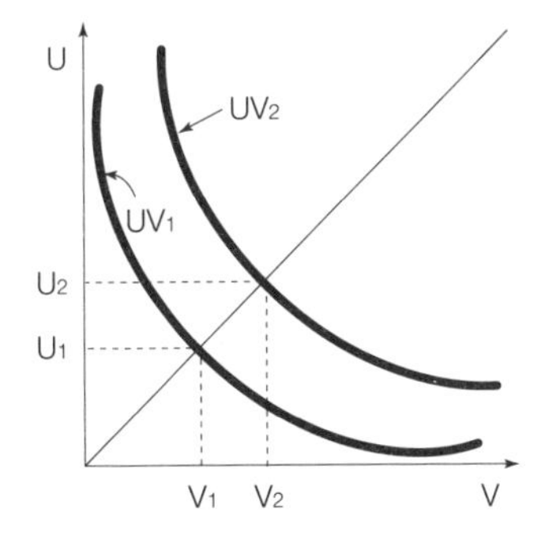

Fig. 13-4. UV Curve

declines overall but increases among those looking for better jobs as favorable job opportunities expand. Unemployment, therefore, never reaches zero. Likewise, when economic conditions deteriorate unemployment rises, but some among a country's different companies will still be looking for employees, so vacancies never reach zero. This is the basis of the UV curve.

If a line is drawn at a 45-degree angle intersecting the points where U and V are equal and it is supposed that unemployment at this point, U1, is, say, 3 percent, vacancies at this point, V1, will also be 3 percent. A 3 percent rate of unemployment requires no immediate government action; any higher, though, is serious. Unemployment up to 3 percent results inevitably from people looking for better jobs or companies looking for better workers—it is regarded as the equilibrium unemployment rate, which is unfixed and fluctuates. The long-term payout of unemployment benefits moves the curve upward and to the right to become UV2. It will move even if unemployment benefits remain unchanged to reflect a change in people's attitudes toward unemployment or jobs.[14] The thinking behind the UV curve is simple yet effective. The application of the UV curve to Japan confirms the shift to UV2.[15]

Despite the clarity and conciseness of UV analysis, it does not explain serious unemployment. Classification of unemployment by degree of severity is needed. In the United States, groups that undergo long periods of unemployment serve, reasonably, as indicators of severe unemployment.[16] If this measure is used in a comparison of the United States and Japan, as in figure 7-3 in chapter 7, Japan is shown to have more long-term unemployed and a larger incidence of serious unemployment. This is because most of Japan's unemployed are older workers. Unemployed older workers in any country have a hard time finding new jobs and remain unemployed long term. Japan's unemployment pattern reflects the methods of dismissal seen in chapter 7. Japanese industry lets go workers whose dismissal entails high costs.

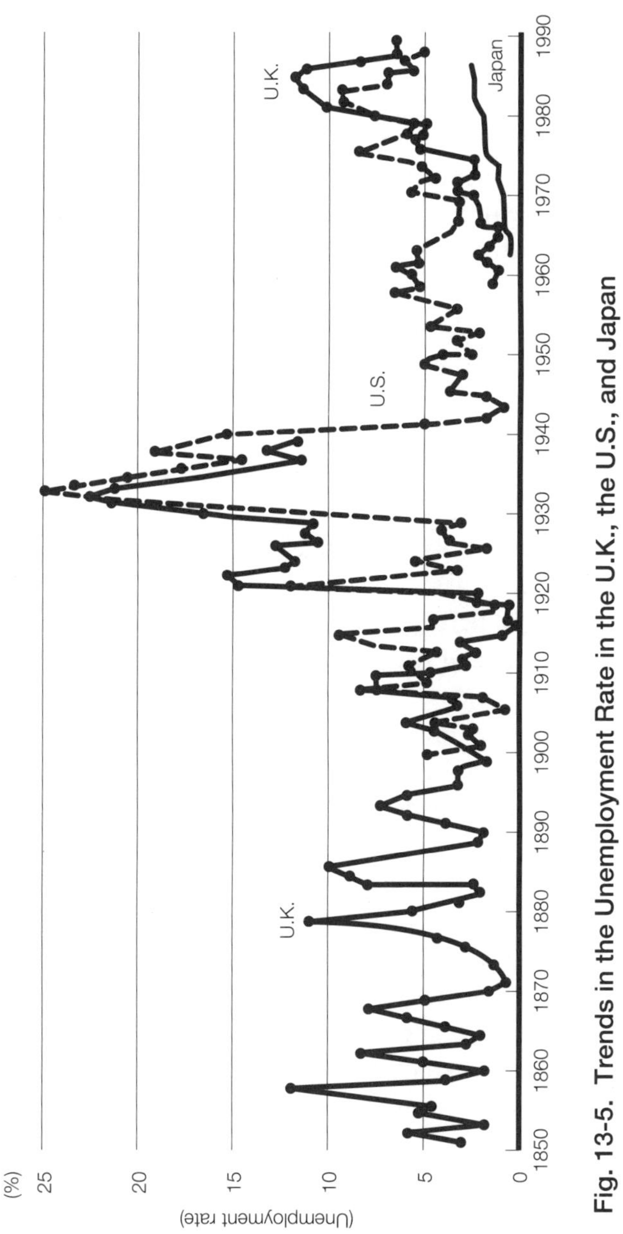

Fig. 13-5. Trends in the Unemployment Rate in the U.K., the U.S., and Japan

Sources: U.K., B. R. Mitchell, *Historical Statistics of the U.K.* (Cambridge University Press, 1962); U.S., Department of Labor, Bureau of Labor Statistics, *Historical Abstracts of the U.S.* (1962); Japan, Management and Coordination Agency, Statistics Bureau, *Rodoryoku Chosa* (Labor Force Survey).

Unemployment Trends

Figure 13-5 traces the unemployment trend back as far as possible. Government statistics on unemployment began around the end of World War I; earlier periods use statistics compiled by U.K. labor unions. Among the main functions of nineteenth-century labor unions was to act as an employment placement service; they thus surveyed unemployment among their members. Although these unions admitted only skilled workers, their data are not far removed from the overall unemployment situation. Union data were combined with later government statistics and plotted in figure 13-5. For ease of reading, the figure includes only the United States, the United Kingdom, and Japan. Only a few other countries have statistics of this sort.

The periods covered in the figure have distinctive features. The first, from the mid-nineteenth century to the beginning of World War I, exhibits textbook economic conditions, with discernable cycles every 7 to 10 years. A bad economy saw unemployment rise to between 7 and 10 percent, but not for long. An improving economy saw unemployment drop to 2 or 3 percent. This is known as frictional unemployment. Modern and Marxist economics use models based on such conditions.

The second period, between the two world wars, reveals mass unemployment that exceeded 20 percent in the 1930s. Not indicated is that unemployment was over 30 percent in vanquished Germany. Mass unemployment remained until World War II. Both world wars saw severe labor shortages.

The third period, from the end of World War II to the oil crisis, saw full employment and excess demand. U.S. unemployment was not especially low, at around 4 to 6 percent, but in Western Europe, represented by the United Kingdom, unemployment was around 1 to 3 percent. Conditions reminiscent of nineteenth-century prosperity lasted for nearly 30 years.

The fourth period, after the energy crisis from the mid-1970s on, saw unemployment shoot up two to three times its previous level and continue to climb. Many Western European countries had unemployment rates exceeding 10 percent, as did the United

Kingdom. These levels, which match those during nineteenth-century depressions, have lasted a long time.

Despite their importance, long-term data on unemployment are seldom published. And efforts to explain them are equally seldom successful. The first period can be explained by the business cycle theory, with its emphasis on capital investment. Various attempts have been made to account for the mass unemployment in the second period, but nothing like an established theory exists for the Great Depression. Likewise, no established theory exists for the third and fourth periods, but the correlation to changes in international trade should be addressed. International trade contracted in the second period as a result of growing isolationism and economic self-sufficiency, as first the United Kingdom, then the United States, France, Germany, and the other industrialized countries withdrew into their economic blocs. After World War II, the opposite happened: the expansion of international trade led to conditions of full employment akin to excess demand. Economics until now has chiefly used a model of a closed economy that omits trade. But long-term trends in unemployment are difficult to explain using such a model.

DISTRIBUTION

Labor's Relative Share in the National Economy

According to classical economist David Ricardo, the distribution of wealth is economics' key issue. This, however, is a complex issue.

The distribution of wealth consists of functional and personal distribution. Functional distribution refers to the distribution of wealth between capital, in the form of profits, and labor, in the form of wages. When business expenses are subtracted from sales, the remainder, or value added, is split between profits and wages. The percentage allotted to each is functional distribution. Personal distribution is the division of income among society's various classes and households. Is wealth concentrated among a select few or distributed equitably? If society comprised only the owners of companies and their employees and wage differentials among employees were small, functional and personal distribution would be the same. Society, however, consists of many different classes, and both aspects of distribution must be tested to determine how wealth is distributed.

Functional distribution, between capital and labor, is usually regarded in terms of labor's relative share of the value added. National economies determine this by dividing employee income by national income. This result, however, is rising, as shown in figure 13-6, because the percentage of self-employed people is decreasing. This is a problem because what is wanted are the shares that go to labor and capital. The formula must therefore eliminate self-employment income, also shown in figure 13-6:[17]

employee income / employee income plus the income of private business corporations

This result is stable over the long term, but short term moves in inverse direction to the economy. It goes down slightly when busi-

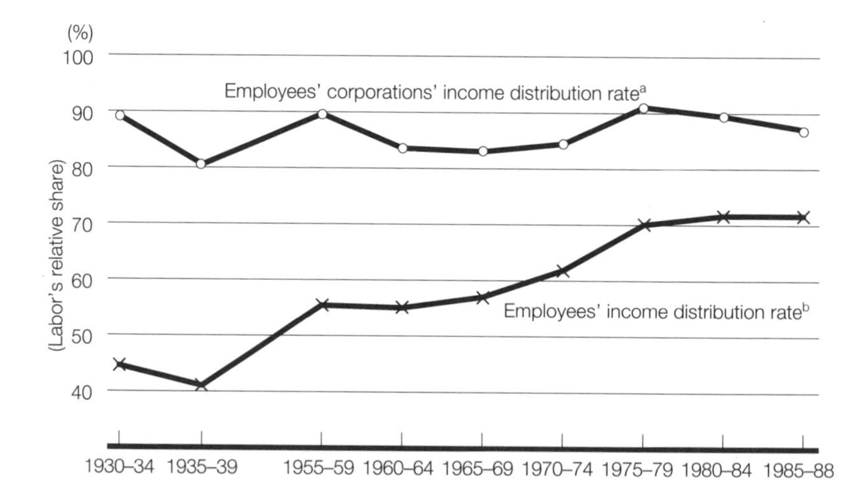

Fig. 13-6. Labor's Relative Share over the Long Term

Source: Hoya Rokuro, *Rodo Bunpairitsu to Shotoku Bunpai* (Labor's Relative Share and Income Distribution), part 2, Rodo Jiho (October 1990), p. 33.

[a] "Employees' corporations' income distribution rate" is obtained by dividing employees' income by employees' income plus the income of private corporations.

[b] "Employees' income distribution rate" is obtained by dividing employees' income by the national income.

ness is good and rises slightly when business deteriorates. This reflects declines in sales and production and a drop in the capacity usage ratio rather than fluctuations in the distribution to labor.

The result obtained using this formula is close to those in Western European countries and only fractionally lower than that in Japan. This does not mean that labor's portion is less in Japan. Labor's relative share is somewhat lower in a growth economy, a phenomenon known as the Kaldor model.[18] This model's main points are readily understandable. When labor's relative share is too high, profits decrease, leaving less to invest in plant and equipment. As a result, long-term growth falls. Less growth puts employment at risk—a high relative share is not beneficial to labor. Labor's relative share is slightly lower in Japan's high-growth economy than in most Western European countries.

Personal Income Distribution

It is perhaps more significant for an industrial society if the incomes of its members are either equal or unequal. A society's stability is at risk if wealth is concentrated among a minority while the majority struggle. An unstable society elicits low productivity. This is the problem of personal distribution.

Simon Kuznets argues that in the initial stages of economic development, income distribution is unequal, but that it later becomes less so. His hypothesis has been confirmed in many countries and is thought to have much in common with the Lewis model.[19]

More recently, Malcolm Sawyer compared personal income distribution in the member countries of the OECD using first-rate data.[20] For Japan, he used the Survey of Nationwide Consumption (*Zenkoku Shohi Jittai Chosa*). The annual Household Survey (*Kakei Chosa*) is also good, but the Survey of Nationwide Consumption is based on superior data compiled every five years.

Table 13-1 offers some of Sawyer's findings. Cited are the rates of income for the 1/5 group and the 5/5 group and the Gini coefficient. The 1/5 group is the bottom 20 percent of a society's household incomes. The object is to find what percentage of the total income for all households is accounted for by this group.

Table 13-1 An International Comparison of Income Distribution (after-tax income)

Period		% of income accounted for by 1/5 group	% of income accounted for by 5/5 group	Gini coefficient
Japan	1969	7.9	41.0	0.316
Sweden	1972	6.6	37.0	0.302
Australia	1966–67	6.6	38.8	0.312
Netherlands	1967	6.5	42.9	0.354
West Germany	1973	6.5	46.1	0.383
Norway	1970	6.3	37.3	0.304
U.K.	1973	6.3	38.7	0.318
Canada	1969	6.0	41.0	0.354
Spain	1973–74	6.0	42.3	0.355
Italy	1969	5.1	46.5	0.398
U.S.	1972	4.5	42.9	0.381
France	1970	4.3	46.9	0.414

Source: Malcolm Sawyer, "Income Distribution in OECD Countries," *Occasional Studies, OECD Economic Outlook* (July 1976), pp. 14 and 17.

Twenty percent indicates equality; the higher the percentage the higher the level of equality in a society. Japan ranks highest in this category. The 5/5 group is the top 20 percent of household incomes. Thus, the lower the percentage the higher the level of equality. Japan ranks among the leaders in this category. A low Gini coefficient indicates an equalizing trend. Here, too, Japan is in the top group. Japan is an egalitarian country.

This is similar to the earlier inference made based on wage structures. Japan has the smallest differential in male white-collar and blue-collar wages among the countries surveyed. Differentials based on educational levels are also small. Japan is often said to have large differentials based on company size, but statistics show that this is not always true. Large differentials between the sexes exist in Japan but do not hinder equality in household income.

High levels of equality likely contribute to the productivity of Japanese workshops. If labor benefited only a handful of wealthy people, few would care about productivity. Nonetheless, steep rises in land prices in large Japanese cities are creating an asset gap between landowners and the landless. This will likely affect workshop morale. The result of this asset gap, however, awaits future examination.

Chapter 14 Basic Theory and the Theory of Stages

BASIC THEORY

Various Hypotheses about the Labor Supply

A basic theory is an abstract model of reality. The value of the real-life elements on which it is based facilitate using it to predict trends. It is a simplification that makes assumptions about a complex reality.

Basic theories on the labor supply assume the following: (1) The only constituents of an industrial society are employers and employees. In fact, the self-employed should also be included, and the borderline between employer and employee is not always clear, but complications are avoided. (2) There is perfect competition: perfect information. People are assumed to know what to do to maximize their advantage. In fact, information is imperfect. (3) There is only a closed, single-country economy, no international trade. (4) There is only a single work skill. This last hypothesis is not essential; it is included to make the discussion more understandable. Under these assumptions, employers and employees act to maximize their own advantages. Basic theory reasons out this behavior and its results.

Economics' most abstract model is the market, where prices are determined by supply and demand. The question of how supply and demand determine wages, which correspond to prices, can be considered in terms of the labor supply.

The common labor supply theory assumes an upward supply function (fig. 14-1-1). In economics, the vertical axis indicates price or wages. Monthly wages are a fine indicator, but hourly

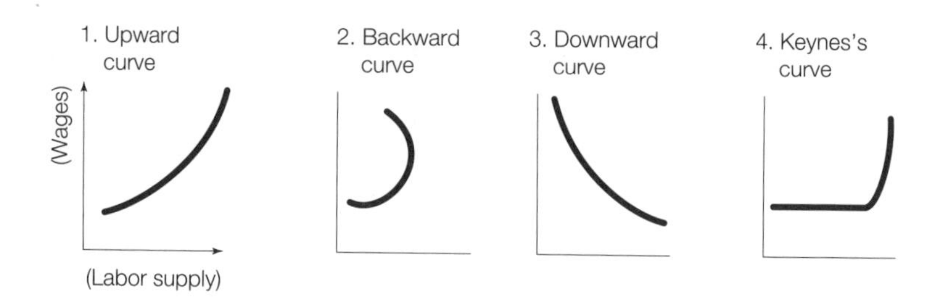

Fig. 14-1. Various Labor Supply Functions

wages are used here. The horizontal axis indicates the labor supply, in number of people or, as here, in working hours. An upward supply function—a function because a change in wages leads to a relative change in the quantity of labor supplied—assumes the existence of income and leisure and occurs as a result of a preference, in economics terms, between them. Both are desirable, but impossible to have together in large amounts. A choice must be made between earning an income and leisure time. Since those who work long hours have little leisure, wages, the thinking goes, must be high to compensate for the sacrifice.

This is a reasonable assumption, as are others about the labor supply. The assumption behind the backward curve in figure 14-1-2 is that a rise in income brings a preference for fewer work hours at the higher hourly wage. The downward curve in figure 14-1-3 presupposes what happens when someone living on their wages is unable, short term, to reduce living expenses. A drop in hourly wages forces the worker to work longer hours for the same monthly income.

The horizontal axis of figure 14-1-4, alternatively, is based on two assumptions. Foremost is Keynes's argument about price rigidity in a downward direction. Keynes noted that even when unemployment rose, money wages did not decline. He offered no explanation other than to say that this is what experience suggests.[1] In chapter 6 it was noted that the implicit contract theory has been proposed to explain this tendency. It appears to assume two contrary situations: that labor unions are strong yet that an enormous surplus population exists and that wages are barely subsistence level in the initial stages of economic development. This is the period of an unlimited supply of labor (chapter 1). The upward or vertical part of the curve indicates tightening of the labor supply and soaring wages.[2]

These assumptions are all reasonable, but which of them is valid, or are they all valid under specific conditions? Because basic theories are formulated as general arguments that are valid under all circumstances, it is hard to determine the labor supply function solely through abstract examination. The supply function is thought to differ for each workforce, so empirical observation is necessary.

Labor Demand

In examining labor demand, it suffices to introduce the downward trend of figure 14-2. Common sense dictates that if wages rise, companies reduce their number of employees, and that if wages fall they increase production and hire more employees. A textbook approach to explaining this, however, requires a number of pages. Figure 14-2 presupposes one company and a short time period, which, in economics, refers to the period when machinery and other equipment is static: for example, a plant's 50 lathes remain unchanged in number. Increases in production from the addition of a worker would diminish. An increase from 49 to 50 workers would contribute significantly to production, but an increase from, say, 80 to 81, would amount to a lesser rise in production. A production increase from the addition of a worker is called the marginal productivity of labor or marginal productivity (MP).

Fig. 14-2. Labor Demand Function

These assumptions result in something so basic as to be omitted from most books.

A company's returns R are what is left when costs are deducted from sales. The sales figure is obtained by multiplying yield Y by product price P. If machinery is ignored and only labor is considered, the figure for costs is obtained by multiplying the number of workers L by wages per person W. The resulting equation is

$$R = P \cdot Y - W \cdot L.$$

Because corporate activity aims to maximize profits, the company should employ enough people to maximize its returns. Time is short, so its machinery is static, only its number of workers can change. How will its returns vary when its number of workers is increased? In other words, if differentiated by the number of workers L, then

$$dR / dL = P \cdot dY / dL - W.$$

In this equation, P and W are constants amid perfect competition, where a single company cannot affect product price. It is assumed that many companies compete. Wages, too, are a given for the company. But, since profit maximization is a situation where returns do not rise if the number of workers rises above a certain level, then $dR / dL = 0$. Thus, if the earlier equation is zero, what results is

$$P \cdot dY / dL = W.$$

Here, dY / dL is the marginal productivity of labor. If it is multiplied by product price P, the value of the marginal productivity of labor is obtained. When this is equal to the market wage W, profits are maximized. In short, a labor demand that meets various wage levels results in a downward curve of marginal productivity.

Difficulty arises when this labor demand curve is combined with the various labor supply curves discussed earlier. When the usual upward supply model is combined with the downward demand model (fig. 14-3-1), employment and the wage level that will result in equilibrium can be determined. Unemployment, however, would exist only during a short adjustment period. This disagrees with the actual unemployment trends seen earlier. When unemployment rose after World War I, economists argued that it was because labor unions had succeeded in winning pay raises that exceeded the equilibrium wage. And, indeed, this discussion is based on that argument.

A downward labor supply curve sometimes causes an even more serious problem. As in figure 14-3-2, when the slope of the demand curve is gentler than that for the supply curve, wages are easy to determine; however, the problem of no unemployment remains. But when the slope of the supply curve is gentler, as in figure 14-3-3, once it moves away from the equilibrium wage it continues to do so, never returning to equilibrium. Suppose, for example, that the equilibrium wage W_0 is ¥200,000 and that equilibrium employment is one million people. Now suppose that for some unexpected reason the market wage W_1 suddenly rises to ¥220,000. The number of people who want to work at that time—the supply—is 800,000, but the demand is 900,000. As a result, the market wage will rise again. As this process repeats itself, wages move further and further away from equilibrium. Even when wages begin below equilibrium, they will move away in the same manner. This is called divergence, a phenomenon noted by Paul Douglas, who was the first to analyze labor supply using statistical evidence.[3] Conversely, in figure 14-3-4 unemployment exists in the horizontal portion of the labor supply line, whereas the steady rise in wages found in actuality cannot be extracted. And the upward portion does not explain the unemployment pointed out earlier.

If the element of time is factored in, another difficulty arises. The preceding dealt with a short period, but with time the number of machines increases and, more importantly, more-efficient machinery is introduced. Demand will thus cease its downward

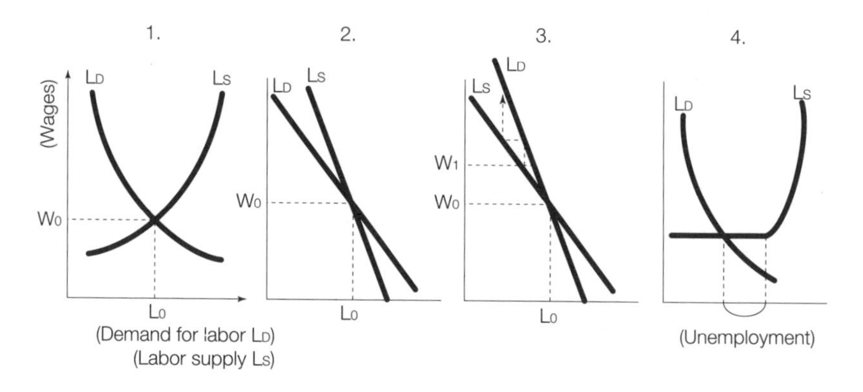

Fig. 14-3. Supply and Demand for Labor

curve, and equilibrium will be difficult to obtain. A worthwhile long-term model for determining wages does not exist, even as basic theory.

Wage Differentials by Occupation

If the fourth hypothesis—of only one work skill—is removed, wage differentials caused by different skills emerge. This problem was addressed 200 years ago by Adam Smith.[4] Smith proposed the law of equalizing net advantage—economic gain, comfort, and so on. By equalizing, he meant, for example, that salaries for highly skilled occupations rise in proportion to the cost of acquiring the skills plus the usual return on investment and that what corresponds to comfort be subtracted from wages. When a job requires higher than average manual dexterity or mental acuity, compensation must be added, especially given the limited distribution of such aptitudes.

This theory views the situation exclusively from the labor supply perspective. In terms of labor demand, companies will raise or lower employment until their marginal productivity matches the supply price. Because the cost of skill acquisition in the wider sense will match marginal productivity, the law of equalizing net advantage agrees with such modern theories as human capital theory.

Supply Models and the Labor Force Participation Rate

Which of these labor supply models approaches reality? Which offers the best way to measure labor supply, working hours, and number of workers? This measurement is usually expressed as

> labor force participation rate = labor force / the total population in the same age group.

The labor force includes all gainfully employed people, the unemployed, and those on leave. The definition of gainful employment is subtle, especially for unpaid family workers of the self-employed, whose treatment varies by country. In Japan, even slightly self-employed people are part of the labor force. The labor force participation rate makes possible observation of changes in the labor supply in response to economic conditions, independent of population trends. The statistics are from the same sources used in earlier discussions of employees and unemployment: Japan's Labor Force Survey and National Census and the U.S.'s *Current Population Survey.* Chapter 1 explains the two methods used to measure employment—usual conditions and actual conditions during a specific week.

Paul Douglas was the first to examine the labor supply statistically. His study of the relationship between incomes and the labor force participation rate in 41 U.S. cities during the 1920s showed that the labor supply function was minus 0.1, a downward, nearly vertical curve.[5]

It has since become clear that the labor force participation rate differs significantly depending on age and sex. Figures 14-4 to 14-7 show trends in the age-sex participation rates for Japan and the United States that are very similar. In the United States and Japan, the participation rate for men in their prime is close to 100 percent and virtually unaffected by economic conditions. The figures show workers aged 35 to 44 or in their early 40s, but the results would be the same no matter the age group during the prime work years. For older, even male, workers, the labor force participation rate drops in both countries. Suppose that wages go up during the period indicated in the figures. The labor supply

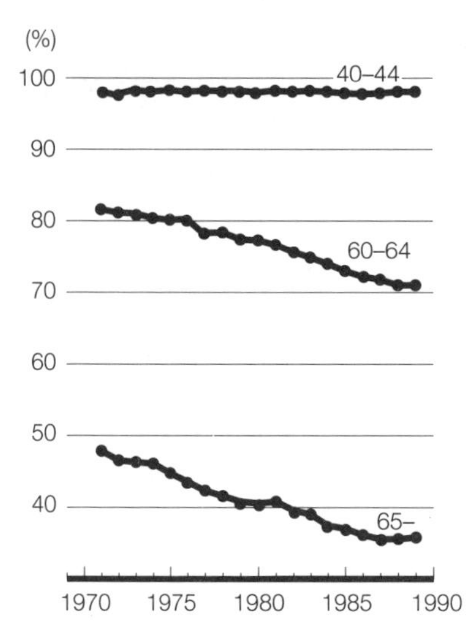

Fig. 14-4. Labor Force Participation Rate for Japanese Males (1971–89)

Source: Management and Coordination Agency, Statistics Bureau, *Rodoryoku Chosa* (Labor Force Survey).

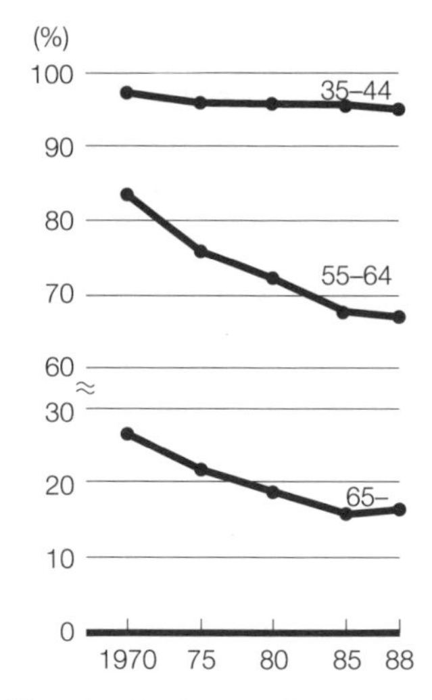

Fig. 14-5. Labor Force Participation Rate for American Males (1970–88)

Sources: *Statistical Abstract of the U.S.*, 1990, p. 378. For raw data, see U.S. Bureau of Labor Statistics, *Employment and Earnings*.

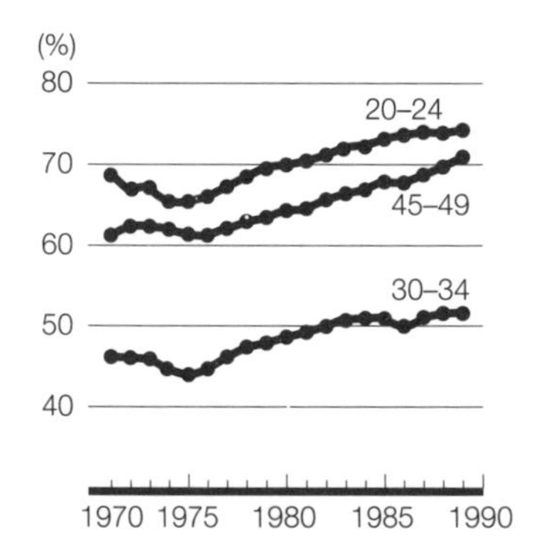

Fig. 14-6. Labor Force Participation Rate for Japanese Females (1971–89)

Source: Management and Coordination Agency, Statistics Bureau, *Rodoryoku Chosa* (Labor Force Survey).

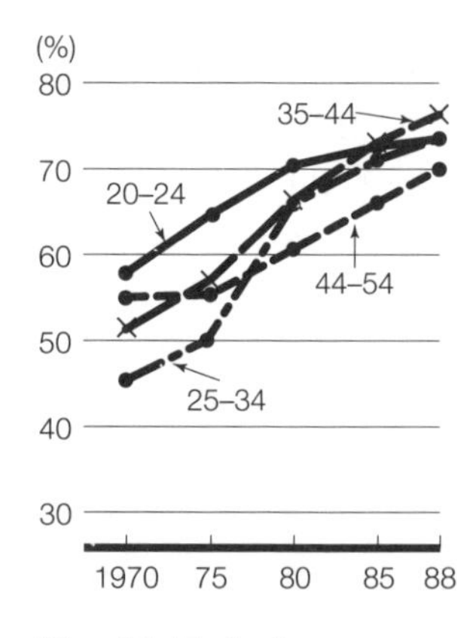

Fig. 14-7. Labor Force Participation Rate for American Females (1970–88)

Sources: *Statistical Abstract of the U.S.*, 1990, p. 378. For raw data, see U.S. Bureau of Labor Statistics, *Employment and Earnings*.

curve will be almost vertical for workers in their prime, but downward for older workers.

For women, the labor force participation rate is rising in Japan and the United States. If, again, it is supposed that wages increase during the period, the supply curve, too, will rise. The labor supply function, however, is far more complicated than this. The function for older workers is affected by factors such as pensions, salary, and self-employment. For women, it is affected by such factors as education and spousal income. This discussion looks at the data only on a time series. Observations of a cross section at the same time are also important.[6] Even from the broadest view, however, it would be a mistake to assume that the labor supply function can be grasped merely by considering the labor force collectively. To classify the labor force, a concept of labor types is needed. This is provided by the theory of industrialization stages.

THE THEORY OF LABOR TYPES

Four Labor Types

A labor type is determined by the skills workers develop during their careers. In economics, including labor economics, work skills have hitherto been classified along the axis of elevation as to their level. This distinguishes between skilled and unskilled workers, but does not consider time. People generally work for many years, improving their skills with experience. If we combine the first axis with another that accounts for change over time, four labor types emerge:

Type A: high skills that do not change over time (skilled worker or craftsman)
Type B: low skills that do not change over time (unskilled worker or laborer)
Type C: high skills that improve greatly over time (internal promotion worker)
Type D: skills that improve slightly over time (semiskilled worker)

Of these four labor types, A and C are especially important.

Type A workers' high skills are acquired over a concentrated period early in their careers and thereafter do not improve. The acquisition period thus should be demarcated from the actual work period and usually is by apprenticeship. The apprentice acquires proficiency in a single trade to emerge a full-fledged craftsman whose skills generally remain static. Consequently, wages are uniform and unchanging for each trade. A labor union, if formed, will bind common interests—likely centered on a single craft or trade—and will exceed the confines of an individual company.

Type C workers, by contrast, improve their skills primarily through on-the-job experience. As seen in chapter 6, OJT is more efficiently and easily implemented within a company. Workers elevate their skills by progressing through a series of related jobs, from easy to complex, and are most concerned with promotion, transfer, and dismissal. Because these are all internal matters, if a labor union is formed it will be based at the plant or company level and will have an industrywide organization.

Two Stages of Industrialization

Abstract descriptions aside, it is best to observe these labor types amid the stages of industrial development in which they played chief roles. These labor types are merely logical inferences, but they are important in describing stages of industrialization.

The history of industrialization since roughly the nineteenth century can be broadly divided into two stages. Between them is the period from the end of the nineteenth century to World War I. The early period can be called stage one, or the stage of private enterprise, and the subsequent period stage two, or the stage of big business.

In stage one, labor types A and B, skilled and unskilled workers, played principal roles, while types C and D had not yet appeared. Present-day perspectives suggest that the economics of stage one centered on small and medium-sized private enterprises that competed locally. The market was small, so the preferred means of production was to turn out single items. Technologically, the precision of machinery was low, and a single machine was used to produce many different items for manual assembly. The all-round manual skills of a craftsman, embodied in type A workers, were thus in demand. The most appropriate labor union for type A workers is the craft union, whose membership is restricted to skilled workers in a particular trade. During stage one, craft unions thrived.

Much of this description applies to the same type of workers today. In Japan, the same logic applies wherever craft unions exist. It is wrong to think that present-day Japanese labor unions are only enterprise unions. Japan's National Federation of Construction Workers' Unions (Zenkensoren), with 500,000 members, is one of the world's largest craft unions. It functions basically as a type A labor union and has much in common with the craft unions of stage one.

In stage two, labor types C and D, internal promotion and semiskilled workers, appeared. Types A and B were also present, but not in leading roles in labor-management relations or labor unions. Economically, stage two witnessed the emergence of large corporations and the growth of the market, facilitating mass production. The larger corporations were able to invest in the huge fixed technology that made mass production a reality. Because mass production promoted a division of labor, higher skills were formed by moving from easy to harder jobs within a company, a system possible only at large firms and that led to the formation of an internal labor market. Since a labor market largely formed within a company, the basic unit of the labor union controlling that market was also based within the company and had an organization that spread not across occupational categories but industrywide, ushering in the age of industrywide unions.

The transition between the two stages of industrialization occurred at different times in different countries. This gave rise to national variations in labor economics and industrial relations.

STAGE ONE—THE AGE OF THE CRAFT UNION

Necessary Skills

Little in-depth information is available for a broad description of stage one. The machine industry in Britain in the latter half of the nineteenth century offers the most detail. It embodies the economic and technological conditions mentioned and has been well researched. Much data is available on the Amalgamated Society of Engineers (ASE), the period's largest craft union.[7]

Economic conditions centered on private enterprise. Most companies had less than 100 employees, and even large concerns had, at most, several hundred workers. By today's standards, most of these firms would be small or medium in size. Contemporary observers depicted the machine industry in competition locally; only gradually did competition spread nationwide. Local markets were small and highly competitive, so mass production would await the development of the larger markets it requires. The companies, moreover, were too small and lacking in capital to install mass-production equipment.

Technologically, little machinery was available, and its performance and precision were low. The British engineering industry manufactured all the then known machines. It boasted workshops to cast and forge the iron and to machine and assemble the parts. In the machine shop, the ASE stronghold, the all-purpose lathe dominated. It made diverse goods and performed a variety of manufacturing operations. Its products built the machinery for the then primary industries: steam engines for the railroad, spinning machines for the textile industry, mining equipment for the coal mines, etc.

Accuracy, however, was so low that machining alone could not be depended on. Finishing touches, such as the filing and fitting of the pistons for steam engines, for example, had to be done manually before the parts could be assembled. From this, it can be inferred that machine shop workers needed high-level manual skills for finishing touches and all-round mechanical skills for using the all-purpose lathe to make diverse products. Detailed studies of machine shop jobs are unavailable, so general descriptions based on the fragmentary evidence of researchers of British labor issues must suffice.

Information on machine shop workers comes from bulletins issued by the ASE. Machine shops had three groups of workers: turners, who used the lathes and did the machine processing; fitters, who filed and chiseled finishing touches; and laborers, who did unskilled, menial chores. Statistics are unavailable for estimating the percentage of unskilled laborers, but evidence suggests that the ratio of fitters to turners was two to one.[8] Low-level machine performance required many workers whose high-level manual skills facilitated fitting parts precisely. Their ability, moreover, to do many jobs required know-how and the knack. The same can be said of turners, who made their own tools, repaired the machines, and made decisions on how best to do jobs. This resembles the way Japanese carpenters work today. Turners and fitters were true craftsmen.

Unions That Foster Skilled Labor

Watching and imitating experienced shop workers is the most efficient way to acquire the skills and know-how to perform a variety of operations. Young people thus apprenticed under skilled workers. Apprenticeships of the period are noteworthy for their length, lasting roughly five to seven years depending on the place, with one or two years of additional training. Normally, apprentices only became craftsmen between ages 22 and 24. Compared with today's schooling, this is not harsh, but compared with the average number of work years at the time it was very severe. In the 1860s, independent craftsmen died on average at around age 37 (usually of tuberculosis). Apprenticeship thus consumed more than a third of a craftsman's active life. The ASE's prominent mutual aid functions provide records of the ages at which craftsmen joined the society and died.

The period's apprenticeship system is also noteworthy for the control skilled workers had in running it. The teaching of apprentices was done exclusively by craftsmen; employers had a say only in apprentices' wages. Through their union, craftsmen governed the number of apprentices and what should be taught, to whom, and how. Control was not confined to the training process. Craftsmen also determined their own jobs and how to do them. Craftsmen, not employers, defined the scope of the jobs in their trade. They decided turners' and fitters' spheres of influence, and employers were unable to effect changes. Who to assign to what job within trades was also decided by craftsmen. In principle, craftsmen could do any job within their trade, in any way, order, and speed.

In today's workshop, such a situation would be inconceivable—management makes all the decisions. Only carpenters appear to preserve the old practices. On the whole, workers' autonomy was first challenged between the end of the nineteenth century and World War I by American Frederick Winslow Taylor.

Among the features of the old system was the separation of skilled and unskilled workers. Unskilled workers seldom became skilled workers without apprenticing. Where labor unions were weak or where demand for labor was strong, a few might be promoted without apprenticing, but generally speaking unskilled workers remained unskilled for life. This is the origin of labor types whose skills remain unchanged over time.

Wage Rates by Occupation

If basic theory is applied to the economic conditions of stage one, where work skills transcended the company level and were common to a particular trade, we can assume, provided that competition existed between buyers and sellers, that wages were determined by occupation. If the seller/worker incurred costs in moving from place to place, and if the buyer was a locally based private enterprise, wages were standardized both by occupation and by locality, with slight differences nationwide, as was the case. Stage one wages have been clarified by statistician A. L. Bowley.[9] Actual wage transactions are illustrated in the Webbs' classic study *Industrial Democracy.*[10] According to these researchers, occupational wages rose rapidly until an apprentice became a craftsman, leveling off thereafter. The local ASE set the standard wage rate for craftsmen based on the weekly wage rate without overtime and would withdraw its members from companies that failed to observe it. Having the union set wages in place of collective bargaining with management may seem remote, but even today Japan's huge construction workers' union Zenkensoren sets and publishes wage rates at a union meeting each spring.[11] Some regional differences are also still evident, but virtually no differences exist between skilled workers in the same trade in the same place.

Stage one wages for unskilled workers, however, were around 60 percent those for skilled workers. Although higher than the wages of most apprentices, wages for unskilled workers did not rise and fluctuated greatly with business cycles. This was because unskilled workers were not organized.

Craft Unions

A precursor to the ASE can be traced back to the 1820s, but the ASE proper was founded in 1851 through the amalgamation of unions in similar trades. Its initial membership of over 10,000 workers climbed steadily to 43,000 by the end of the 1870s and to over 90,000 by the end of the 1890s. It was by far the largest labor union of its day.

To have an impact on wage determination, a union must organize, on a wide scale, workers who compete with one another. During stage one, competition existed within each trade among workers in similar occupations. Because the companies that bought workers' services had much in common and the quality of the workforce was similar, the conditions for determining wages were universal. It was thus advantageous for workers to form a union.

The ASE covered the skilled occupations in general, including those of making and repairing machines, but centered on machine shop fitters and turners. Because its members included the fitters and turners in the machine and repair shops of the period's major industries, spinning and coal mining, it was able ultimately to expand to all industries. Unskilled workers could not become union members because they did not compete with skilled workers. Not until after World War I did the ASE embrace other than craftsmen. The ASE's unionization rate was so high that it is said that companies in the major manufacturing centers that needed new fitters or turners would visit local union halls.

As the labor market spread through areas by occupation instead of by company, the ASE set up district committees and branches in each area that it made the center of its local operations. Its national headquarters was in London. Japanese subsequently mistakenly believed that a labor union should be organized by occupation and locality to be considered real. Organizations like the ASE, however, apply only under special conditions for a certain workforce.

The ASE's function was to allow workers to determine working conditions for themselves rather than through collective bargaining with management and to then ensure that the conditions were observed. The Webbs called this "union rule."

Bolstering this function was an outstanding system of mutual aid. In the absence of social security, the ASE provided benefits for such as illness, job loss, and retirement. Sick members received benefits that amounted to one-third of their wages during the first six months of a yearlong illness and about one-fifth during the second. Members who lost jobs initially received one-third of their wages. This was then gradually reduced to one-fifth, but coverage was for 30 weeks. During strikes, members were paid unemployment benefits as a kind of strike benefit. To maintain its mutual aid system, the ASE collected as much as 3 percent of members' wages as union dues. Today, union dues in Japan are thought high at around 1 percent, but are lower than in Europe.

ASE activities, moreover, were supported especially by volunteer officials. To reduce the cost of maintaining its mutual aid, the ASE had few full-time, salaried officials. Its backbone was volunteer members in its branch offices and local districts.

From the perspective of today's labor unions, the activities of the craft union seem strange. But given the conditions of the day, especially the presence of type A workers, it was a splendid system. The continued presence of type A workers ensures the existence of modern-day craft unions. The Builders' Union in the United States, the Pattern-Makers Union in the United Kingdom, and Zenkensoren in Japan continue to function as craft unions.[12] Regrettably, conventional wisdom in Japan overlooks much of this.

Laissez-faire

In general, government was noninterventionist, or laissez-faire, during stage one. It did not intervene in determining wages or labor conditions or protect the labor unions handling these issues. Nevertheless, misconceptions about government's role are long-standing in Japan. According to what can be called the social policy argument, government laws are important in protecting working conditions and legally sanctioning the formation of labor unions, but Japan does not discharge its responsibilities in this area very well. This argument assumes, incorrectly, that nineteenth-century laws to protect workers protected all workers and provided legal safeguards for the formation of labor unions and for working conditions.

In fact, the only workers protected by law were women and minors; adult male workers had no legal protection. Likewise, safeguards for working conditions extended only to working hours, and, again, applied solely to women and minors. And labor unions were active decades before the laws recognizing them were passed. Contrasting and mistaken views appear in books on social policy that are an exam subject on Japan's government employees examination.

The first laws cited by these books as examples of labor protection legislation are those that set limits on working hours. An 1847 British law established the 10-hour day. Debate continues on why this limit was set and made law by Parliament, whose members were predominantly employers. Arguments include humanism; the reason of total capital, which considers industrial society as a whole; labor disputes; and business competition. Okochi Kazuo's reason of total capital theory is well known.[13] The law, however, applied to women and minors only. It is thought, however, that because women and minors worked alongside men in the factories, the law would eventually extend to men too. But the male craft unions had already won a 10-hour workday some 10 years before 1847, indicating their power. By contrast, no laws protected the wages of women or minors.

The Trade Union Act was passed in Britain in 1871, but craft unions had existed since the 1830s and were approaching their heyday before the law. The law was enacted not to govern the formation of labor unions but to provide them with legal status in light of a secretary's disappearance with union funds. Laissez-faire was a special feature of stage one.

STAGE TWO—THE AGE OF THE INDUSTRIAL UNION

The Establishment of an Internal Labor Market

Stage two differs from stage one in that its model is the heavy and chemical industries in the United States. Much has already been said here about these industries. Chapters 4 and 12 dealt, respectively, with workshops in the U.S. steel industry and with present-day U.S. labor unions. Chapter 6, moreover, developed the rationale for this model, including theories about the internal labor market and OJT.

A key point is the relationship between U.S. labor practices and the theory of Japanese uniqueness. The idea that labor economics and industrial relations are different in Japan has long been the mainstream view in Japan. Recent research has weakened this argument, but not dislodged it. Westerners, meanwhile, are increasingly using this argument against Japan in pressing their demands. The Japan-is-different argument, found primarily in the United States, is an example. It asserts that international trade with Japan is impossible because Japan is different and lacks market competition. It shares roots with the theory of Japanese uniqueness.

The theory of Japanese uniqueness says that skills should transcend individual companies, that workers should be able to move freely from company to company, that wages should be determined by occupation, and that labor unions should be a cross-section based on occupation or industry. Japan's reality, however, is permanent employment that ties workers to companies and workers with only seniority-based, company-specific skills; wages that differ significantly depending on the company and on the worker's age; and enterprise unions that are not unions at all.

The standard by which Japan is judged unique is found in Western practices. It actually corresponds to stage one, but stage one developed under unique circumstances. Ignorance of how stage two evolved in Japan and the West results in misunderstanding the West today and a belief in Japanese uniqueness. All countries have distinctive features worthy of attention. But the theory of Japanese uniqueness extends far beyond these differences to assert that Japan is uniquely unique. Stage theory is indispensable to test this assertion.

The economic condition necessary for stage two was the appearance of big business. Increased company size made securing a market and acting with a long-term view possible. And more capital made investing in large machinery and other fixed equipment possible. These two factors made mass production feasible, leading, in turn, to a division of labor within large organizations that created many jobs, some easy, some difficult. Companies that took advantage of this by having workers gain experience gradually, from easy to more difficult jobs within a cluster of related jobs, reduced their cost of skill formation and formed internal labor markets. Type C, internal promotion, workers followed steep career paths, while type D, semiskilled, workers followed shallow career paths. Type A and B, skilled and unskilled, workers, existed, but not in prominent positions.

Most noteworthy about stage two was that the responsibility for skill formation and for determining what skills would be formed and in what ways was transferred from craftsmen to companies. Companies then wrested control from workers over how and at what speed jobs should be done. The Taylor system symbolizes these changes. From the end of the nineteenth century to World War I, Frederick Taylor, an American, proposed more-efficient work methods based on time-motion studies.[14] This enabled managements to examine and break down work procedures, eliminate unnecessary operations, and establish standard movements thought to be the most efficient. Workers opposed Taylor's methods, but methods based on his ideas gradually spread worldwide from the United States.

In addition to the Taylor system, since the 1960s attention has been paid—primarily in Japan and Sweden—to workshop workers and their ideas. In the 1980s, Japanese methods attracted widespread attention, especially quality control circles and such practices.[15] Chapter 8 revealed that intellectual skills underpin these practices. Different from the worker-initiated system of stage one, all this is a phenomenon of stage two.

The Establishment of an Internal Wage Structure

With skills being formed primarily within companies, compensation for skills also came to be decided there, leading to an internal wage structure. Enterprise-specific skills account for only a small portion of workers' skills. With labor types and especially occupations similar, general wage levels and a general wage structure transcend the company level and are shared industrywide. A type C workforce, found mainly in large companies, shares a more or less upward wage curve, but wages paid to individual workers for specific jobs may vary by industry and company. Some method is needed to regulate wage payments for the various type C jobs.

The internal wage structure uses the pay-for-job and the pay-for-job-grade plans. The pay-for-job plan sets pay at one rate for each job, with no raise while a worker is on the same job. The pay-for-job-grade plan sets pay on a range by job grade so that raises are possible while a worker is on the same job. Usually, pay raises within the range occur as yearly increments subject to merit ratings.

Production workers at U.S. Steel in the early 1940s provide an example of the pay-for-job plan.[16] Until then, U.S. Steel, then the world's largest company, had allowed each of its establishments to set wages. When problems arose over wage discrepancies for similar jobs depending on the establishment, a job classification plan was adopted. Principal jobs were classified by such as the degree of skill, intelligence, and responsibility involved, and evaluations were made based on the number of points assigned to each classification. Blue-collar jobs had nearly 30 grades, each with a single wage rate. There were no pay raises within each grade.

The pay-for-job-grade plan encourages skill formation of high-level skills over the long term among type C workers. First, compensation increases in line with a worker's progression to upper grades. Second, it rises in accordance with a worker's skill development at a single job. Third, compensation accords with differences in high-level skill development among individuals by means of merit ratings.

The pay-for-job plan, too, seems suitable for encouraging skill formation among type C workers over the long term, particularly through job-grade promotion, provided, however, that it is not governed by seniority. Under both plans, wages slowly rise with achievement and length of service, forming a wage profile of height and length. But when promotion is based exclusively on length of service, as at U.S. steel companies, the absence of merit ratings means the absence of competition among workers. Applied to blue-collar workers, the pay-for-job plan usually lacks merit ratings.

The pay-for-job-grade plan is widespread for white-collar workers in Western Europe and North America, ranging from 50 to 60 percent for professional and managerial employees.[17] Its Japanese feature is its application to white-collar and to blue-collar workers in large corporations. Evidence, again, of white collarization. The difference, if any, between its application in the West and Japan is in range, which seems slightly larger in Japan, where it is likely to take longer to reach the ceiling. Conclusions, though, must be withheld for lack of sufficient data.

The Increasing Role of Government

When a society enters stage two, the role of government increases in two respects. First, government's support rises for places that lack the conditions necessary for independent negotiations. Workers' negotiate independently with management to determine working conditions, but only through an organization. Where a labor union, for example, does not exist, minimum working conditions are determined by law. In Japan, the Labor Standards Law defines minimum working conditions. What distinguishes stage two from stage one is that laws once limited to women and minors now also apply to adult males. Take the minimum wage system for instance. Since approximately World War I, minimum wages in most industrialized countries have been determined by law. Japan, however, did not enact minimum wage legislation until after World War II.

The lack of a labor organization does not imply poor working conditions. Even fair-sized companies with industrywide unions may not have an organization at each establishment. In such situations, laws encourage the creation of an employees' association to serve as a management participation organization (see chapter 12). This is not a legal requirement in Japan and the United States, but such organizations are widespread in Western Europe and Scandinavia.

Weak organizations, though, may be stifled by management. Laws thus stipulate that certain actions constitute unfair labor practices; the dismissal or mistreatment of a labor official is an unfair labor practice subject to legal sanctions. Such laws are notably evident in the United States, where labor unions were late in developing.

Laws prohibiting discrimination against women and minorities, for whom joining unions was difficult, began in the United States with the Civil Rights Act of 1964 and spread to Western Europe in the 1970s. Such legislation all went into effect late in Japan with the Equal Opportunity Law of 1986.

The concerns of working people extend, naturally, outside the workshop to living conditions. Thus the craft unions' mutual aid systems in stage one. The advent of stage two made this the second area where government's role increased when it established social security, including social insurance and public aid. Participation in social insurance is compulsory by law, but no penalties are involved. Everyone pays the insurance fees, and the benefits are paid to the needy. It encompasses principally health insurance, workers' compensation, unemployment insurance, and old-age pensions. Social security differs among the industrialized countries, but the German system is the oldest and the pattern for Japan. In Germany, management and labor split the fee payments; employers pay only the full cost of workers' compensation. Health insurance was introduced in Japan in the 1920s, not much later than in Europe; pensions were introduced in 1942; and unemployment insurance came after World War II. Public assistance provides support to the needy at public expense without fee payments.

Government's increased role probably stems from the decline in the class system at the workshop and government levels. In stage one, skilled workers created craft unions and were able to maintain their livelihoods through them. Unskilled workers, however, lacked the means to protect their livelihoods. Their recourse was the church and other charitable organizations. In stage two, it became possible to advance from unskilled to skilled jobs, such that distinctions between these workers merged somewhat. To protect their own interests, skilled workers had to give way to protect the class beneath them.

At the government level, voting rights spread in stage two to the lower classes. They are said to have done so in stage one, but they were confined to skilled workers, who could own homes. Their spread in stage two to unskilled workers meant that thereafter governments that disregarded that group found it difficult to retain power.

CHANGEOVER—AN EXPLANATION OF NATIONAL DIFFERENCES

The Existence of Differences

Apart from general trends common to all countries are many different trends, even among industrialized countries. A look at the relative weight of each basic labor type discloses the differences in table 14-1. No statistical evidence on labor types is likely ever to be available, so these findings emerge from case studies of related matters.[18] Data for Japan, the United States, and the United Kingdom are mainly for large companies because of abundant studies. Workers have been divided into white-collar workers; blue-collar workers in the direct production departments of the process industry; blue-collar workers in the machine and other industries; and, somewhat less reliably, blue-collar workers in small and medium-sized companies.

In white-collar workshops in all three countries, internal promotion, type C workers are thought to be the mainstream. They

Table 14-1 Sphere of Existence for Labor Types

			Japan	U.S.	U.K.
Large companies	White collar		C	C	C
Large companies	Blue collar	Direct production departments of the process industry	C	C	C
Large companies	Blue collar	Machine industry, etc.	C	DAC	AD
Small and medium-sized companies	Blue collar		D	D	DA

Legend:
Type A: high skills that do not change over time (skilled worker or craftsman)
Type B: low skills that do not change over time (unskilled worker or laborer)
Type C: high skills that improve greatly over time (internal promotion worker)
Type D: skills that improve slightly over time (semiskilled worker)

are also the majority in all three countries' blue-collar workshops in the direct production departments of the process industry. The countries diverge, however, regarding the last two categories. In the machine industries, type C blue-collar workers are the majority at large companies in Japan, but in the United States most workers are semiskilled, type D workers, along with skilled, type A and some type C workers. In British machine industries, many type A workers are found alongside type D workers. Type C workers are thus most widespread in Japan, followed by the United States, and least so in the United Kingdom. Just the opposite is true of type A workers.

Changeover Costs

Sufficient evidence is unavailable to account for national differences, so a hypothesis, first stated more than 30 years ago and unrevised since, must suffice.[19] It argues that differences stem from variations in changeover costs, which are highest for switches in labor types.

Changeover costs are also high for equipment and machinery. In the textile industry, the main equipment used in stage one was the spinning mule, operated primarily by skilled male workers and developed by the British into an unprecedented size. With the shift to stage two, the textile industry's main equipment became the spinning ring. The immense cost to the British spinning industry of scrapping its spinning mules delayed the changeover there. The

Japanese textile industry also used spinning mules, but its shift to stage two occurred before state-run factories in the large fiefs, such as Shimazu, had fully developed. The switch to the spinning ring was easily made by Osaka Textiles—later Toyobo—helping to launch the Japanese textile industry into international competition. The transition to stage two involved few difficulties for late-developing countries.

People, unlike machines and equipment, cannot be scrapped. The more changeover involves humans rather than machines, the higher the costs. A labor type is a kind of social system. As such, it should be influenced by environment, such as economic and technological conditions. Yet, it appears that labor types can exist independent of the environmental conditions that created them.

Labor types depend on the skill formation process during workers' careers. Older workers, who morally cannot be discarded if their skills become obsolete, can acquire new skills in their stead, but at tremendous cost. The time required to form the old skills—most of a worker's career—will be lost. And the costs are not restricted to one generation. Skill formation is possible only when there is a teacher and a pupil. This condition is best met within a social organization, such as an apprenticeship system or within a company. Once an organization forms, it tends to perpetuate itself. If labor unions are involved in skill formation, they become entrenched as social systems and independent of such as technological change. In industrial society, a labor union consists primarily of skilled workers. It protects its members' interests through protecting their skill formation methods from change. Labor types thus continue to exist despite technological and generational changes. Changeover entails much time and cost.

The Progressive Nature of Japanese Industrial Relations

Given the above, national differences in changeover timing and in labor economies can be explained. Stages one and two have the appropriate economic and technological systems and the appropriate social systems, including labor type, labor union, labor-management relations, and so on. Stage one had skilled workers, apprenticeship, and a craft union. Internal promotion, however, is appropriate for stage two. It encourages the stage's suitable labor type and company-level labor-management relations. Stage one's length ensured that its social system developed thoroughly. Consequently, discarding this system with the advent of stage two entailed formidable changeover costs, delaying the diffusion of stage two's social systems. Only countries whose industrial development was late made the transition more easily—a phenomenon known as the latecomer effect.

Stage one flourished earliest in Britain, yielding strong craft unions that impeded the spread of internal promotion there in stage two. In Japan, where industrialization occurred late, at around the transition between the two stages, stage one was so short that its systems never took root and were thus easy to discard. Stage two systems, however, developed thoroughly in Japan. U.S. industrialization occurred somewhere between industrialization in Britain and Japan, as did the spread of internal promotion there.

Similar developmental patterns are evident within countries. In Britain, the engineering industry, which flourished in stage one, yielded the country's most powerful craft union. Skill formation and industrial relations appropriate to the machine industry in stage two were thus late to develop, and many stage one institutions remain. By contrast, the process industries, especially those such as the chemical industry that developed in the twentieth century, have less of a craft union tradition and more internal promotion than other industries in the United Kingdom today. The same is true of the steel industry.

Because stage two social systems are thoroughly established in Japan, the country's skill formation and industrial relations have put it a step ahead of world trends. However, when stage three begins there is a distinct possibility that Japan may fall behind.

Simply pointing to the latecomer effect as the basis for Japan's success ignores the world's many other late-developing countries. Why is it that only Japan is a step ahead? The answer seems to be the fortunate congruence of Japan's internal development and the timing of its changeover to stage two. Most other countries embarked on industrialization after stage two was considerably advanced and thus were too late to take the lead. It is unknown when, where, or in what form stage three will begin.

Epilogue: The Future of Japanese Work Methods

The good features of Japan's work methods are likely to continue to spread worldwide. They will be refined and altered to such an extent that Japan may need to relearn them.

Globalization is the wave of the future. It differs from internationalization in that it involves direct investment suited to local needs. Companies are no longer simply importing and exporting goods; they are producing their products locally in the markets where they will be used. In fact, companies are localizing all their economic activities—planning, development, research, and even marketing—by hiring and tapping the know-how of local talent. To sell their products, companies must understand local needs and develop appropriate products. In this regard, they differ significantly from the old multinationals, which largely tended to follow the dictates of their head offices. This practice no longer suffices amid globalization.

Globalization demands that more attention be paid to the way jobs are done. The transferability abroad of work methods is increasingly crucial. Globalization transcends the mere movement of goods; firms must invest directly and plan, develop, and produce goods locally. Efficiency depends on skills. Determining which work methods from one country to develop in different parts of the world and how much of a foundation must be laid to develop them into efficient skills have never been more important.

Japanese work methods are distinguished by intellectual skills and long-term competition—workshop skills and the competitive system that stimulates their formation. Because intellectual skills are akin to technical knowledge, countries that show interest in introducing them by preparing the necessary conditions should have no difficulty doing so. Long-term competition, however, will prove harder to export because of its close relation to social systems and the time needed for the social systems in other countries to change. It will be especially difficult to establish long-term competition where short-term competition is firmly entrenched or where there is no competition, as in union-controlled production workshops in the United States and Western Europe. But the situation is not hopeless; long-term competition has been adopted in U.S. and Western European offices. And it is likely to be adopted more readily in countries where workshop systems are not yet established.

A more serious problem lies in the negative effects arising from misunderstandings about these methods. Intellectual skills are invisible, and competition takes a long time to take hold. Results, therefore, are not immediately obvious. Few intellectuals, moreover, in Japan and elsewhere make the effort to see what is not readily apparent. The good in Japan's work methods are thus misunderstood, such that no one bothers to foster the best of those methods. Fortunately, the solid achievements of Japanese companies abroad are doing much to diminish misunderstandings.

Japan must do more to clarify for people of other countries the nature of its work methods. It must do so thoroughly and repeatedly. Explanations should be in the target languages. Many countries throughout history have been active in other countries, most in their own languages. The United Kingdom, the United States, and France are examples. Japan has the opportunity to be one of the first to operate in the languages of the countries in which it does business.

All this notwithstanding, Japanese methods are not problem free. Developing leaders is a problem that companies wishing to practice long-term competition must face. Companies that consider workers' long-term performance records in selecting leaders will be slow to make decisions. The leader of a large firm should, preferably, be someone with experience in all its important posts. The longer the selection process the less time for such a person to acquire that experience. The slow but steady development of leaders is weak in Japanese companies. This shortcoming will remain hidden only so long as normalcy prevails in industry worldwide; a dramatic change, such as war or problems arising from globalization, will expose it for all the world to see. The impact of such a shortcoming will be significant, and Japan must be prepared to bear the costs.

As globalization proceeds, other problems are also likely to arise in the selection of leaders. Promotion amid long-term competition is ultimately affected by the performance appraisal of an immediate superior. Workers assigned overseas for a long time, especially in a remote place that few from the company ever visit, lack opportunities to impress their superiors. As a result, those people who devote themselves to globalization are left out in the cold. Talented workers who might otherwise contribute to globalization will thus refuse overseas postings, and long-term competition will fail.

What is needed is a practice of employing in key posts at head offices in Japan only those who have spent at least five years working abroad. Then, perhaps, Japan's time in the sun will last a little longer.

Appendix

All of the important reference works are cited in the endnotes. Here, I will single out the most noteworthy for a more extended discussion.

Umemura Mataji's *Chingin, Koyo, Nogyo* (Wages, Employment, Agriculture) (Tokyo: Daimeido, 1961) has had a profound impact on Japanese labor economists. No other work has more revolutionized the study of labor issues in Japan. Worthy of being read and reread, this book is written in a clear, unpretentious style that belies the in-depth study of evidence on which it is based. Moreover, despite its easy, narrative flow it presents conclusions that are a stark contrast to previous assumptions.

International comparisons are indispensable for an understanding of the situation in Japan. The best of these is Shiba Masaji's *A Cross-National Comparison of Labour and Management with Reference to Technology Transfer* (Tokyo: Institute of Developing Economies, 1973). No other work that I am aware of offers a better international comparison of workshop labor practices. Mr. Shiba's thorough study of electrical generating plants resulted from his spending two months in a plant in each of eight countries in Asia, including Japan, and in North America. He analyzed his observations and expressed his findings numerically in such a way that it is hard to imagine his book ever being surpassed. However, Ronald P. Dore's *British Factory, Japanese Factory* (Berkeley: University of California Press, 1973) compares favorably with Mr. Shiba's work. It details work at a Hitachi factory and at a British electrical machinery plant and provides an especially clear sense of work at a British factory.

Final mention must go to Inoki Takenori's *Keizai Shiso* (Economic Thought) (Tokyo: Iwanami Shoten, 1989). Labor economics initially may seem like a narrow field, but because it is an area of human behavior the organizations that arise from it are closely related to social systems. Mr. Inoki's book observes these relationships in as much breadth as possible. As a general rule, studies of economic thought begin with Britain, France, and Germany at the outset of the modern period. Mr. Inoki, however, starts with the Greeks and Romans. Just as a knowledge of the Chinese classics facilitates a thorough analysis of Japanese classical literature, an examination of Greek and Roman classics makes possible rich insights into economic phenomena. Mr. Inoki's work has turned a longtime dream of Japanese intellectuals into reality. It is a splendid achievement.

Notes

Chapter 1: Various Worker Groups

1. Umemura Mataji, *Sengo Nihon no Rodoryoku* (The Postwar Japanese Labor Force) (Tokyo: Iwanami Shoten, 1966). The issue is examined in the first chapter of this virtually unparalleled work.
2. Koike Kazuo, *Chusho Kigyo no Jukuren* (Skill Formation in Small and Medium-Sized Companies) (Tokyo: Dobunkan, 1981). Chapter 3 deals with this problem.
3. Arthur W. Lewis, "Economic Development with Unlimited Supply of Labor," *Manchester School of Economics and Social Studies*, vol. 22 (May 1954).
4. John C. H. Fei and Gustav Ranis, *Development of the Labor Surplus Economy: Theory and Policy* (Homewood, Ill.: R. D. Irwin, 1964); originally published as "A Theory of Economic Development," *American Economic Review*, vol. 56 (Sept. 1961).
5. Minami Ryoshin, *Nihon Keizai no Tenkanten* (The Turning Point in the Japanese Economy) (Tokyo: Sobunsha, 1971); a book that developed out of the following article published in a leading economics journal: "The Turning Point in the Japanese Economy," *Quarterly Journal of Economics*, vol. 82 (August 1968).
6. Taira Koji, *Economic Development and the Labor Market in Japan* (New York: Columbia University Press, 1970).
7. Yasuba Yasukichi, *Keizai Seichoron* (Economic Growth) (Tokyo: Chikuma Shobo, 1980), chapter 5.
8. Umemura Mataji, *Chingin, Koyo, Nogyo* (Wages, Employment, Agriculture) (Tokyo: Taimeido, 1961), chapter 3.
9. The increase in the wage differentials before the war might be attributed to the appearance of a new type of skilled worker with a higher level of skills. In the case of the older skilled labor categories, such as carpenters, the differentials are in fact shrinking. This new type of highly skilled worker is thought to be the prototype for the internal promotion labor type to be discussed later.

Chapter 2: Examining the Seniority Wage Lenged

1. Ujihara Shojiro, *Nihon Rodo Mondai Kenkyu* (A Study of Japanese Labor Issues) (Tokyo: Tokyo Univ. Press, 1966), part 3, chapter 3. First published as an article in 1951.
2. OECD, *Development of Industrial Relations Systems: Some Implications of Japanese Experience* (Paris: OECD, 1977).
3. There are two or three careful comparative studies of worker attitudes and outlooks. Among them, the most comprehensive are those done by the All Japan Federation of Electric Machine Workers' Unions (Denki Roren), which come to rather the opposite conclusion from what is popularly believed. Denki Roren, "10-kakoku Denki Rodosha no Ishiki Chosa" (Survey of the Attitudes of Electrical Workers in 10 Countries), *Chosa Jiho* (Bulletin), vol. 212, and "Nichibei Denki Rodosha no Ishiki

Hikaku Chosa" (Survey Comparing the Attitudes of Japanese and American Electrical Workers), *Chosa Jiho* (Bulletin), vol. 232.

4. The first but clearest attempt to distinguish between these two concepts was an article that appeared in a mimeographed pamphlet: Umemura Mataji, "Nenrei to Chingin" (Age and Wages) in Tokei Kenkyukai, ed., *Chingin Kozo no Jittai Bunseki* (An Analysis of Wage Structure) (Tokyo: Tokei Kenkyukai, 1956).
5. For American companies, see, for example, Koike Kazuo, *Shokuba no Rodokumiai to Sanka—Roshikankei no Nichibei Hikaku* (A Comparative Study of Industrial Relations on the Shop Floor in the United States and Japan) (Tokyo: Toyo Keizai, 1977).
6. See Robert Martin Blackburn, *Union Character and Social Class: A Study of White-Collar Unionism* (London: Batsford, 1967), pp. 71–75. An example of salary schedules used during this period by large British banks can be found in Koike Kazuo, *Chingin—Sono Riron to Jissai* (Wages—Theory and Practice) (Tokyo: Diamond Inc., 1966), pp. 199–201.
7. See Koike Kazuo, "Nihon no Hoshu Seido" (Pay Systems in Japanese Industry), *Keiei Shirin* (Bulletin), vol. 31, No. 2, 1994.
8. A very general account of the salaries for management at large British companies can be found in Myron J. Roomkin, ed., *Managers as Employees: An International Comparison of the Changing Character of Managerial Employment* (New York: Oxford University Press, 1989), pp. 43–44.
9. See Umemura, "Nenrei to Chingin" and "Nenrei-shotoku Purofiru no Kokusai Hikaku" (An International Comparison of Age-Wage Profiles), *Keizai Kenkyu* 22, 3 (1971). Statistics on the United States are printed in Wladimir S. Woytinsky et al., *Employment and Wages in the United States* (New York: Twentieth Century Fund, 1953).
10. For a careful analysis of the differences in white-collar wages in EC member countries, see Muramatsu Kuramitsu, "Kinzokubetsu Kyuyo Kozo Kara Mita Naibu Rodo Shijo no Ruikeika" (The Type in an Internal Labor Market as Seen from the Structure of Wages by Length of Service), *Nanzan Keizai Kenkyu*, October 1988.
11. Shimada Haruo, *Earnings Structure and Human Investment: A Comparison between the United States and Japan* (Tokyo: Kogakusha, 1981).
12. Ibid. In addition, other evidence may be relevant. When we compare the age-wage profiles between the results of the 1980 Census of Population and the 1960 Census of Population, it is distinct that, in the United States, the profiles for college graduates and for high school graduates become slightly steeper in 1979 than in 1959. (See Koike, "Amerika no Howaito Kara" (White-collar Workers in the United States) (Tokyo: Toyo Keizai Shimposha, 1993), p. 83.
13. Ono Akira, *Nihonteki Koyo Kanko to Rodo Shijo* (Japanese-Style Employment Practices and the Labor Market) (Tokyo: Toyo Keizai Shinposha, 1989).

Chapter 3: Examining the Permanent Employment Theory

1. Statistics on separation rates for the United States were found in *Employment and Earnings*, put out monthly by the Bureau of Labor Statistics, Department of Labor, and, for easy reference, the statistical tables published at the end of the *Monthly Labor Review*, the Department of Labor journal. However, since both were discontinued in the middle of 1982, the figures for 1981 are given. Because the figures were based on reports from establishments, they ought to be compared with Japan's Monthly Labor Statistics (*Maigetsu Kinro Tokei*), which collects statistics from establishments. Such statistics in Japan are compiled for establishments with 30 or more employees, however, whereas the statistics for the United States give no indication of establishment size. The Survey of Employment Mobility (*Koyo Doko Chosa*) also contains statistics on separation rates for Japan; it is very detailed and provides valuable information, such

as cross-references by age and by company size. For time-series examinations, the Monthly Labor Statistics are better, however.

2. In the Survey of Employment Mobility, the category for "regular" workers includes some "temporary and casual" labor. For statistical purposes, "regular" includes not only those who are "nominally regular" (a category that corresponds to regular employees) but also "nominally temporary and casual" workers who have worked more than 18 days in the two previous months. Separation rates for "nominally regular" workers only are not known, but it is inconceivable that the distribution rate would be so low as to be close to zero. Separation rates for workers in their late 20s and older are thought to refer almost entirely to "nominally regular" workers.
3. The data are found in Koike Kazuo, *Nihon no Jukuren* (Skill Formation Systems in Japan) (Tokyo: Yuhikaku, 1981), pp. 114–15.
4. Robert E. Hall, "The Importance of Lifetime Jobs in the United States," *American Economic Review*, Sept. 1982. See also the 1993 edition of *Employment Outlook*.
5. OECD, "The Importance of Long Term Job Attachment in OECD Countries," *Employment Outlook*, Sept. 1984. See also the 1993 edition of *Employment Outlook*.

Chapter 4: The Carreers of Workers at Large Companies

1. Koike Kazuo, *Shokuba no Rodokumiai to Sanka—Roshikankei no Nichibei Hikaku* (A Comparative Study of Industrial Relations on the Shop Floor in the United States and Japan) (Tokyo: Toyo Keizai Shinposha, 1977), chapter 2. Case studies of other American industries are also given. A few other studies have been done in this area. In particular, some excellent recent research on white-collar workers has appeared, notably the work by Rosenbaum (see chapter 11). But these works, which are primarily in the field of sociology, are concerned mostly with the promotion and selection process and do not examine jobs and skills. That is the reason I rely mainly on my earlier study. As a guide to these works, see Nakamura Megumi, "Amerika no Kyaria Kenkyu" (A Survey of the Studies on Careers in the United States), in Koike Kazuo, ed., *Daisotsu Howaito-kara no Jinzai Kaihatsu* (Human Resource Development of College Graduates in Industry) (Tokyo: Toyo Keizai Shinposha, 1991).
2. Koike, *Shokuba no Rodokumiai to Sanka*.
3. Kikuchi Kozo and Ishida Mitsuo, *Gendai Igirisu no Roshi Kankei* (Industrial Relations in Contemporary Britain) 2 (Tokyo: Tokyo Daigaku Shuppankai, 1988).
4. In some cases the worker is invariably rehired. This is called a temporary layoff, and it refers to a shutdown of operations to replace equipment or to do other repairs. Because workers are assured of being rehired, usually within 30 days, layoffs are not in reverse order of seniority, and only those who are affected by the equipment change are laid off.
5. Because management can easily dismiss workers during the three- to six-month period after hiring, the probationary employment system is superficially the same as in the United States, but few dismissals seem to be made in Japan even during the probationary period.
6. A number of case studies are discussed in the following three books. Koike, *Shokuba no Rodokumiai to Sanka*; Koike Kazuo and Inoki Takenori, *Skill Formation in Japan and Southeast Asia* (Tokyo: Tokyo University Press, 1990, originally published in Japanese in 1987); Aichi Prefecture, Department of Labor, *Chiteki Jukuren no Keisei-Aichiken no Kigyo* (The Formation of Intellectual Skills at Companies in Aichi Prefecture) (Nagoya: Aichiken Rodobu, 1987).
7. A few statistical studies have examined how widespread this sort of rotation is. Highly recommended is Koyo Shokugyo Sogo Kenkyujo, *Kigyonai Rodoryoku no Yuko Katsuyo ni kansuru Jittai Chosa* (Survey of the Effective Use of the Labor Force within Companies) (Tokyo: Koyo Shokugyo Sogo Kenkyujo, 1982), chapter 4. But if I may add a note of caution based on my own experiences, questionnaires do not always reveal the true extent of rotation. I once conducted a survery that tried to determine

rotation in small and medium-sized businesses. When I interviewed respondents to my questionnaire, however, in some cases no rotation existed even though the respondent had replied "yes" on the questionnaire and vice versa. Unless the question is well formulated, information is difficult to obtain. See Koike Kazuo, *Chusho Kigyo no Jukuren* (Skill Formation in Small and Medium-sized Companies) (Tokyo: Dobunkan, 1981). The questionnaire is given in chapter 1 and the interviews in chapter 2.

8. Koike Kazuo, Yamamoto Ikuro, and Muramatsu Kuramitsu, "Kojo no Naka no Ido to Kojo no Naka no Rodokumiai" (Internal Mobility and Plant-Level Unions), in Nagoya University *Keizai-gakubu, Chosa to Shiryo* (Surveys and Sources), no. 58 (1976). This study is a detailed analysis of the moves of workers between workshops in a large machinery factory in the Nagoya area and of labor union regulations regarding them.
9. A detailed analysis of temporary transfers can be found in Nagano Hitoshi, *Kigyo Gurupunai Jinzai Ido no Kenkyu* (Research on Transfers within Groups of Companies) (Tokyo: Taga Shuppan, 1989)

Chapter 5: Intellectual Skills

1. For the first two sections of this chapter, see Koike and Inoki, *Skill Formation in Japan and Southeast Asia* (Tokyo: Tokyo University Press, 1990). Chapter 1 of that book deals with the theory of skill formation systems; other chapters contain detailed discussions of workshop practices in Japan, Thailand, and Malaysia.
2. The separated system was often found when I visited 18 small and midsize companies in the Osaka area in 1982, but in some places both systems could be observed even within the same company. Osaka Prefecture, Industrial Labor Policy Promotion Commission, *Maikuro Erekutoronikusu-ka ni tomonau Koyo Rodo eno Eikyo to Taio ni tsuite* (The Impact on Workers as a Result of Advances in Microelectronics) (Osaka: Osaka Prefecture, 1983), pp. 106, 113, passim.
3. See Koike Kazuo, "Nihon no Off-JT" (Off-JT in Japan), in Koike Kazuo, ed., *Gendai no Jinzai Keisei—Noryoku Kaihatsu o Saguru* (Contemporary Human Resource Development—An Examination of Skill Formation) (Kyoto: Minerva Shobo, 1986).
4. Ibid.
5. The case study used is from Aichi Prefecture, Department of Labor (1987). It is based on interviews conducted by Muramatsu Kuramitsu, Hisamoto Norio, and Koike Kazuo at three large companies and eight small and medium-sized companies in Aichi Prefecture during 1986.

Chapter 6: Current Theories

1. Gary S. Becker, *Human Capital: A Theoretical and Empirical Analysis, with Special Reference to Education* (New York: Columbia University Press, 1964).
2. Walter Y. Oi, "Labor as a Quasi-Fixed Factor of Production," *Journal of Political Economy*, December 1962.
3. Peter B. Doeringer and Michael J. Piore, *Internal Labor Markets and Manpower Analysis* (Lexington, Mass.: Heath and Company, 1971).
4. Koike Kazuo, *Nihon no Chingin Kosho—Sangyobetsu Chingin Kettei Kiko* (Collective Bargaining in Japan—Wage Determination by Industry) (Tokyo: Tokyo University Press, 1962). This work studied intercompany wage differentials in three different industries as thoroughly as possible given the limited availability of data.
5. Ohashi Isao, *Rodo Shijo no Riron* (The Theory of Labor Markets) (Tokyo: Toyo Keizai Shinposha, 1990). Chapter 1 contains a survey of the most recent research on this issue.
6. Sidney and Beatrice Webb, *Industrial Democracy* (London: Longmans, Green & Co., 1920, first published in 1897).
7. Clark Kerr, "The Balkanization of Labor Markets," in E. Wight Bakke et al., ed., *Labor Mobility and Economic Opportunity* (New York: John Wiley & Sons, Inc., 1954).
8. John T. Dunlop, "The Task of Contemporary Wage Theory," in John T. Dunlop, ed., *The Theory of Wage Determination* (Macmillan, 1957).

9. Doeringer and Piore, *Internal Labor Markets*.
10. Oliver E. Williamson, *Markets and Hierarchy* (Free Press, 1975). Chapter 4 especially, and this cites only one of Williamson's many works on the subject.
11. Many scholars have written in this area. Here, we cite E.P. Lazear, "Why is There Mandatory Retirement?," *Journal of Political Economy*, December 1979. For a more detailed analysis, see Ohashi, *Rodo Shijo no Riron*.
12. The standard works are Martin Neil Baily, "Wages and Employment under Uncertain Demand," *Review of Economic Studies*, January 1974, and Costas Azariadis, "Implicit Contracts and Underemployment Equilibria," *Journal of Political Economics*, December 1975.
13. Inoki Takenori, *Keizai Shiso* (Economic Thoughts) (Tokyo: Iwanami Shoten, 1987), especially pp. 211ff. of this splendid study.
14. Although somewhat dated, for a study of intercompany wage differentials see Koike, *Nihon no Chingin Kosho*, which, within the limits of the available data, attempts to compare wages by age and length of service among textile, steel, and private railway companies. Data for wage comparisons within industry are so astonishingly rare that few studies have been made on this subject in Japan, and even fewer elsewhere. The only groups to compile and publish information of this kind are the industrial unions.

Chapter 7: Adjustment to Change: Dismissal and Unemployment

1. Shimada Haruo, "Kajo Koyo o Kangaeru" (Some Thoughts on Surplus Employment), *Nihon Keizai Shimbun*, April 11–12, 1976.
2. Shinozuka Eiko, *Nihon no Koyo Chosei—Oiru Shokku Iko no Rodo Shijo* (Employment Adjustment in Japan—The Labor Market after the Oil Shock) (Tokyo: Toyo Keizai Shinposha, 1989), chapters 1 and 2.
   Particularly excellent comparative studies are Abraham and Houseman's two works. In one, the ratio of elasticity of employment to output for German blue-collar workers is shown to be far less than for U.S. blue-collar workers but barely different from the figure for U.S. white-collar workers: K. G. Abraham and S. N. Houseman, *Job Security in America—Lessons from Germany* (Washington, D.C.: the Brookings Institution, 1993). In the other study, the figure for Japanese blue-collar workers is shown to be not much different from that for U.S. white-collar workers: Abraham and Houseman, "Job Security and Work Force Adjustment: How Different are U.S. and Japanese Practices?" *Journal of the Japanese and International Economies*, vol. 3 (1989).
3. For a more detailed account, see Muramatsu Kuramitsu, *Nihon no Rodo Shijo Bunseki* (An Analysis of the Japanese Labor Market) (Tokyo: Hakuto Shobo, 1983). This work is a rigorous analysis of employment adjustment practices in Japan. This is the most important study on the subject.
4. Hisamoto Norio, *Koyo Chosei o Meguru Nishi-Doitsu Roshi Kankei no Kenkyu* (A Study on Employment Adjustment in West German Industrial Relations) (Shokugyo Kunren Daigakko, 1989).
5. Ibid.
6. The German word *soziale*, in relation to labor, has the connotation of welfare.
7. For blue-collar workers, see Hisamoto, *Koyo Chosei;* for white-collar workers, see Koike Kazuo, *Nihon no Koyo Shisutemu* (Employment Systems in Japan) (Tokyo: Toyo Keizai Shinposha, 1994), chapter 4-2. In German, the early retirement system is referred to by the term *Aufhebungsvertrag*, literally, "severance agreement."
8. An excellent study on blue-collar workers at large steel companies is Kikuchi and Ishida, *Gendai Igirisu* (1988). For white-collar workers, see Koike, *Nihon no Koyo Shisutemu*. See also Alison L. Booth, "Extra-Statutory Redundancy Payments in Britain," *British Journal of Industrial Relations*, vol. 25, no. 3 (1987). Booth gives an overview of the diffusion of voluntary redundancy in contemporary Britain.
9. Ministry of Labor, *Koyo Hendo Sogo Chosa* (Comprehensive Survey of Employment Fluctuations), 1979. This survey is based on a questionnaire sent to 9,300 private

establishments with five or more full-time employees. All establishments with 500 or more employees were included in the survey, while smaller companies were included on a sample basis.

10. See Koike Kazuo, "Rodo Undo no Tenkai" (The Development of the Labor Movement) and "Miike," Iida Tsuneo et al., ed., *Gendai Nihon Keizaishi—Sengo 30nen no Ayumi* (Economic History of Modern Japan—Developments during the 30 Years since the End of the War), 1–2 (Tokyo: Chikuma Shobo, 1976).
11. Koike Kazuo, "Kaiko Kara Mita Gendai Nihon no Roshi Kankei" (Contemporary Japanese Industrial Relations from the Perspective of Dismissals), Moriguchi Chikasi et al., ed., *Nihon Keizai no Kozo Bunseki* (A Structural Analysis of the Japanese Economy) (Tokyo: Sobunsha, 1983).
12. Muramatsu Kuramitsu, "Kaiko, Kigyo Rieki to Chingin—Ote Kosaku Kikai Meka 13sha ni Kanshite" (Dismissals, Corporate Profit, and Wages—A Study of 13 Large Machine Tool Manufacturers), *Academia,* no. 89 (March 1986).
13. For more details, see Koike, "Kaiko Kara Mita Gendai Nihon."
14. In 1988, Toyota produced 3.96 million cars domestically compared with 3.94 million for Ford. The types of cars were not the same, however, so the figures can only be said to be roughly similar. Ford had 350,000 employees, more than 60 percent of whom were in the United States. These figures include employees in Ford divisions in the space industry, plastics, steel, glass, finance, etc.

Chapter 8: Workers at Small and Medium-Sized Companies

1. For a thorough examination of the extensive material on this subject, see Odaka Konosuke, *Rodo Shijo Bunseki* (An Analysis of the Labor Market) (Tokyo: Iwanami Shoten, 1984), especially chapter 3: "It would be fair to say that the wage differentials by company size came into existence in 1920" (p. 116). See also, Odaka's article, "Chingin Keisha Kozo no Choki Hendo" (Long-Term Changes in Wage Differentials by Company Size), *Nihon Rodo Kyokai Zasshi* (Journal of the Japan Institute of Labor) (July–August 1970). Sano Yoko, "Dainiji Taisenmae no Kigyo Kibokan Kakusa" (Wage Differentials by Company Size before World War II), *Mita Gakkai Nenpo* (Mita Academic Annual), no. 4, 1962, examines extensively local municipal government sources; Nishikawa Shunsaku, "Menboseki-gyo no Chingin Hendo to Chingin Kakusa" (Wage Differentials and Wage Changes in the Cotton and Spinning Industry), *Mita Shogaku Kenkyu* (Mita Business Studies), vol. 3, no. 5 (December 1960), analyzes the situation in the cotton and spinning industry, which has the most complete data for the prewar period. Taira, *Economic Growth and Labor Markets,* analyzes the prewar situation using basic data.
2. Koike, *Nihon no Chingin Kosho,* analyzes competition among companies in the product market through the exhaustive use of available evidence.
3. Melvin W. Reder, "The Theory of Occupational Wage Differentials," *American Economic Review* (December 1955). This essay has been included in many anthologies.
4. Lloyd G. Reynolds and Cynthia Taft, *The Evolution of Wage Structure* (New Haven: Yale University Press, 1956).
5. For changes in wage differentials in prewar Japan, see Koike Kazuo, "Sen'i Sangyo no Chingin Suijun to Sono Susei" (Wage Levels and Their Trends in the Textile Industry), *Febian Kenkyu* (Fabian Studies), vol. 17, no. 7 (August 1966).
6. Koike, *Chusho Kigyo no Jukuren*, chapter 2.
7. Aichi Prefecture, Department of Labor, *Chiteki Jukuren no Keisei.*
8. Koike, *Chusho Kigyo no Jukuren*, chapter 1.
9. National Institute of Employment and Vocational Research (Koyo Shokugyo Sogo Kenkyujo), *Kigyonai Rodoryoku no Yuko Katsuyo ni Kansuru Jittai Chosa* (Investigation into the Effective Utilization of the Labor Force within Companies) (Tokyo: Koyo Shokugyo Sogo Kenkyujo, 1982).
10. Aichi Prefecture, Department of Labor, *Chiteki Jukuren no Keisei.*

Chapter 9: Women and Older Workers

1. Future population estimates for Japan are based on the Ministry of Health and Welfare, Institute of Population Problems' *Nihon no Shorai Jinko Suikei* (Future Population Estimates for Japan), published at the time of each National Census. They are found in the institute's journal, *Jinko Mondai Kenkyu* (Research on Population Problems). The most recent estimates were made in December 1986 based on the 1985 National Census. They must be used with caution, since estimates of the birthrate on which they are based are likely to change.
2. See Ministry of Labor, *Koyo Kanri Chosa* (Survey of Employment Systems). These data are good for observing the mandatory retirement system in a time series. They only date from the end of the 1960s, however. For the period before that, the Chuo Rodo Iinkai (Central Labor Relations Committee)'s *Taishokukin, Teinensei oyobi Nenkin Jijo Chosa* (Survey on Retirement Pay, the Mandatory Retirement System, and Pensions) traces data for large companies back every other year to the immediate postwar period.
3. Ibid.
4. The basic data on employment conditions for older workers are found in the Ministry of Labor's *Konenreisha Shugyo tou Jittai Chosa* (Survey on the Employment of Older Workers) for 1981, 1985, and 1990 and *Konenrei Rodosha Koyo Jittai Chosa* (Survey of the Employment of Older Workers) for 1976.
5. Ministry of Labor, Survey of Employment Systems.
6. On the skills of older workers, see Matsuyama Mihoko and others, Kikai Shinko Kyokai (Japan Society for the Promotion of the Machine Industry), *Kikai Kogyo ni okeru Nenrei to Shokumu ni kansuru Chosa Kenkyu* (Survey on Age and Work in the Machine Industries) (Tokyo: Japan Society for the Promotion of the Machine Industry, 1978), and Koike Kazuo, "Konensha no Rodo Noryoku" (Work Skills of Older Workers), in Kanamori Hisao and Ibe Hideo, ed., *Koreika Shakai no Keizaigaku* (Economics in an Aging Society) (Tokyo: Tokyo University Press, 1990).
7. On the employment of older workers at large companies in the United Kingdom and West Germany, see Koike Kazuo, *Nihon no Koyo Shisutemu* (Employment Systems in Japan) (Tokyo: Toyo Keizai Shinposha, 1994), chapter 4-2.
8. ILO, *Yearbook of Labour Statistics,* and EC, *Labour Force Sample Survey*. The former prints the government statistics for each country as is, with no attempt to reconcile the methods used; the latter adopts the actual method, based on responses during a given week.
9. Edmund S. Phelps, "The Statistical Theory of Racism and Sexism," *American Economic Review* (September 1972), pp. 659–61, and *Inflation Policy and Unemployment Theory: The Cost Benefit Approach to Monetary Planning* (New York: Norton, 1972). In addition, see Joseph E. Stiglitz, "Approaches to the Economics of Discrimination," *American Economic Review* (May 1973).
10. For a detailed account of the equal opportunity laws in the United States and other countries, see Kuwabara Masahiro, *Danjo Koyo Byodo no Unyo Kijun* (Operating Standards for Sexual Equality in Employment) (Tokyo: Sogo Rodo Kenkyujo, 1985).
11. See Koike Kazuo, "Futatsu no Michi" (Two Routes), in Koike Kazuo and Tomita Yasunobu, ed., *Shokuba no Kyaria Uman* (Career Women in the Workshop) (Tokyo: Toyo Keizai Shinposha, 1988).
12. In doing research on women workers, their job content and skills are extremely important, but hard to investigate. On these points, the following documents provide valuable information: Wakisaka Akira, *Kaishagata Josei—Shoshin no Nekku to Raifu Kosu* (Company Women—Life Course and Impediments to Advancement) (Tokyo: Dobunkan, 1990); Tomita Yasunobu, "Ogata Kourigyo ni okeru Kino Keisei" (Skill Formation in Large-Scale Retail Businesses), in Koike Kazuo, *Gendai no Jinzai Keisei—Noryoku Kaihatsu o Saguru* (Contemporary Human Resource Development) (Kyoto: Mineruva Shobo, 1986); Nakamura Megumi, "Ote Supa ni okeru Josei

Kanrishokusha, Senmonshokusha" (Female Managers and Professionals at Large Supermarkets), in Koike and Tomita, *Shokuba no Kyaria Uman* (1988).

13. Richard S. Belous, "How Human Resource Systems Adjust to the Shift toward Contingent Workers," *Monthly Labor Review* (March 1989), p. 11.
14. Shinozuka Eiko, *Nihon no Joshi Rodo* (Japanese Women Workers) (Tokyo: Toyo Keizai Shinposha, 1982), pp. 94–95.
15. Belous, op. cit. (1989).

Chapter 10: The Transferability Overseas of the Japanese Way of Working

1. Thailand's deficit with Japan was between 3 and 4 percent of GNP in the early 1980s; the United States' was less than 1 percent.
2. It is impossible to review all of the sources here, so a general introduction to the literature includes the following two: Koike Kazuo, "Kaigai Nihon Kigyo no Koyo Seido" (Employment Systems of Japanese Companies Abroad) in Kansai Keizai Kenkyu Senta, ed., *Kokusai Kankyoka ni okeru Koyo Mondai* (Employment Problems in an International Environment) (Osaka: Kansai Keizai Kenkyu Senta, 1988), and Koike Kazuo, "Nihon Kigyo no Kaigai Tsuyosei—Manager-so ni Shoten o oita Bunken Sabei" (Transferability Abroad of Japanese Companies—A Survey of the Literature with a Focus on the Managerial) (Kokusai Sangyo Rodo Kenkyu Senta, 1989). Vast numbers of studies continue to be published. Few careful studies have been done, however, and most of them have already been cited. As an example of the view that the methods used at Japanese companies are radically different, see Michael Yotaro Yoshino, *Japanese Multinationals* (Cambridge, Mass.: Harvard University Press, 1976).
3. Takamiya Makoto, *Japanese Multinationals in Europe* (Berlin: International Institute of Management, 1979). It was later included in the following work: Keith Thurley and Takamiya Susumu, *Japan's Emerging Multinationals* (Tokyo: Tokyo University Press, 1985).
4. Malcolm Trevor, *The Japanese Management Development Systems: Generalists and Specialists in Japanese Companies Abroad* (London: Dover, 1986).
5. Michael White and Malcolm Trevor, *Under Japanese Management* (London: Heineman Educational Books, 1985).
6. Ibid.
7. Shimada Haruo, *Human Wea no Keizaigaku* (The Economics of Human Ware) (Tokyo: Iwanami Shoten, 1988).
8. Ishida Mitsuo et al., ed., "Amerika Gasshu Koku ni okeru Nikkei Shinshutsu Kigyo ni tsuite no Kenkyu (Chukan Hokoku)" (Research on Japanese Companies in the United States of America, An Interim Report), *Doshisha Amerika Kenkyu*, Supplement 13, 1990; in particular, part 1, by Ishida, and part 2, by Ishida and Kagawa Kozo. Although no direct comparison was made, the following work is cited for its detailed observations of Nissan in the United Kingdom: Peter Wickens, *The Road to Nissan: Flexibility, Quality, Teamwork* (London: Macmillan, 1987).
9. Wickens, op cit. (1987), p. 123.
10. Koike and Inoki, *Skill Formation in Japan and Southeast Asia*
11. Odaka Konosuke, ed., *Ajia no Jukuren—Kaihatsu to Jinzai Keisei* (Skills in Asia—Development and Skill Formation) (Tokyo: Ajia Keizai Kenkyujo, 1989). This work looks at the quality of skills at local companies in various Asian countries. It is a careful study, but it relies primarily on questionnaires and makes very few observations of workshop practices; the authors were not aware of the distinction between integrated and separated systems.
12. Koike Kazuo, *Nihon no Koyo Shisutemu* (Employment Systems in Japan) (Tokyo: Toyo Keizai Shinposha, 1994), chapter 7-2.
13. See Aichi Prefecture (1987), pp. 22–25. According to a comparative study of U.S. and Japanese managers done primarily by Baba Masao, job descriptions and the limits of workers' duties were more frequently put into writing at Japanese firms than at

American ones. The study was based on perceptions rather than facts, but it is a careful work and extremely valuable. Japan Productivity Center (Nihon Seisansei Honbu), *Nichibei Kanrishoku Kodo Hikaku Kenkyu Chosa Hokokusho* (Research Report on a Comparative Study of the Behavior of Japanese and American Managers) (Tokyo: Nihon Seisansei Honbu, 1984), pp. 75, 78, 88, 89.

14. OECD, Development Assistance Committee, *Economic Cooperation Review*.
15. Koike and Inoki (1990), chapters 5 and 6.
16. For more details, see Koike and Inoki (1990), chapter 4, pp. 55–70.

Chapter 11: College Graduates in Industry

1. The Ministry of Labor's Statistical Survey of Wage Structure includes comprehensive statistics for employees by educational level and traces changes in this area since 1954. The old higher school system refers to the three-year higher professional schools that students entered after completing six years of elementary school and four to five years of middle school. Most higher schools were national and are the antecedents of many national universities, excluding the imperial universities. It is thus appropriate to group them together with universities.
2. The youngest to be surveyed were in their early to mid-20s, but college graduates make up only a small part of this age group, and their exact percentage is not known.
3. The dissatisfaction of white-collar workers in nonmanufacturing companies was noted in Trevor, *Japanese Management Development Systems*. See also, Hayashi Kichiro, *Ibunka Intafeisu Kanri—Kaigai ni okeru Nihonteki Keiei* (Cross-Cultural Interface Management—The Japanese Economy Abroad) (Tokyo: Yuhikaku, 1985).
4. When Tomita Teruhiko conducted a questionnaire survey of British managers at 20 Japanese manufacturing companies in the United Kingdom, they clearly rated their Japanese companies highly. The reasons they gave were good prospects for promotion and the opportunity to make good use of their skills. The assessments of the British managers were considerably higher than those given by Southeast Asian managers. Tomita claims that the higher the level of industrialization in a country the higher the assessments. Tomita Teruhiko, "Transferability of Japanese Style Management to Britain," in Tuvia Blumenthal, ed., *Japanese Management at Home and Abroad* (Ben Gurion: Ben Gurion University Press, 1991).
5. Malcolm Trevor, *The Japanese Management Development System: Generalists and Specialists in Japanese Companies Abroad* (London, Dover, N.H.: F. Pinter, 1987).
6. James E. Rosenbaum, *Career Mobility in a Corporate Hierarchy* (Orlando: Academic Press, 1984). The main points were made in an article that appeared in 1979: "Tournament Mobility: Career Patterns in a Corporation," *Administrative Science Quarterly*, vol. 24, pp. 220–241.
7. J. Benjamin Forbes, "Early Intraorganizational Mobility: Patterns and Influence," *Academy of Management Journal*, vol. 30, no. 1, 1987.
8. The case of a Malaysian bank is described in Koike and Inoki (1987), chapter 10. Other interviews were conducted at four banks and three manufacturing companies in the United States, six large corporations in France, eight large corporations in West Germany, three banks in Italy, two banks in Belgium, four banks in Austria, and six large corporations in the United Kingdom.
9. An interview with the chief of head office personnel at a large French company about the hiring of college graduates disclosed that of the 120 persons hired that year, 100 were graduates of *grande e'coles* and the other 20 were graduates of the University of Paris and other ordinary universities. Since May 1968, the company, he said with pride, had become more democratic and had begun hiring graduates of ordinary universities. Most of the graduates of *grande e'coles* were from not the famous schools but from around 30 professional schools; only 1 or 2 came from the famous schools. Graduates of *grande e'coles* who were hired by the firm majored in such fields as mechanical engineering, electrical engineering, aeronautics, and computer science. Judging from the

numbers involved, *grande e'coles* could be considered on a par with the old prewar Japanese university system.

10. Japan Productivity Center, *Nichibei Kanrishoku Kodo Hikaku Kenkyu Chosa Hokokusho* (A Comprehensive Study of Managers' Behavior in the U.S. and Japan) (Tokyo: Nihon Seisansei Honbu, 1984). This questionnaire survey of managers in the United States and Japan analyzed the responses of 917 Japanese and 482 American managers and obtained noteworthy results. Both had roughly the same views about the role of length of service as a criterion for promotion, and American managers, although not as many as their Japanese counterparts, also agreed that length of service should be included in merit ratings to determine salary. The analysts were surprised that length of service was accorded such importance in the United States, but as my book has shown, it is not surprising at all.

    For vivid descriptions of white-collar employment practices at American companies, see Halloran Fumiko, *Ekuzekutibu Ofisu no Asa* (Morning in the Executive Suite) (Tokyo: Nihon Keizai Shinbunsha, 1985), and Matsuura Hideaki, *Beikoku Sarariman Jijo* (The American Salaryman) (Tokyo: Toyo Keizai Shinposha, 1981).
11. Greg Bamber and Ed Snape, "Britain," in Myron J. Roomkin, ed., *Managers as Employees: An International Comparison of the Changing Character of Managerial Empowerment* (Oxford, New York: Oxford University Press, 1989).
12. Cyril Sofer, *Men in Mid-Career, A Study of British Managers and Technical Specialists* (Cambridge: Cambridge University Press, 1970).
13. Ibid., pp. 245–46.
14. Koike Kazuo, *Daisotsu Howaito-kara no Jinzai Kaihatsu* (Human Resource Development of College Graduates in Industry) (Tokyo: Toyo Keizai Shinposha, 1991). Several other outstanding studies have been done on this subject. Particularly worth noting are the series of articles by Vladimir Pucik and Hanada Mitsuyo: Vladimir Pucik, "Managerial Career Progression in Large Japanese Manufacturing Firms," *Research in Personnel and Human Resources Management* suppl. 1 and "Promotion Patterns in a Japanese Trading Company," *The Columbia Journal of World Business*, vol. 20, no. 3, 1985; Hanada Mitsuyo, "Jinji Seido ni okeru Kyoso Genri no Jittai—Shoshin Kanri Shisutemu kara Mita Nihon Kigyo no Jinji Senryaku" (The Competition Principle in Action in the Personnel System—Personnel Strategy at Japanese Corporations as Seen in the Promotion Administration System), *Soshiki Kagaku*, vol. 21, no. 2. Both authors make use of careful analysis, but their critical awareness is focused on when the selection is made and not on skill formation, so neither considers breadth of experience.

    The work by Inoue Shozo, especially "Naibu Rodo Shijo no Keizaiteki Sokumen" (Economic Aspects of the Internal Labor Market), *Nihon Rodo Kyokai Zasshi* no. 282, September 1982, should be singled out. The data are outstanding, and the analysis meticulous. Inoue analyzed the internal careers of 1,115 male white-collar workers at a large steel manufacturer. His findings showed that most white-collar college graduates moved within a single specialized area, but he also makes it clear that a considerable number moved to related areas.

    In addition, the international comparison of engineers done primarily by Imano Koichiro and Sato Hiroki is worth noting. Although mainly dependent on a questionnaire, the study is also based on interviews. Japan Productivity Center, *Nihon no Gijutsusha, Eikoku no Gijutsusha—Kyaria to Noryoku Kaihatsu* (Japanese Engineers and British Engineers—Careers and Skill Development) (Tokyo: Nihon Seisansei Honbu, 1990) and *Kenkyu Kaihatsu Gijutsusha no Shogu ni Kansuru Chosa Hokoku* (Research Report on the Treatment of R&D Engineers) (Tokyo: Nihon Seisansei Honbu, 1985).

    The painstaking work of Wakabayashi Mitsuru should also be mentioned. For example, "Daisotsu Shinnyushain no Kyaria Keisei Katei o Miru" (Looking at the Career Formation Process of Incoming College Graduates), *Gekkan Rikuruto*,

February and March 1986. Wakabayashi analyzes the career records of college graduates employed in Japanese department stores and claims that performance in the early stages of a career determines future advancement; in short, that Japan, too, has an early screening system. The basis for this assertion rests on a high correlation between early performance and subsequent promotion. But this alone is not sufficient reason to accept this premise. If a worker is outstanding, his or her performance is likely to be good from the outset; but it cannot be said that this alone will determine someone's future career. An essential element of the early screening system is that those whose early performances are good are separated out from the rest at the beginning of their careers. For a thorough overview of this research, see Yashiro Atsushi, "Kigyonai Shoshin ni kansuru Jurai no Kenkyu Doko" (Research Trends in the Area of Internal Promotion), *Koyo to Shokugyo* no. 66, Winter 1988.

15. Kuwahara Yasuo, "Kanrisha, Keieisha Kyaria Keisei no Mekanizumu" (Career Formation Mechanisms for Managers and Business People), in Koshiro Kazuyoshi and Kuwahara Yasuo, eds., *Gendai Howaito-kara no Rodo Mondai* (Tokyo: Nihon Rodo Kyokai, 1988), analyzes the careers of executives at a large Japanese corporation, noting their degree of specialization and the late screening process. It makes no mention, however, of their breadth of specialization.

Chapter 12: Labor Unions in the Workplace

1. For the United Kingdom, see Hugh Armstrong Clegg, *The Changing System of Industrial Relations in Great Britain* (Oxford: Blackwell, 1979).
2. Government statistics on labor disputes in various countries are readily accessible in the ILO, *Yearbook of Labour Statistics*. For unionization rates, see the OECD, *Employment Outlook* (Paris: OECD, July 1991). Chapter 4 offers figures since 1970.
3. This issue is thoroughly examined in Nakamura Keisuke, Sato Hiroki, and Kamiya Takuhei, *Rodo kumiai wa honto ni yaku ni tatte iru no ka?* (Are Labor Unions Really Useful?) (Tokyo: Sogo Rodo Kenkyujo, 1988).
4. Richard B. Freeman and James L. Medoff, *What Do Unions Do?* (New York: Basic Books, 1984). For Japan, see Muramatsu Kuramitsu, "The Effect of Trade Unions on Productivity in Japanese Manufacturing Firms," in Aoki Masahiko, ed., *The Economic Analysis of the Japanese Firm* (Amsterdam, New York: North Holland, 1984).
5. Albert O. Hirschman, *Exit, Voice, and Loyalty: Responses to Decline in Firms, Organizations, and States* (Cambridge, Mass.: Harvard University Press, 1970).
6. In the context of a comparison with practices in the United Kingdom, Milton Derber, *Labor-Management Relations at the Plant Level under Industry-wide Bargaining: A Study of the Engineering (Metalworking) Industry in Birmingham, England* (1955), calls this a uniquely American practice.
7. See chapters 1–3 of Koike, *Shokuba no Rodokumiai to Sanka* (1977).
8. Thomas A. Kochan, Harry C. Katz, and Robert B. McKersie, eds., *The Transformation of American Industrial Relations* (New York: Basic Books, 1986). The standard work on American industrial relations is probably Kochan, *Collective Bargaining and Industrial Relations: From Theory to Policy and Practice* (Homewood, Ill.: Richard D. Irwin, 1980).
9. For an examination of this point, see Koike Kazuo, "Amerika no Rodokumiai" (American Labor Unions), in Okazaki Hisahiko et al., eds., *Amerika no Seiki no Seisui* (The Decline and Fall of the American Century) (Tokyo: Nihon Keizai Shinbunsha, 1984).
10. Koike Kazuo, *Rodosha no Keiei Sanka—Seio to Nihon* (Labor Participation in Management—Western Europe and Japan) (Tokyo: Nihon Hyoronsha, 1978), contains detailed observations on how this system actually operates.
11. Hisamoto Norio offers a careful study of why a management participation system of this kind was established in West Germany at that time. See "Sengoki (1945–1952) Nishi Doitsu Kyodo Kettei Ronso" (The Dispute over Codetermination Systems in

Post-War [1945–1952] West Germany), *Nihon Rodo Kyokai Zasshi* (October 1986), and "Nishi Doitsu Kyodo Ketteisei no Keisei" (The Formation of the Codetermination System in West Germany), *Keizai Ronso* (November/December 1986).

12. Basic statistics on labor unions are found in the Ministry of Labor's *Rodo Kumiai Kihon Chosa* (Basic Survey on Labor Unions) as the survey was called prior to 1982. Since 1982, it has been consolidated with other surveys, and statistics can be found in *Roshi Kankei Sogo Chosa* (Comprehensive Survey of Industrial Relations).
13. Richard Price and George Sayers Bain, "Union Growth Revisited: 1948–1974 in Perspective," *British Journal of Industrial Relations*, vol. 14, no. 3 (November 1976).
14. A detailed analysis of the functions of industrywide labor unions in Japan is given in Koike Kazuo, *Nihon no Chingin Kosho—Sangyo Reveru no Chingin Kettei Kiko* (Wage Negotiations at the Industry Level in Japan) (Tokyo: Tokyo University Press, 1962).
15. For a risk-sharing model of industrial relations, see Koike Kazuo, "Kaiko kara Mita Gendai Nihon no Roshi Kankei" (Japanese Industrial Relations from the Perspective of Dismissals), in Moriguchi Chikashi et al., eds., *Nihon Keizai no Kozo Bunseki* (A Structural Analysis of the Japanese Economy) (Tokyo: Sobunsha, 1983).

Chapter 13: Changes in Wage Levels and Unemployment

1. A. W. Phillips, "The Relation between Unemployment and the Rate of Change of Money Wage Rates in the United Kingdom, 1861–1957," *Economica* (November 1958).
2. Richard G. Lipsey, "The Relation between Unemployment and the Rate of Change of Money Wage Rates in the United Kingdom, 1862–1957: A Further Analysis," *Economica* (February 1962).
3. Otto Eckstein and Thomas A. Wilson, "The Determination of Money Wages in American Industry," *Quarterly Journal of Economics*, vol. 76 (August 1962).
4. Sano Yoko, *Chingin Kettei no Keiryo Bunseki* (An Econometric Analysis of Wage Determination) (Tokyo: Toyo Keizai Shinposha, 1970). Sano's findings are summarized in chapter 5.
5. Koshiro Kazuyoshi, *Tenkanki no Chingin Kosho* (Wage Negotiations at the Turning Point) (Tokyo: Toyo Keizai Shinposha, 1978).
6. An example is the work on the productivity of global automobile manufacturers by a group at the Massachusetts Institute of Technology: James P. Womack, Daniel T. Jones, and Daniel Roos, *The Machine That Changed the World* (New York: Rawson Associates, 1990).
7. See, for instance, the excellent study by Magota Ryohei, *Jisshitsu Chingin no Kokusai Hikaku* (An International Comparison of Real Wages) (Tokyo: Rodo Hogaku Shuppan, 1963). This information is also found in Nihon Keizai Chosa Kyogikai, ed., *Chingin no Kokusai Hikaku* (An International Comparison of Wages) (Tokyo: Toyo Keizai Shinposha, 1964).
8. Umemura, *Chingin, Koyo, Nogyo* (1961).
9. Ibid., chapter 1.
10. For the most detailed analysis of the small differences in definitions used in unemployment surveys by various countries, calculations of unemployment rates that adjust for these, and even a list of unemployment surveys for each country, see Constance Sorrentino, "International Comparison of Unemployment," U.S. Department of Labor, Bureau of Labor Statistics bulletin no. 1979 (1978).
11. In the United States, the labor force survey is called the Current Population Survey and is found in *Earnings and Employment,* published monthly by the Bureau of Labor Statistics. Japan's survey, the *Rodoryoku Chosa* (Labor Force Survey), is published monthly by the Management and Coordination Agency's Statistics Bureau. A formal difference is that in the United States the week chosen for survey purposes is in the middle of the month, whereas in Japan it is the last week of the month.

12. Tomita Yasunobu, *Shitsugyo Tokei o meguru Shomondai* (Various Problems Related to Unemployment Statistics) (Osaka: Osaka Furitsu Daigaku Keizai Gakubu, 1989).
13. J. C. R. Dow and L.A. Dicks-Mireaux, "The Excess Demand for Labour, A Study of Conditions in Great Britain, 1946–56," *Oxford Economic Papers*, vol. 10, no. 1 (February 1958).
14. Damodar Gujarati, "The Behaviour of Unemployment and Unfilled Vacancies in Great Britain, 1958–71," *Economic Journal* (March 1972).
15. Yoshida Kazuo and Endo Hiroshi, "Sekiyu Kiki iko no Shitsugyo Kozo no Henka" (Changes in the Structure of Unemployment since the Energy Crisis), *Kikan Gendai Keizai*, no. 51 (Winter 1982). The series of articles by Mizuno Asao is also valuable.
16. Julius Shiskin, "Employment and Unemployment: The Doughnut or the Hole?" *Monthly Labor Review* (February 1976).
17. Hoya Rokuro, "Rodo Bunpairitsu to Shotoku Bunpai (1, 2, 3)" (Labor's Relative Share and Income Distribution [parts 1–3]), *Rodo Jiho* (September, October, November 1990), calculates various examples of labor's relative share in Japan.
18. Nicholas Kaldor, "Alternative Theory of Distribution," *Review of Economic Studies*, vol. 23 (1955).
19. Simon Smith Kuznets, "Economic Growth and Income Equality," *American Economic Review* (May 1955); also see Kuznets, *Modern Economic Growth: Rate, Structure, and Spread* (New Haven: Yale University Press, 1966).
20. Malcolm Sawyer, "Income Distribution in OECD Countries," *Occasional Studies, OECD Economic Outlook* (July 1976).

Chapter 14: Basic Theory and the Theory of Stages

1. John Maynard Keynes, *The General Theory of Employment, Interest and Money* (London: Macmillan, 1936), chapter 2, p. 9.
2. Gary Becker's household production model can be cited as another example of a labor supply theory that has gained attention recently. In contrast to earlier theories that only considered commodities sold in the market, Becker's model assesses the importance of the nonmarket within the household, such as housework; in other words, commodities that cannot be sold. Becker's model reasons that when women enter the labor market, their thoughts and actions are affected not simply by the size of their salaries but also by housework. See Chuma Hiroyuki, "Rodo Kyokyu" (Labor Supply), in Ohashi Isao et al., eds., *Rodo Keizaigaku* (Labor Economics) (Tokyo: Yuhikaku, 1989).
3. Paul H. Douglas, *The Theory of Wages* (1st ed. 1934; New York: A. M. Kelley, 1957) The distinction of being the first to approach wage determination based on statistical evidence belongs to Douglas.
4. Adam Smith, *An Inquiry into the Nature and Causes of the Wealth of Nations* (1776).
5. Douglas, *The Theory of Wages* (1957).
6. For the United States, the standard work is T. A. Finegan and William G. Bowen, *The Economics of Labor Participation* (Princeton: Princeton University Press, 1969). Many studies are available for Japan, but cited here is Higuchi Yoshio, *Nihon Keizai to Shugyo Kodo* (The Japanese Economy and Employment Behavior) (Tokyo: Toyo Keizai Shinposha, 1991).
7. For an authentic account of the union, the basic work thus far is James B. Jefferys, *The Story of the Engineers 1851–1945* (London: Lawrence & Wishart, 1947). See also, M. L. Yates, *Wages and Labour Conditions in the British Engineering Industry* (London: Macdonald, 1937); Tokunaga Shigeyoshi, *Igirisu Chinrodoshi no Kenkyu* (A Study of British Labor History) (Tokyo: Hosei Daigaku Shuppankyoku, 1967); Kurita Ken, *Igirisu Rodo Kumiaishiron* (A Historical Treatise on the British Labor Unions) (Tokyo: Miraisha, 1973). Much of this section is based on Koike, *Chingin* (1966), chapter 2.
8. Jefferys's book contains the percentages of new members in the Amalgamated Society of Engineers by occupation at the end of the nineteenth century. Because the member-

ship rate for this union is thought to be quite high, the figures do not seem to be overestimates.

9. A. L. Bowley, "The Statistics of Wages in the U.K. during the Last 100 Years, part 10–14," *Journal of the Royal Statistical Society,* vol. 68–69.
10. Webb and Webb, *Industrial Democracy* (1897).
11. The National Federation of Construction Workers' Unions (Zenkensoren), Agreed Wage Schedule for Craftsmen in the Building Trades, (Zenkensoren, Tokyo Federation: March 14, 1990), exemplifies wage determination by a union. It states that the agreed wage for craftsmen in the building trades (effective April 1) will be as follows:
    One day ¥26,000
    Except as given hereunder:
    stonemasons ¥30,000
    molder ¥28,000
    The average number of workdays for said craftsmen will be 22 days (= 1 month).
12. For workers in the building trades in Japan, see Takanashi Akira, ed., *Kensetsu Sangyo no Roshi Kankei* (Industrial Relations in the Construction Industry) (Tokyo: Toyo Keizai Shinposha, 1978). For an analysis of wage fluctuations and other aspects of the external labor market, see Muramatsu Kuramitsu, "Kensetsugyo ni kansuru Koyo to Chingin no Doji Kettei Moderu—Seizogyo tono Hikaku" (Employment in the Construction Industry and a Simultaneous Wage Determination Model—A Comparison with the Manufacturing Industry), *Nanzan Keizai Kenkyu* (February 1990).
13. According to the Okochi theory, individual companies pursue profits to the extreme, paying no attention to the results in the long run. They attempt to lengthen working hours to earn more, leaving no healthy workers in the long run because of fatigue, ultimately endangering the whole system. Okochi predicts the need for an invisible headquarters to check this individual, selfish behavior by regulating working hours with legislation. Okochi cites this invisible headquarters as "the reason of total capital." Okochi Kazuo, *Shakai Seisaku no Kihon Mondai* (Basic Issues of Social Policy) (Tokyo: Nihon Hyoronsha, 1940).
14. Most of Taylor's articles were later collected and published in Frederick Winslow Taylor, *Scientific Management* (New York: Harper, 1947).
15. Daniel Roos, James P. Womack, and Daniel T. Jones, *The Machine That Changed the World* (NY: Rawson Associates, 1990).
16. Jack W. Stieber, *Steel Industry Wage Structure: A Study of the Joint Union-Management Job Evaluation Program in the Basic Steel Industry* (Cambridge, Mass.: Harvard University Press, 1959), analyzes the introduction of the precursor of the American job-classification plan at U.S. Steel. This is the standard work on this subject.
17. See Martin E. Personick, "White-Collar Pay Determination under Range-of-Rate Systems," *Monthly Labor Review* (December 1984).
18. Many studies on British white-collar workers are available. An example is Blackburn, *Union Character* (1967), which observes staff in the British banking industry. For the British steel industry, see Kikuchi and Ishida, *Gendai Igirisu* (1988); K. G. J. C. Knowles et al., eds., "Wage Differentials in a Large Steel Firm," *Oxford Institute of Statistics Bulletin* (August 1958); W. H. Scott et al., *Technical Change and Industrial Relations: A Study of the Relations between Technical Change and the Social Structure of a Large Steel Work* (Liverpool: Liverpool University Press, 1956). For workshops in the chemical industry, Shirley Lerner, *Workshop Wage Determination* (1969); for the electrical machinery industry, Ronald P. Dore, *British Factory, Japanese Factory: The Origins of National Diversity in Industrial Relations* (Berkeley: University of California Press, 1973). Clear data on the automobile industry are not available, but see Herbert Arthur Turner et al., *Labour Relations in the Motor Industry: A Study of Industrial Unrest and an International Comparison* (London: Allen & Unwin, 1967).

U.S. findings are mainly based on interviews: Koike, *Shokuba no Rodokumiai* (1977). And many other excellent studies have been done on Japan in addition to the work just cited.

19. Koike Kazuo, "Chingin, Rodo Joken Kanri no Jittai Bunseki" (Analysis of the Administration of Wages and Working Conditions), in Susuki Shinichi and Ujihara Shojiro, eds., *Romu Kanri* (Personnel Management), 1967, and Koike Kazuo, "Nenko Chingin no Naiyo to Konkyo" (The Substance and Grounds of Seniority Wages), *Keizai Semina* (November 1961).

Index

N

O

P

Q

R

S

W

Y

The LTCB International Library Foundation Statement of Purpose

The world is moving steadily toward a borderless economy and deepening international interdependence. Amid this globalization of economic activities, the Japanese economy is developing organic ties with the economies of individual nations throughout the world via trade, direct investment, overseas manufacturing activities, and the international movement of capital.

As a result, interest in Japan's politics, economy, and society and in the concepts and values that lie behind Japan's socioeconomic activities is growing in many countries.

However, the overseas introduction and dissemination of translations of works originally written in Japanese lags behind the growth of interest in Japan. Such works are not well known outside Japan. One main reason for this is that the high costs involved in translating and publishing materials written in Japanese hinder the undertaking of such activities on a commercial basis. It is extremely important to overcome this barrier to deepen and broaden mutual understanding.

The LTCB International Library Foundation has been founded to address this pressing need. Its primary activity is to disseminate information on Japan in foreign countries through the translation of selected Japanese works on Japan's politics, economy, society, and culture into English (and other languages) and the publication and distribution of these translations. To commemorate the completion of The Long-Term Credit Bank of Japan, Ltd.'s new headquarters and its 40th anniversary, LTCB has provided the LTCB International Library Foundation with an endowment.

We sincerely hope that the LTCB International Library Foundation will successfully fulfill its mission of promoting global understanding and goodwill through enhanced cultural exchange.

March 1, 1994

The founders of the LTCB International Library Foundation